CAMBRIDGE STUDIES IN AMERICAN LITERATURE AND CULTURE

Cross-Cultural Reckonings

Continued after page 190

Cross-Cultural Reckonings

A Triptych of Russian, American, and Canadian Texts

BLANCHE H. GELFANT
Dartmouth College

CAMBRIDGE
UNIVERSITY PRESS

Published by the Press Syndicate of the University of Cambridge
The Pitt Building, Trumpington Street, Cambridge CB2 1RP
40 West 20th Street, New York, NY 10011-4211, USA
10 Stamford Road, Oakleigh, Melbourne 3166, Australia

First published 1995

Printed in the United States of America

Library of Congress Cataloging-in-Publication Data

Gelfant, Blanche H., 1922–

Cross-cultural reckonings : a triptych of Russian, American, and
Canadian texts / Blanche H. Gelfant.

p.   cm. – (Cambridge studies in American literature and
culture : 84)

Includes index.

ISBN 0-521-44038-6

1. American literature – 20th century – History and criticism.
2. Russian literature – 20th century – History and criticism.
3. Canadian literature – 20th century – History and criticism.
4. Literature, Comparative – American and Russian.   5. Literature,
Comparative – American and Canadian.   6. Literature, Comparative –
Russian and Canadian.   I. Title.   II. Series.

PS159.R8G44   1995

809'.04 – dc20   94-9763

                                                                CIP

A catalog record for this book is available from the British Library.

ISBN 0-521-44038-6 hardback

Once again for Nina and Alan,
And now, also, for Sam,

Contents

Acknowledgments

I thank, first of all, the various writers – Russian, American, and Canadian – whose books have inspired these essays and infused them with whatever life they may have. I have tried to express my thanks through the essays' form by giving precedence to the books rather than to comments made about them by various critics. I thank these critics also, and numerous others, theorists and biographers, all of whom have provided the many perspectives discussed or alluded to in my voluminous notes.

Then, of course, I have colleagues, friends, librarians, and various others to thank. I cite them in the notes to the essays to tell specifically where and how they have helped me, but I am happy to name some of them here, again. I thank my colleague Professor Louis Renza for reading drafts of various essays and offering cryptic and complex comments I always found illuminating. His way of thinking is at once incisive and involuted, and always intellectually energizing. I thank my colleague Professor William Spengemann for reading an almost final version of The Capitalistic Will, which, after his uninhibitedly skeptical comments, became a preliminary draft seeking an identity his criticism helped me find. I thank Professor Eric Sundquist, Editor of Cambridge Studies in American Literature and Culture, the series in which this volume appears. Professor Sundquist encouraged me to gather together these cross-cultural critiques because he believed they would make an unusual and interesting volume of open-ended literary reckonings. I have only myself to fault if they do not.

I thank with special appreciation Professor David Stouck of Simon Fraser University, with whom I share a longstanding interest in Willa Cather and in the Canadian writer, Ethel Wilson, the subjects of the last two essays. I share his interest in Wilson only because he introduced me to her fiction many years ago. He introduced me, too, to other Canadian writers who have considerably enriched my pleasure as a reader, while he has enlarged my understanding of friendship and of cross-cultural connections. Professor Stouck kindly read The Captialistic Will essay and, aside from specific suggestions, gave me some sense of confidence that what I was saying about the concept of Canadian cultural identity was not egregious.

Here I can thank in public the two patient and wonderfully forebearing librarians at Dartmouth College in charge of interlibrary loans. Patricia Carter and Marianne Hraibi have relentlessly hunted down books I needed, hunted me down when the books were long overdue, and with kindness and good humor understood when I needed them a little bit longer. I thank also Julie Low, a student who began as a research assistant tasked to fetch and carry books and became an endearingly indefatigable inquisitor about my work. Finally, I thank Dartmouth College for encouraging literary scholarship by providing funds for research activities and fostering the intellectual interests of its faculty.

To my daughter and my son, both thousands of miles away, I offer thanks for long-distance encouragement and love.

Introduction: On Waywardness

Il n'est pas subject si vain qui ne merite un rang en cette rapsodie.

Montaigne

The waywardness of the essays in this volume has endeared them to me – but only after it had surprised me, troubled me, and caused me considerable struggle. Seen in retrospect, the struggle seemed to be over linearity, a traditional aspect of the essay hardly worth contention, one would think, though it has troubled feminist critics considerably. Linearity troubled me because the essays I was writing stubbornly refused to follow a single direction – a single theme or purpose – that would lead them to a clearly defined destination. They followed instead unpredictably wayward paths that met and diverged, crossed and collided. Some of the paths broadened into highways that allowed congenial or contending texts to travel together, engaging in dialogues which their critics, confined to the bypath of notes, could comment upon but not control. Some paths crossed boundary lines that defined the oppositions within binary cross-cultural comparisons. Others simply continued – resisting, if only by implication, the closure toward which a linear critical essay conventionally moves.

For example, the first essay, Days of Reckoning, refused to reach conclusions even though the texts it discussed, and the various reckonings made within and about them, seemed to demand a final reckoning or judgment. It argued that such a reckoning would be artifactual, produced by the contingencies of a binary cross-cultural critique. By assuming a triadic form it sought to avoid these contingencies and to multiply its meanings. Perhaps it only made meaning itself more indeterminate, but it did not equate indeterminacy with unreadability. On the contrary, it declared itself readable in a number of different ways: horizontally, vertically, elliptically, and crisscross. This became possible, it argued, once it rejected the linearity traditional to academic essays and, by analogy, turned itself into a triptych. As in a painting, a single frame, the essay as a whole, contained and was constituted by three discrete parts or panels, each panel consisting of a cross-cultural critique that was complete in itself but capable of combining with the others to form a multifaceted argument moving in several directions at once. A reader following one direction could be diverted to another that ran parallel to or intersected with it, or that cut it off from or changed its destination. One panel read in conjunction with another – the first with the third, for instance – produced a specific cross-cultural comparison, while any combination of panels modulated the meaning of the essay as a whole. Thus meanings became more than usually multiple, coexistent, and cognizant of each other. They deferred to their differences while recognizing their similarity as artifactual products of the shifting contexts the essay created. The shifts took place as the essay's focus changed from panel to panel, and changed again as panels were compared, contrasted, or combined. Each shift defined particular critical issues which, like a triptych's panels, were at once discrete and interconnected – issues pertaining to cultural identity, historical change and continuity, literary representations of gender, postmodern theories skeptical of the truth of fiction (and of truth itself), and testimonials to the writer's truth.

The triadic form that held these issues together gave the essay latitude to rethink oppositions generated by binary comparisons and to resist the teleology of linear arguments. As it tried out – or essayed – a multifaceted criticism, the triptych sought to loosen strictures that conventional forms of academic discourse have placed upon waywardness and the intellectual freedom it can afford. Seeking freedom of form, Days of Reckoning began to question the cross-cultural approach it was taking and to engage in literary reckonings that would not come to a final account. In the novellas that the essay discussed, characters literally reckoned; they counted, calculated, and made accountings. The essay itself used reckoning as a metaphor that called to mind the etymological meaning of *essay* as an *exagium* or weighing. Trying to weigh arguments freely and let the scales tip as they would, Days of Reckoning allowed in subjects it had not intended to include, adopting as it went along the famously carefree and originary attitude of Montaigne's *Essais:* "Il n'est pas subject si vain qui ne merite un rang en cette rapsodie."[1] Such an attitude makes an essay wayward.

The inherent waywardness of the novel itself as a literary form turned out to be a submerged motif of the last essay in the volume, The Capitalistic Will. The essay argued that the novel's waywardness allowed the writer to resist a reader's desire for clarity. Unexpected twists and turns of plot and characterization, as well as strange elisions, produced mystification, an effect the essay refused to deplore. On the contrary, The Capitalistic Will proclaimed a critic's love of textual mysteries, her appreciation of their involuted purposes, and her pleasure in their obfuscating tactics which, the essay argued, criticism could not completely counter. The essay described reckonings made within the texts only to question their validity and deny their finality. It skeptically recalculated the final reckonings that characters had made and declared them obfuscations serving personal, cultural, and literary purposes. These purposes were reinforced by the novels' self-reflective expository passages, which the essay traced to sources of unearned authority – to writers or narrators with a vested interest in the culture of capitalism. Such passages, the essay argued, represented the texts' murky attempts at a final reckoning that would account for events the essay considered unaccountable. In a succession of long notes, the essay provided space for a diversity of critical judgments, but it found their finality questionable, necessarily so because the complexities of the texts – concealed by their serene and superficially simple styles and obfuscated by their self-serving explanations – demand a continuous re-reckoning. The inconclusiveness of the reckonings produced in The Capitalistic Will represented the essay's resistance to a demand for final judgment implicit in critical processes that seek a settlement of accounts – an accounting that, as we say, closes the books.

In *essaying* an open-ended critique, I found myself appropriating for the second time an art form that evoked waywardness by drawing the eye in various directions rather than across a single linear plane to a prescribed endpoint. Previously, in a book called *Women Writing in America,* I had borrowed the collage, using it in my subtitle to justify a lack of closure. Like the triptych, the collage is a multifaceted art form that induces the eye to wander over disparate pieces held together in juxtapositions that jar the aesthetic sensibility and open the mind to a re-reckoning of fundamental cultural assumptions – assumptions about what is and is not of intrinsic artistic value, or of intrinsically consequential difference, or of a hierarchical order that could, and perhaps should, be democratized. For once diverse and diversely valued fragments have been placed upon the canvas of a collage, junk and high art interact with indifference to their culturally defined differences. Seeing this interaction, I offered the collage as an analogue for an open-ended feminist criticism by suggesting that diverse women's voices, rather than visual images, could be placed upon an equal, equalizing, and expandable plane. One essay in *Women Writing* mimetically reproduced the form of a collage by painting the portrait of a writer with fragments of prose set off from each other by different discursive modes and different typographies, the jagged pieces coming together to reveal the wholeness of a self created out of a woman's fragmented and multiple roles. Another essay described a novella as a literary collage, a story constructed of fragments and found objects – actual junk and junked lives – which had been salvaged, put together, and redeemed by the writer's art.

Though the form of the triptych seems more strictly prescribed than that of the collage, it has considerable freedom to vary its triadic pattern or to exceed it by becoming a polyptych. Generically, the triptych is a type of polyptych, a multifaceted art form that has no fixed number of panels and no single design. Some polyptychs place beneath their main panels a secondary series of small interconnected pictures. Such pictorial sequences have the qualities of discreteness and connectedness I see in the endnotes, which simultaneously support the essays and stand apart from them as autonomous elements. If they maintain their double stance properly, these notes should justify their length as commentaries interesting in themselves. The essays' increasing reliance upon notes to introduce the arguments of literary theorists may reflect an increasing reluctance to concede to theory a space which could be occupied by practical criticism. The earliest essay I wrote, The Hidden Mines, is the least annotated and the most personal. In it, an "I" speaks directly to the reader. Subsequent essays, more directly concerned with theory and its proliferation, invent the fiction of a critic with two voices, a personal voice that speaks in the essays to address the texts, and another voice, heard in the notes, that converses with critics about literary and cultural contexts.

This marked separation between essay and essayistic notes invites readers to enjoy a certain waywardness in their choice of what to read and in what sequence. One can read the essays without the notes for self-contained arguments about the texts. One could read the notes first for background material and arguments of their own. One could read the essay and notes conjointly, turning from the texts to various contexts. All of these possibilities are adumbrated in a highly wayward discussion of notes that I read after I had written this apologia for my essays. I refer to Derrida's lucubrations in the published version of his spoken comments, entitled "This is Not an Oral Footnote."[2] Echoing Derrida as he echoes Magritte, I can say that this book is not a book, since one can read its collected essays in any order, though the first, Days of Reckoning, establishes a theoretical scaffolding for the volume as a whole. For this reason, I have placed it first though it was written after the two essays that follow, Speaking Her Own Piece, and The Hidden Mines. Because Days of Reckoning discusses most explicitly issues I see implicated in postmodern cross-cultural criticism as theorized and practiced, it can serve as a introduction to the concerns of the other essays, though it can be read also, I would suggest, as an inconclusive conclusion to the volume as a whole. Its segmented form and inferential argument allow it to be read in a reverse order, since its concluding pages reflect upon what it originally intended and so serve as a preamble or beginning as well as an end.

I have a vision I have not been able to realize – of a critical essay divided into two parts: an explicatory essay and a set of notes that would constitute a secondary essay when read continuously. This master diptych would have two horizontal panels, one focused upon literary texts, and the other upon critical contexts. Each horizontal panel could be read independently as a self-contained essay, or both could be read together as vertically continuous, thus assuming the conventional form of a footnoted critique. All I could achieve was a rather idiosyncratic bifurcation which, however, did allow me to pursue an interest in individual texts while I explored a variety of contexts – literary, cultural, biographical, historical. All the essays express a self-conscious concern with a critic's choice of contexts for the study of literature. This concern arose with the conception of each essay, since each was written in response to an invitation that defined explicitly, if generally, the setting for which the essay was destined – distinct and different settings pointing to national culture as a context for literary criticism. To explain why the essays redefined the terms of their invitations and how they engaged interactively in a process of continuous cross-cultural reckonings, I introduce each essay with a short account of the particular context in which, and about which, it was written. This adds another voice to the volume, reminiscent, self-reflective, and occasionally rueful.

Notes

1 The quotations from Montaigne that serve as epigraphs for prefactory notes come from a 1962 edition of *Essais,* ed. Maurice Rat (Garnier Frères, 2 vols.).
2 Jacques Derrida, "This Is Not an Oral Footnote," in *Annotation and Its Texts,* ed. Stephen A. Barney (New York: Oxford University Press, 1991), pp. 192–205. The temptation to digress is strong, since one could wander into another bypath by pursuing Derrida's account of the footnote. Derrida declares that if he wanted "to be sure" that any polemical attack he might make "would be read and not passed by," he "would put it in a footnote, conferring on it the principal role, so that what is apparently the main text would become an auxiliary pretext for the footnote" (p. 198). To explain this apparent inversion, Derrida engages in a "digression," and to avoid further digression, I leave him here with the last word. To do otherwise would be to demonstrate once more the critic's inexhaustible capacity to comment, argue, and annotate. Perhaps, as Montaigne has said, this capacity testifies to our inexhaustible desire for knowledge (le desir de connoissance), made tangible by our swarming textual commentaries. In his essay "De L'Experience," Montaigne observed that "il y a . . . plus de livres sur les livres que sur autre subject; nous ne faisons que nous entregloser." In his (not) oral footnote, Derrida elaborately glosses himself.

Panel I: On Breaking Up

veu la naturelle instabilité de nos meurs et opinions, il m'a semblé souvent que
les bons autheurs mesme ont tort de s'opiniastrer à former de nous une constante and solide contexture

Montaigne

In the summer of 1990, I was on my way to Russia, carrying with me indispensable items for the trip, chewing gum and lipsticks and a set of lectures on
Russian and American short fiction. The lipsticks were for Russian chamber-
maids, and the lectures were for a group of American and Canadian college
alumni, mature men and women, on a tour – an educational tour, the brochure
said – of Soviet Russia. I was to educate the group about modern Russian and
American literature, and my counterpart, a Canadian historian from McGill
University, was to educate us about the history of the Soviet Union. This history, long, involuted, and astonishing, had led to a time of heightened promise.
In the summer of 1990, the Soviet Union – and the world – seemed to be moving toward a future in which Cold War fears would become a mere memory
the past. This was the promise, many believed, held out by Gorbachev and his
policy of *glasnost*.

As I imagined myself cruising up the Volga River, leisurely combining edifying conversation with vodka cocktails, I could not foresee the incessant worry
that my happy and ignorant plunge into cross-cultural criticism would bring. For
one commitment led to another. By coincidence, I was asked that summer to
write an essay on teaching literary texts from a cross-cultural perspective – a nice
coincidence, I thought, since I was already engaged in drawing cross-cultural
comparisons. Two years later, I was still writing the essay, which I thought I
might never finish and, because of its length, never publish. My unending reading and writing became an end in itself, fulfilling an ideal of scholarship I would
not abnegate though, clearly, it could impede a professional career. I kept writing, and the world kept changing. As we know, Gorbachev lost his luster and
his position, and the Soviet Union was fragmented into a "former" state. Sud-

7

denly the road to a peace was turning in the direction of disillusion, violence, and tragedy. Why, I now wonder, did a lifetime of reading leave me unprepared for such twists and turns? Why did I not foresee the possibility of the tragic ironies that I knew could complicate any plot, including those of politics? In the summer of 1990, I shared the celebratory mood of our group in spite of what we could not avoid seeing and hearing, even on a carefully guided tour. We saw the long lines in front of shops with quickly emptied shelves. We heard grievances and complaints from our Russian guides. We added our complaints as we recoiled from the grubbiness of railroads and grew weary waiting for planes that were hours late. But we understood that discomfort, disorder, and stories of discontent were part of the packaged tour. We were on the outlook for wonders, and we saw them ahead on a historical road to the future that was straight and unalterable.

At the time, I thought the road ahead of me was clear. I had accepted fairly straightforward assignments I would fulfill in a fairly straightforward way by comparing *this* with *that* to show the heuristic value of bringing together exemplary texts from different national and cultural contexts. My first assignment was going well, I thought. The texts I had chosen aroused interest. The lectures I gave raised long and hot arguments – perhaps because they often followed the cocktail hour, but more likely, because they emphasized textual and cultural indeterminacies rather than the certainties my celebratory readers expected. I wanted to be straightforward and affirming, but I was zigzagging my way through a range of critical problems that were to become more confounding as I tried to fulfill my second assignment. How could I answer a call for a methodological essay on teaching literature from a cross-cultural perspective when I was beset by doubts about distinctions between text and context, definitions based upon binary oppositions, and divisions drawn by national boundaries which, presumably, art could transcend? I doubted the legitimacy of critical responses based upon a reading of translations. I doubted the validity of cultural generalizations based upon exemplary particulars. How exemplary of cultural difference, or of anything, were the particular texts I had chosen? I suspected that the clear and cogent reasons I could give for my choices did not expunge their essential arbitrariness.

As my doubts emerged, the essay that became Days of Reckoning began to display its waywardness. It refused to stay within the limit of pages assigned, thus becoming unsuitable for the collection for which, presumably, it was being written. It refused to develop a linear argument, to allow a binary comparison, and to entertain certain conclusions. It began to fragment and then to reassemble itself into a triadic form that enacted its developing argument about essayistic form itself – that this form was essentially inconstant and artifactual, a product of disparate pieces. I began to think that the effort to make of pieces one constant and solid fabric – "une constante and solide contexture," as Montaigne had put it – was misplaced when applied to a cross-cultural literary essay. Indeed, the effects of this effort would be specious because they were produced by the contingencies of a particular method and design – by a binary comparative structure, a linear form, and a partisan selective process. After all, my discommoding essay wanted to argue, comparing *this* with *that* – as compared, say, to comparing sets of *this and that* – was an arbitrary, if simple and conventional, way of performing cross-cultural literary criticism. Comparison could assume a multiple as well as multiplicity of forms; it could be read in crisscross ways or up and down, rather than only linearly. It could reproduce rather than erase "la naturelle instabilité de nos meurs et opinions" that Montaigne believed the essay morally bound to reveal.

As its arguments prevailed, the essay gave up its original assignment to pursue a dogging question: How could the literary critic apply postmodern theories to novels valued for their realistic representations of a cultural milieu when these theories defined culture as a text inseparable from a language that was, essentially, self-referential? When Solzhenitsyn wrote about Stalin's *gulags,* did his words refer to other words or to a real world? Such a question would have disconcerted his readers on the summer cruise up the Volga, since they naively assumed that the words he, and they, used referred to actual social realities.

Meanwhile, the changing circumstances of Russian everyday life were suggesting the inability of an essay, no matter how widely or wildly extended in form, to accommodate a subject of such scope as cross-cultural literary criticism. Indeed, the social and political tumult in the now former Soviet Union revealed the inadequacy of any list of literary texts to represent a cultural context. Context itself began to seem to me a site of uncertainty and pieces: historical uncertainties, critical uncertainties, pieces left from what had been broken up – a country or, how less significantly, a literary form – and pieces out of which to make a new, if inconstant, whole. Moreover, wholeness seemed to me inherently elusive, an unattainable, and perhaps undesirable, ideal. No text could tell the whole story even of the slightest historical happening upon which it was based. This is not to deny that the texts of Days of Reckoning have important historical relevance to their times – the relevance is inseparable from their importance. But the Russian novellas elided the ethnic diversity of the Soviet Union and the devastating political issues inherent in this diversity, while the American novellas focused exclusively upon a white, urban middle class. Pointing this out, my lectures discomforted an audience eager to believe that a few selected literary texts could give a trustworthy view of the culture from which they came. Clearly, the view would be partial and slanted, and it required the critic to find a position from which to essay its value. The question of what this position might be, raised tentatively in my lectures, moved to the foreground of the essay to produce the fragmented but paradoxically coherent form of a literary triptych.

One value of this triadic form, as I saw it, was that it opened a space for women's new and neglected writings alongside well-known works written by and about men. The first panel considers two such works: *One Day in the Life of Ivan Denisovich* by Alexander Solzhenitsyn and Saul Bellow's *Seize the Day*. In contrast, the second panel presents much less known novellas, *Sofia Petrovna* and *The Girl*, which happen to have much in common. Both were conceived in a time of crisis, both were long left unpublished, and both are now getting the attention they were long denied. Both are moving testimonials to their times and to two extraordinary radical women – Lydia Chukovskaya and Meridel Le Sueur. The third panel brings the triptych into the present with Natalya Baranskaya's novella "A Week Like Any Other" and Arlene Heyman's prize-winning "Artifact," works currently attracting comment for their incisive portrayals of contemporary women.

Each of these sets of novellas occupied a space within the essay that was both discrete and overlapping, since each panel was separated from the others and, at the same time, melded with them to form a single encompassing critique. Within any one panel, a comparison between an American and a Russian novella revealed striking similarities in the novellas' literary form and themes, and in their critical reception. These similarities threw into relief differences that may, or may not, have been culturally inscribed. When I was lecturing on the novellas as we traveled up the Volga – I write this nostalgically – I began to find myself mystified by a certain lack of difference in the emotions that the books aroused. Everyone seemed to feel the same about different characters. Everyone disliked Bellow's hapless Tommy Wilhelm and Heyman's strangely unsatisfied Lottie (we did not read *The Girl*). American, as well as Canadian, readers found these characters' desires, whether for money, love, self-identity, or an ineffable Truth, petty and ungracious, even grating. In contrast, everyone admired Solzhenitsyn's prisoner for his quiet acceptance of his fate, seeing it as heroic rather than, as some critics claim, merely accommodating. Almost without exception, the women in the audience, whom I would have thought distanced from Baranskaya's desperately rushing heroine, embraced the Russian character because her story reminded them of their own or their daughters' lives. I found this equation of literature and life refreshing, if disconcerting, as it affirmed a proposition denied by postmodern theories and evoked by the epigraph that introduces Days of Reckoning – namely, that Truth is "Something big," something one can come close to, look at, and recognize within the disguises of fiction.

Days of Reckoning in Russian
and American Novellas:
A Cross-Cultural Triptych

> Oh, this was a day of reckoning. . . . a day . . . he would take a good close look
> at the truth.
>
> Something very big. Truth, like.
>
> *Seize the Day*

In Saul Bellow's novella, *Seize the Day,* Tommy Wilhelm, a preposterously superfluous, suffering man, articulates a belief in truth that postmodern literary and
cultural critics generally disavow. Wilhelm conceives of truth as a vaguely reified
"Something" – an object of size, located in space, and accessible to the human
gaze. Throughout his fateful day of reckoning, Wilhelm hotly pursues this oxymoronic reification, following small and seemingly foolish signs, like a man's hat
bobbing up in a crowd, until at last he discovers the ultimate reality he has been
seeking – truth simultaneously embodied and disembodied by death. This ambiguous representation affects Wilhelm profoundly, consummating "his heart's
ultimate need" but sundering his physical being. His vulnerable creaturely body
convulses and seems to come apart, its disjunct segments independently bending,
bowing, twisting, shaking, crippling, swelling, nodding, being clutched.[1] These
bodily contortions apparently signify Wilhelm's deliverance from this world to
another, a higher, freer, world of "happy oblivion" where he can forget his
earthly troubles. In the novella's final tableau, an ecstatically sobbing Wilhelm
enters this transcendent realm in his own perverse way: instead of rising to its
heights, he sinks. Thus, he completes the drowning action with which the
novella begins by losing – and finding – himself in an undefinable depths. There,
murkily, mortality evokes self-love as the essence of truth.

This hyperventilated denouement, comic in its outrageous excess of rhetoric
and emotion, reveals a contentious aspect of Wilhelm's truth: its power to trans-
port an ordinary mundane person – ordinary even if, like Wilhelm, ludicrous –
out of historical time and place, the situating circumstances that contextualize
cultural criticism. Cultural criticism, however conceived or practiced, is ir-

refragably circumstantial. Though it may vary among disciplines, invariably it locates its (human) subjects within a particularized site – geographic, historic, social, or artifactual – and then contextualizes them within a culture. More precisely, the culture itself is the densely circumstantial context within which human activities and their products are to be described.[2] *Described* may be misleading, since it suggests an account of existent social realities which, like Wilhelm's reified truth, are waiting to be discovered. In postmodern critiques, *description* usually melds into *interpretation* or *construction*.[3] All three terms are antithetical to truth as transcendent and, thus, as ahistorical or uncircumstanced. All three are linked by their inseparability from the language by which they are constituted. Unlike truth, descriptions, interpretations, and social constructions cannot be ineffable; they must have utterance in words.[4] Hence the centrality given to language and writing in postmodern cultural theories, specifically, in the discipline focused directly upon culture: descriptive anthropology or ethnography. Having become self-reflective about what they do, ethnographers now declare that they write: "The ethnographer 'inscribes' social discourse; *he writes it down*" (original emphasis).[5] Appropriating from literary critics the term *text* as the polysemous product of writing, ethnographers emphasize the textuality of both the object and product of their activity, of the cultural forms they study and their written accounts of these forms. They subject both texts to interpretation, since they view one as inscribed with social meanings the other explicates. This conceptualization of culture as "semiotic" and "interpretive," an artifact of discourse, valorizes meaning or, rather, a plurality of possible meanings.[6] Thus the purposes of postmodern literary critics and anthropologists coincide as both engage with texts in order to construe meanings rather than discover truth.

I begin with truth because its elision on theoretical grounds from the practice of cross-cultural literary criticism raises for me an intractable question of purpose: Why should one pursue the involuted process of reading a literary text within the context of a cultural critique that is also a text, an artifact of language, since neither text nor context can offer more than words?[7] The question affirms, rather than impugns, the primacy of language by seeking its relationship to knowledge and to social action. These relationships assume particular urgency in criticism of fiction valued for its representation of a real world embedded in circumstances that are knowable and presumed to contain or constitute historical truth. This essay discusses six such novellas, American and Russian, each in its own way claiming to be true – that is, to represent accurately the historical circumstances of its time and place – and all critically acclaimed for this representation. Moreover, all thematize a quest for truth as their characters seek to distinguish truth from the false appearances, deceptions, and lies they see as all-surrounding. If Bellow's Wilhelm is not the most admirable character among those seekers, he is the most dogged and desperate in his pursuit, and in this respect, the most exemplary. He is also the most "visionary," willing to project himself "past words, past reason, coherence" (p. 117) to attain a preternatural glimpse of ultimate being, stripped, stark, and undistractable. Other characters, as we shall see, seek truth within the distractions of daily events, culling it from the minutiae of their personal lives or from the public and political revelations of the daily newspapers. My purpose is not to contrast a fictional character's belief with the skepticism of critics or real people, an opposition made pointless, I would think, by ontological difference. Rather, I wish to locate certain problems in literary cross-cultural criticism and explore the possibilities of practice within the multifaceted form of a triptych. At the end of this essay, I discuss what I have found these possibilities to be and I make an attempt to weigh their value for cross-cultural criticism.

Despite the skepticism of postmodern theorists, notable contemporary writers and their critics have evinced a belief in truth and claim it can be found in fiction. Recent Soviet Russian fictions, in particular, have been considered astounding instances of truth in fiction – astounding because writers like Alexander Solzhenitsyn and Lydia Chukovskaya dared tell of terrors made commonplace in Stalin's time, because their accounts were published or promised publication in Soviet Russia (if subsequently repressed or long delayed), and because they and their work have survived. Critics who believe that words create rather than refer to a world may find themselves unsettled by Solzhenitsyn's *One Day in the Life of Ivan Denisovich* or Chukovskaya's *Sofia Petrovna,* or any literary text richly invested with documentary value. If they ignore the autobiographical and historical matrix of fiction insistent upon its factualness, they politicize criticism by their very indifference, though they may argue that they are (in their view, properly) depoliticizing literature. Realistic literature weighted with the authority of actual experience seems to me to place postmodern literary theories, particularly cross-cultural criticism, upon tenuous grounds no matter how it resolves the issue of truth – whether, in the abstract, it assumes or it denies its existence, and whether, in practice, it considers Solzhenitsyn's novella a true account of Soviet prison life or a text to be interpreted rather than believed.

Having described a shaky ground, I am going to set upon it only lightweight objects – some hats, some newspapers, a hook from a lady's belt. These have been taken from the six novellas whose truth I shall not preemptively deny though I pursue their meanings. I propose to "take a good close look" (Wilhelm's phrase) at small, ordinary things in order to discern their verbal and thematic designs – literary purposes and patterns that may adumbrate cultural patterns. A close reading that concentrates upon small "inspectable" details conflates cultural and literary interpretive modes, that of "thick description" with formal analysis. Both methodologies involve an examination of "microscopic" or "miniature" elements as clues to a grand signifying design.[8] Paradoxically, both reinstate truth while denying its apprehensibility, if not its essence. For, "thick description" proceeds from "local truths to general visions" of a "cultural landscape" (p. 21), while formal literary analysis discovers "fictional truth" within a text's tautological verbal patterns.[9] Concentrating upon minute indices, a gesture or a word, neither approach seems to share Wilhelm's assumption that truth is to be sought in "something very big." Nevertheless, both methods involve the critic in processes of detailed reckonings similar to those that occupy Wilhelm throughout his fateful day.

Reckoning, the versatile signifier for counting, calculating, figuring, drawing up or settling accounts, for estimating, dealing with, or judging, evokes an eschatological vision in *Seize the Day*. The Day of Reckoning, as Wilhelm designates the time spanned in the novella, is the day of final judgment in which revelation of truth would, presumably, coincide with the end of the world. The constant acts of reckoning in which Wilhelm engages as he figures his monetary value on New York's commodities market prefigure an ultimate accounting of human and moral values. Thus, the end of the novella, like the end of the world, attempts a grand summing up, a final accounting in which, unaccountably, the platitudes of everyday life become synonymous with truth. *One Day in the Life of Ivan Denisovich* also ends by converting the ordinary into the visionary as it conflates a simple arithmetical calculation with a final reckoning. Both novellas imply that its day is emblematic of all days, and in this respect, the minutiae of daily life, which constitute the realistic content of the fictional accounts, create and represent a context that is at once social, political, historical, cultural, and, as judgment ensues, moral. What precisely characters count, besides money, a conspicuous item, offers insights into the multifarious levels of reckonings in which they and the text are involved, and which will involve the critic who must take these reckonings into account.[10] Money is, of course, a traditional and universal symbol of exchange useful for cross-cultural comparison, but it is, perhaps, too weighty a matter for this essay. I move on to lighter items that figure in the novels' verbal and cultural semiotic systems – to hats, newspapers, and hooks.

Hats: Solzhenitsyn and Bellow

> when a man is wearing a hat . . . it is harder to find out how he feels
>
> *Seize the Day*

> he . . . put his hat on (with his number on a patch of cloth at the front)
>
> *One Day in the Life of Ivan Denisovich*

To compare *One Day in the Life of Ivan Denisovich* by Alexander Solzhenitsyn with Saul Bellow's *Seize the Day* is to contemplate extremes – characters *in extremis* trying to survive within cultural settings that represent the extremities within – and extreme differences between – the Soviet state under Stalin and

American urban society. As individuals, Solzhenitsyn's Ivan Denisovich Shukov and Bellow's Tommy Wilhelm could hardly be more antithetical: a Russian peasant imprisoned in a forced labor camp, and an unemployed salesman, formerly a Hollywood extra, on the loose in the streets of New York. But, as we shall see, with the passing hours of their day, distinctions between these antipodal characters begin to blur. Bellow's Wilhelm, a free man, feels imprisoned by bourgeois society and seeks freedom as obsessively, and foolishly, as he does easy money. Solzhenitsyn's Shukov, the prisoner, achieves a form of freedom through means that may inspire admiration for his person but troubling questions about his political efficacy. If, as critics have argued, these contrasting characters, each in his own way, prevail against their constrictive circumstances – their real or symbolic imprisonments – they do so by acts of transcendence. Such acts imply that culture itself is a context from which, paradoxically, even the imprisoned can be freed.

As a literary form, the novella has advantages for both the critic and the writer concerned with cultural contexts, however described or construed. It gives greater visibility than the novel to the miniature details that allow for cultural "thick description," and greater scope than the short story for creating a social matrix out of its details. For the writer it may serve as "an initial exploration of a reality in the search of the great forms appropriate to it" – a description accorded Solzhenitsyn's novella and applicable to *Seize the Day*.[11] The compressed form of the novella intensifies the struggle for freedom that Bellow and Solzhenitsyn were to make a noetic theme of their novels. Both tightened the form by restricting the time of their stories to a single day. Each follows an ordinary man through the course of this day, beginning with morning and ending at night with a final reckoning – the character's attempt to sum up an entire way of life that constitutes the culture within which he has been shaped and judged and upon which he delivers judgment.[12] Though individualized by idiosyncrasies – a lisp caused by toothlessness, for example, or a shuffle – both Shukov and Wilhelm conform to cultural stereotypes as Soviet worker-prisoner and footloose American. Distanced from these characters, Bellow and Solzhenitsyn enter their consciousness through an indirect discourse that reproduces the speech heard in American city streets and Soviet prison camps. Each colloquial style is aesthetically calibrated to produce distinctive effects and tonalities. The febrilely excited tone of *Seize the Day* reaches a pitch of exasperation as its protagonist falls into comically perverse misadventures. Even the novella's title – *Seize the Day* – evocative of lyrical love poetry, becomes frenetic as Wilhelm applies it to himself as an importunate lover falling in love with himself as the fated victim of time. In contrast, the prose of *One Day in the Life of Ivan Denisovich* seems low-keyed and understated, often ploddingly explanatory. The ordinariness of its language makes its extraordinary horrors seem matter-of-fact, as though their deep entrenchment in Soviet life has become a commonplace. At the same time, the novella's language strategically contains and conceals a daring counterpoint be-

tween blunt prison jargon and subtle (and seriously censurable) religious overtones.[13] Both texts include many and varied forms of reckoning, but neither is
unambivalent in its attempted final judgment of the society it depicts; nor is its
depiction, whether of the Soviet state or American capitalistic society, unambiguous. Both have been praised, not unequivocally, for their moral incisiveness
and for prefiguring the writers' long and extraordinary careers. As we know,
these careers were honored when, within a few years of each other, both Bellow and Solzhenitsyn received the Nobel Prize for literature.

Strange as it may seem, hats figure immediately in the two texts of this panel as
they enter into the reckonings of the main characters. I begin with *Seize the Day*
since Tommy Wilhelm unmistakably places significance upon hats, though he
is mistaken (as usual) in the significance he sees. His initial belief in the efficacy
of his hat is patently nonsensical, indicative of a train of thoughts he pursues in
a quest for money that is incongruously intermixed with a quest for truth. Wilhelm's day begins with his attempt to hide his money troubles with a hat: "When
a man is wearing a hat," he tells himself, "it is harder to find out how he feels"
(p. 3). This remark introduces an inner discourse that follows Wilhelm's zigzagging thoughts through qualifications and erasures that correct his usual lies. "He
had once been an actor," he thinks and then adds, "no, not quite, an extra" (p.
3). This is the first of many revisions in which one word replaces another to
change the tenor of a statement. To say he hopes, rather than believes, admits
uncertainties usually denied, among them doubts about his appearance. As a former actor (if only an extra), a former salesman – and a former husband, lover,
and dog owner – Wilhelm is now a man besieged by troubles, a failure who is
necessarily "worried about his appearance": "he believed – he hoped – that he
looked passably well" (p. 3).[14] In the commercial atmosphere of New York, Wilhelm knows that he must appear to be a success if he is to survive his failures.
Seize the Day begins, thus, with a discrepancy between appearance and reality,
a universal literary theme that American urban novels, in particular, develop
through a character's fixation upon clothes. The anonymity of city life gives
clothes significance as the sign of social worth that can be immediately identified and subjected to reckoning. In the streets of *Seize the Day,* as in the Siber-
ian cold of *One Day in the Life of Ivan Denisovich,* clothes are vital to sustain life;
they are – or seem – indispensable to Wilhelm's survival in the commodities
market where he makes a living selling while he is, in turn, being sold. But like
all appearances, that presented by clothes may be deceptive, as Wilhelm discovers through his ludicrous relationship with "a gray straw hat with a wide cocoa-
colored band" (p. 57) that makes an independent odyssey through the city
streets, stopping along the way at a men's toilet.

This hat belongs to the elusive Dr. Tamkin, an advisor on financial, psychological, and spiritual matters – and a "confuser of the imagination" (not unlike

Bellow). Undoubtedly a charlatan, he may also be the savior who will rescue the sinking Wilhelm from a sea of troubles. Bellow seems to be reenacting Dr. Tamkin's con game with a hat that now you see and now you don't. When Wilhelm first sees the gaudy hat, he does not see Tamkin, though they are face to face. Later, he equates hat and man as he waits for the man outside a toilet door above which he sees a "a gray straw hat with a cocoa-colored band" (p. 105). But when "the hat was taken down" and the door opened, "a stranger came out who looked at him with annoyance" (p. 105). This comic-strip moment typifies the mistakes Wilhelm will make during the day by confusing arbitrary social signs with realities to which they do not refer. Confusion inheres in a world where everything is distorted or transmogrified – the Hotel Ansonia, an American landmark, looking like a huge Hungarian palace, or "like marble or like sea water . . . [or] like the image of itself" (p. 5). Thus, when Tamkin is conjured out of the city crowd like "a benevolent magician," Wilhelm marvels at his strangeness: "What a creature Tamkin was when he took off his hat" (p. 62). Seen without his hat and from Wilhelm's muddled view, Tamkin is a baffling artifact – part animal, part human, part thing, and part impossibility: he has a "gull's nose," "eyes brown as beaver fur and full of strange lines," "peculiarly formed bones" shaping his shoulders into "two pagoda-like points," and weirdly loose and clawlike fingernails (p. 62). Wilhelm studies these bizarre features to discover Tamkin's character, which may be revealed, if one can believe it, by Tamkin's pigeon-toed stance, "a sign perhaps that he was devious or had much to hide" (p. 62).

Wilhelm's account of the man he entrusted with his last cent leads to soul-searching as well as quixotic questions: "was Dr. Tamkin honest?"; was his heavy red underlip "possibly foolish" (pp. 62–63)? Always of "two minds," Wilhelm ends with equivocation – honest and a crook. He listens to Tamkin's tales of miraculous cures and pronounces them "Sensational, but . . . dull . . . Funny but unfunny. True but false" (p. 66). He laughs at Tamkin's contraptions but defends Tamkin as an "inventor" and true American: "Everybody wants to make something. Any American does" (p. 41). Among the inventions (if indeed they exist) is a hat for truck drivers who drive by night, so devised that its electrical apparatus will awaken the wearer with a shock when he begins to drowse (p. 41). Ridiculous – and yet possibly practical and paving a way to fortune.

Wilhelm's inconclusive reckonings end in reversals of past views, reversals subject to future reversal. He realizes, for example, that "Tamkin was on my back, and I thought I was on his" (p. 104); and that his father, rather than he, "is the salesman. He's selling me" (p. 13). Both reversals define Wilhelm as a victim fleeced in New York's commodities market, where he is an investor and an investment. He has invested the last of his savings in partnership with Dr. Tamkin, his surrogate father, while to his real father, Dr. Adler, he has been an investment that has failed. Within a culture that figures value by profit or loss, he has been measured by a materialistic yardstick and reckoned worthless. Accordingly, both fathers abandon him, and he is left with only a flashy hat to lead him to "the consummation of his heart's ultimate need" (p. 118).

After Tamkin disappears along with Wilhelm's money (invested in lard, a suitably incongruous choice for the novella's muddled Jew), Wilhelm follows what he takes to be Tamkin's straw hat on its bobbing path through Manhattan's streets until he loses it in a funeral parlor. In the presence of death, the concealing hats of deceivers like Wilhelm and Tamkin give way to "dark homburgs." Each homburg is indistinguishable from the other, as is the ineluctable end that awaits each human being. As a cliché might put it, in the end all wear the same hat. This is a realization that the residents of the phantasmagoric Hotel Gloriana, where Wilhelm's day begins, have deliberately tried to ignore. Not only proud Dr. Adler, who refuses to be reminded of death, but all the elderly residents of the hotel, painted old women and damaged dapper men, will face the eviction that Wilhelm experiences as actual and symbolic. His notice that he must leave the hotel, having failed (among other failures) to pay his rent seems to him a fateful sign of permanent future dispossession. Stripped of every social appurtenance – reduced to "bare unaccommodated man" – Wilhelm confronts himself in the stranger lying in the coffin, a "sunken" figure who calls to mind the drowned Lycidas. Remembering that Lycidas was raised from his watery grave "through the dear might of him that walk'd the waves," Wilhelm imagines his own resurrection in the form of financial recovery. Throughout the day, the hope that "recovery was possible" had kept him afloat in a sea of sorrows. The same hope sustains the gambler through his losses, the investor in a falling stock market, the down-and-outer who will not relinquish a belief in possibilities, the quintessentially American dream of rising in the world. Wilhelm believed – or rather, he hoped – that, like Lycidas, he could rise from his watery grave by recovering his money and position. Instead, unaccountably, he recovers long-lost remnants from his college days as "involuntary memory" brings to mind some lines of poetry and a hat – Wilhelm's college "beanie." Worn with a raccoon coat, the beanie represented a role that Wilhelm thought he could appropriate as a socially acceptable identity. If in the way of his world, clothes made the man, then the beanie typified him as a college student. But Wilhelm discarded this role as thoughtlessly as the hat, quit school, and headed for Hollywood, where role playing (changing hats) is a consummate art. As with all his conscious decisions, his departure had been a mistake, made possible only because he had once been valued for his "striking looks." Now, years later, he remembers the beanie and some desultory lines of poetry from Shakespeare, Milton, and Keats, quotations that arrest and coalesce the disparate motifs roiling in his mind: sorrow, death, and love. Unabashedly, Wilhelm identifies his lumbering self with the sad lady of Keats's "Endymion," with Milton's Lycidas, and with the lover of Shakespeare's sonnet. In the funeral parlor, he surrenders to sorrow, confronts his mortality, and, before a crowd of strangers, calls forth love within and for himself as one who must "love that well, which [he] must leave ere long."

After a day of reckoning in which Wilhelm re-counts his losses, he finds he can count only upon his feckless and mistaken self. He has no one else and nothing, a man completely wiped out – no cash, no credit, no home, no family, no friends, no hope of help or rescue. Though he possessed innate charm, he has stubbornly refused to make himself socially acceptable by meeting the standards of American middle-class success. He has alienated his father, who (understandably) "wants a young, smart, successful son" (p. 45). He has alienated his wife, leaving her because marriage was "choking" him to death, only to remain a "slave" begging for the freedom of divorce she refuses to give. He has lost the woman he loves. He has even lost his dog. He had wanted to find "a way out" of "the world's business," a phrase he reiterates to suggest a cultural setting in which all critical questions are compressed into two interrogatives: "Buy? Sell?" (p. 87). In effect, Wilhelm sought to change the currency of his bourgeois society from money to free-flowing love – a mystically appealing alternative that would reinstate him as a valuable human being even though he has, and does, nothing. A dream of unconditional love seems to him responsive to the human condition as it has been defined by time. Wilhelm's way of reckoning time is that of the lyric poet who urges love as a response to the transience of life, a motif evoked by the novella's title and sustained by its setting, a hotel where residence is temporary. Under the pressure of time as well as of the world's business, Wilhelm sees himself engaged in the essential effort of "trying to stay alive" (p. 99). He ends up, however, embracing as truth the platitude that, like the Hotel Gloriana's residents, all retired – no longer engaged in the business of life – "he's going to die too" (p. 53).

Death cancels the losses he has reckoned up during the day by equalizing, through an ironically democratic gesture, the rich and the poor, the successes and the failures, the winners and a loser like Wilhelm. At least, so Wilhelm concludes in a final visionary moment when he transcends his mundane troubles to contemplate ultimacy – the end and the purpose of human life. In keeping with his character, his vision is astoundingly muddled and appealing, evoking from a college dropout the classic tradition of English poetry and from a hapless Jew the hope of Christian redemption. To describe Wilhelm in his moment of truth is to laugh helplessly. For what rejoinder can one make to Wilhelm, a rebellious bungler who bungles into the consummate American role as rebel? In stripping himself of material possessions, Wilhelm acts out his rebellion against the values of American capitalistic society. His "mistakes" have all been studied and purposeful: to repudiate success as socially defined and demand a recognition that makes failure irrelevant. A creature of his culture, Wilhelm tries, as do other Bellow protagonists, to project himself beyond a culturally circumstanced situation into a moral realm where final judgments are uninfluenced by historical contingencies. In his historical time and place, Wilhelm is judged by other characters, and by his readers, as a colossal and culpable failure. When he sees himself as others see him, Wilhelm concurs in this judgment. "Ass! Idiot! Wild boar! Dumb mule! Slave! Lousy, wallowing hippopotamus!," he calls himself, obliging his exasperated readers (p. 55). At the same time, by willing himself to failure, Wilhelm raises questions that have become increasingly urgent in contemporary American society: What is the worth of a man who has no money and no home? How is he to be judged? As for himself, Wilhelm had already decided that "there was no figure or estimate for the value of this load" (p. 39). In a bathetic conclusion, Wilhelm desists from judgment and falls back upon compassion as he evokes love for all humankind, including its fools. The conclusion is outlandish, comic, defiant, and bafflingly ambiguous, traits characteristic of Bellow's fiction. Whether they are representative American traits one may wonder but, I think, forbear from asserting. One can say, however, that as a grand failure who has just lost his hat in the commodities market, Wilhelm reenacts a historically originating role of the American as rebel. If his cause is elusive, it is because Tommy Wilhelm is, as he says, a "visionary creature," seeking a glimpse of a truth that, contrary to his belief, cannot be reified.

As both fool and poet, lowman and everyman, Bellow's Tommy Wilhelm has a long literary lineage, too intricate to trace here.[15] To say that Wilhelm is a traditional wise fool, however, would be to grant *Seize the Day* a thematic closure that it denies by sharing its character's indecisiveness. Like Wilhelm, a man "divided in his mind," the novella does not choose between the alternatives it creates. Moreover, while its rhetorical strategy is to qualify assertions by *but* or *and yet,* it countermands its own exceptions by a recurrent and recuperative *and* that connects opposites. Its inconclusive conclusion is "True *and* false" – truth contaminated by irradicable lies, humankind a mixed bag of spiritual aspiration *and* an inescapable creatureliness called to mind by animal allusions. A cultural critique of *Seize the Day* seems to me to require backtracking and qualification, so that it, too, would be littered with phrases like *and yet* – two words that can introduce Ivan Denisovich Shukov, the protagonist of the second novella in this panel, Alexander Solzhenitsyn's *One Day in the Life of Ivan Denisovich.*
    As a Soviet prisoner, Shukov is compliant, bending as he must to the rigid schedule of his day, *and yet,* as the day proceeds he appears self-determined, a man who achieves dignity and independence by exercising the freedom he has created for himself by a continuous process of reckoning. Reckoning is crucial to Shukov's survival and to the moral accountings made by the novella in which Shukov figures as a person who counts, in the various senses of the word, and a person being counted. Again and again, Shukov will stand in line before guards who count and re-count the prisoners shivering before them in the cold. Shukov will join in this counting because his well-being depends upon the number of prisoners lined up ahead to rush into the dining room or sleeping quarter, places

where life can be temporarily sustained. Every minute of warmth counts toward survival; every bowl of food counts, and Shukov counts the bowls, the food trays, the number of prisoners still at the dining table, each reckoning of portentous significance. Numbers constitute much of the novella's text, which sometimes becomes a succession of numbers or of numerical calculations introduced by such verbs as *reckoned, figured, calculated, counted,* and *re-counted.* As the guards relentlessly count and re-count the prisoners – "They'd counted 462. Ought to be 463" – so do the prisoners: "They turned and stood on tiptoe to see whether there were two men or three in the back row. It was a matter of life or death to them now."[16] An elaborate and explicit counting of bowls that continues for pages would seem almost farcical if it, too, were not a matter of life and death (pp. 77–80).[17] Shukov will end his day, as he spent it, in calculation. Last seen, he is re-counting his "many strokes of luck" in a brief synoptic review of the day that has just become the past. Then, Shukov counts the days ahead in the future: "Three thousand six hundred and fifty-three days . . . three extra days" – the time still to be served in his prison sentence (p. 158).

As this precise reckoning indicates, Shukov calculates carefully. Unlike Wilhelm, who is convinced that "the making of mistakes expressed the very purpose of his life" (p. 56), "Shukov made no mistakes" (p. 95). An inviolate moral code determines his choices, and strange as it may seem (to repeat the phrase that introduced Wilhelm's hat), Shukov's prison cap reifies his code. Indeed, to follow his cap through the text is to define Shukov's moral "nature," an innate quality that, presumably, circumstance cannot alter: "eight years in a camp couldn't change his nature" (p. 105). His nature leads Shukov to resist the pressures placed upon him by time and place as adamantly as Wilhelm, as deviously, but much more adeptly. The extremity of Shukov's circumstances calls for consummate skill, since for him the ultimate consequence of mismanagement is death, not a symbolic death like Wilhelm's metaphoric drowning, but an actual end to his life. Wilhelm can bungle through his day, equivocate, and survive, at least temporarily. Shukov survives, temporarily, through decisiveness and managerial enterprise: "Shukov knew how to manage anything" (p. 18). Even in prison, Shukov manages to make money by doing "private jobs" (p. 139). He is constantly engaged in business, bartering and buying, carrying out transactions that promise a personal profit. How, one might wonder, has Shukov developed managerial skills that the feckless Wilhelm, living an entrepreneurial world, has either never learned or never learned to value? How has he acquired the practical knowledge (the pragmatism commonly attributed to Americans) with which he can manage to sustain himself and his moral integrity? Perhaps Shukov's enterprise represents "the practical guile native to the Russian peasant," a claim that would support Shukov's own intuitions about national characteristics.[18] Figuring ways to make money, however, can hardly be singled out as a trait that particularizes the Russian peasant. I would suggest that Shukov's hat, inscribed with an identifying number, S 854, may provide a clue to his character as at once singular and representative – to Shukov as an individual as well as a cipher in a system, a person as well as Soviet peasant and prisoner.

Shukov himself pays close attention to a "new regulation" concerning prisoners' hats: "You had to take off your hat to a guard five paces before passing him, and replace it two paces after." Knowing that "prisoners had been thrown into the guardhouse because of that hat business," Shukov avoids punishment by avoiding the guards (p. 30). "Smart" or canny by "nature," he is also deliberately calculating, seizing opportunities when they appear and making them serve his own purposes. His ultimate purpose is, like Wilhelm's, to survive, but to survive with dignity. Unlike Wilhelm, he resists self-pity and self-abasement. He contrasts himself with "that jackal" Fetiukov, whose wheedling (not entirely unlike Wilhelm's) he detests: "he would never lower himself like that Fetiukov" (p. 40). *That* Fetiukov" represents what Shukov does not want to become, while other prisoners show him how to maintain a moral identity – how to choose to be free though imprisoned. Since prison obviously limits the individual's freedom to choose, Shukov can make decisions only over seemingly infinitesimal matters which, in the course of the day, become weighted with moral import. Thus, Shukov's decision to wear or not to wear a hat reflects his moral code: "however cold it might be, he could never bring himself to eat with his hat on" (p. 28). Men he admires, like his squadron leader Tiurin, observe the same decorum, as Shukov notes: "He too hadn't learned to eat with his hat on" (p 86). Like Tiurin, Shukov will suffer discomfort for the sake of a decorum that he pragmatically equates with survival. This equation is personified by the old *zek*, a famous character almost always cited by critics, who has survived successive prison sentences with dignity. Shukov takes a *close look* at the old man (as though he is being granted Wilhelm's "good close look at the truth"), and he sees what time can and cannot effect. The old *zek* has lost his hair and his teeth; his face has been drained of life, *and yet* he has managed to retain his will: "he wasn't going to give in" (p. 138).[19] Nor was Shukov. On the contrary, "the longer he spent at the camp the stronger he made himself" (p. 142).

Under dire Soviet conditions, Shukov defines himself in American terms as a self-made man – *and yet,* he acknowledges his dependency upon others: his squad leader, his fellow prisoners in the 104th squadron, his co-workers. His first squad leader, Kuziomin, had taught him that "even here people manage to live" (p. 18).[20] Managing for Shukov means following rules other than, if in addition to, those of the prison guards. Among Shukov's self-made rules is unquestioning obedience to his squad leader Tiurin, a character, like the old *zek,* who is seasoned, strong, and admirable. Epitomized in the text as "a true son of the GULAG," Tiurin is a "father" to Shukov and his squadron, a man upon whom they depend for their survival. Supported by a surrogate father, son, and brothers, members of his squadron, Shukov is sustained by a close family life denied to Wilhelm. Joining his fellow prisoners for a few blissful moments of warmth and leisure, Shukov feels himself within his family: "The shop was quiet. Zeks who had tobacco were smoking. The light was dim, and the men sat gazing into the fire. Like a big family. It was a family, the squad" (p. 86). In this family Shukov finds a young prisoner, Gopchik, to replace the son he lost years ago. Shukov appreciates the "cunning" that the "puppy" Gopchik has already learned, while, on his part, Gopchik admires and wants to learn from the older, seasoned zek. The bond the two men form as surrogate father and son affirms the irrefrangible structure of the Soviet family, which can survive separation of its members and reconstitute itself regardless of circumstances. In effect, Shukov has the family protection and support for which Wilhelm pleaded in Seize the Day, only to discover that time itself, as well as personal incompatibility, had broken the link between generations.[21] Wilhelm describes his father as "a stranger" (p. 93), while Dr. Adler denies his son by saying, "I come from a different world" (p. 49). Seize the Day implies that emotional ties cannot hold the American family together once it has lost its economic function in a capitalistic society, a view sustained in longer novels, like Mr. Sammler's Planet, which also portray the alienation between self-made fathers, who had worked hard to make money, and their feckless children.

Shukov can produce the "hard work" to which Dr. Adler in Seize the Day attributes his all-American success. As a respected, even happy, worker, as well as a family man (wife and daughters apparently nonessential to the construction of his family), Shukov represents an ideal Soviet citizen. He knows his craft, and he is crafty about when to exert himself and when to fake his motions. In the course of the day, he shows others how to plaster efficiently and how properly to cut a piece of roof felting. In his work, as in his survival skills, he is exemplary, a model prisoners from whom others, like the young Gopchik, can learn. A single sentence, given emphasis as a separate paragraph, defines his role as teacher: "He showed them how to do it" (p. 67).[22] Shukov shows fellow prisoners and he shows the reader. In effect, Solzhenitsyn has written a how-to book, an instruction manual on how to succeed that contrasts with Bellow's manual on how to fail. One Day in the Life of Ivan Denisovich often addresses the reader directly, evoking a "you" to whom it offers instructions, explanations, and, occasionally, emphatic asides: "You'd make jokes if you were in his shoes" (p. 61, original emphasis). Shukov's knowledge is practical and can be learned; it tells "you" how to live, concentrating upon means. Wilhelm's knowledge is eschatological, to be intuited rather than learned; it focuses upon the mysterious nexus between love and death in order to apprehend the end of being.[23] In the final scene of Seize the Day, Wilhelm's mawkish weeping over his own mortality may satisfy his heart's desire for love, but like his troubles, the world about him remains the same – a world in which, as he has said, "money makes the difference" (p. 55). At the end of One Day in the Life of Ivan Denisovich, Shukov has his dignity, but he still faces an interminable prison sentence. Time will effect no change in his world, as static in its own way as Wilhelm's moiling city. For the prison camp represents Soviet society during the Stalin decades, and Shukov's day – ironically, "an almost happy day" – is exemplary of the days ahead of him and for the Russian people.[24]

"One word of truth shall outweigh the whole world" – the Russian proverb with which Solzhenitsyn concluded his Nobel Lecture summed up his exalted view of the writer in the modern world and of his own writing.[25] Solzhenitsyn ascribed to literature the power to prevail over violence, the rampant and officially rationalized violence of the Soviet state. This prevailing power inheres in the truth that the writer – only the writer, Solzhenitsyn said – representatively articulates: writers are the "articulators of the national tongue, . . . who] give expression to the national soul." "Who else but writers," Solzhenitsyn asked rhetorically, "shall condemn their incompetent rulers . . . who else shall censure their respective societies?" (p. 496). In *One Day in the Life of Ivan Denisovich,* the hero, a peasant and prisoner, believed that "there was little sense in writing. Writing now was like dropping stones in some deep, bottomless pool. they drop; they sink – but there is no answer" (p. 48). In time, Shukov gave up writing even the monthly letter home that he was allowed. Not writing, he completes his isolation from the world outside that will remain silent, as he expects, but that he silences because it cannot answer letters it does not receive. Shukov observes a privileged prisoner writing a poem, and he hears educated prisoners arguing over the art of the theater; but no character in the novella assumes the artistist's heroic role of articulating a truth that would reveal the violence of political oppression to the world at large.[26] None speaks out to "defeat the lie!" – the lie that, in his Nobel Lecture, Solzhenitsyn linked to violence as its inevitable accomplice. Critics have praised Shukov's "personal heroism" and "spiritual resistance" to physical violation; but though he is an exemplary Soviet prisoner who can show a generalized *you* how to survive in a prison camp, he has no voice that can be heard by those beyond his prison walls. He may be heroic as a person, but as a political force, he lacks the power, and the will, to destroy these walls.[27] He accepts the paternalism of a social system always ready to become, if it is not already, totalitarian. Solzhenitsyn's own political views have been scrutinized to see whether they conserve or challenge institutions through which the state, or any paternalistic power, maintains a hold upon its people.[28] "Must truth be reactionary?" – this question has been raised in specific response to Solzhenitsyn's Nobel Prize acceptance speech.[29] It evokes another question: If the writer, as Solzhenitsyn asserts, speaks the truth in defiance of lies, then who is to deliver final judgment upon the words spoken? A reckoning remains to be made, *and yet* the ascertainment of truth about a text – or a culture – seems to require indefinite deferral. Two hats – one meant to conceal and deceive, and the other to identify categorically (different categories to prison guard and to prisoner) – suggest various and divergent possibilities of interpretation and, consequently, of judgment. I propose to defer judgment by moving to the next panel, for its juxtaposition expands the possibilities of interpretation. Set against the novellas of the first panel, those of the second provide an unforeseen perspective upon the acts of transcendence by which Shukov and Wilhelm survive, rather than impinge upon or transform, the circumstances that have defined their day.

Newspapers: Chukovskaya and Le Sueur

The newspapers filled her with a vague terror

Sofia Petrovna

she would . . . tell them not to believe what was in the papers

The Girl

The similarities notable in the publishing histories of Lydia Chukovskaya's novella *Sofia Petrovna* and Meridel Le Sueur's *The Girl* – both written in 1939, both considered at the time unsuitable for publication, both published decades later – may be coincidental, a matter of chance. If so, they are interesting merely to note. On the other hand, they may be significant to a cross-cultural consideration if they reflect an underlying similarity in the conception of both novellas – in their origins and in the ideas by which they are informed. Both Chukovskaya and Le Sueur trace their texts to an originative desire to tell the "true history" of their times and to a view of writing as an act of "telling" or indictment.[30] In their novellas they both juxtapose the truth of fiction to the lies, distortions, and deceptive omissions of newspapers whose accounts of contemporary events they include. Both describe newspapers manipulating the public mind and participating in a studied subversion of their countries' ideals: the ideal of a socialistic state and of a democracy. In *Sofia Petrovna*, newspapers represent the state, and in *The Girl*, sinister class interests, but this difference is offset by their similarity "as powerful forces of falsehood" ("Author's note," *Sofia Petrovna*, p. 2). Complaints about mass media mystification are familiar, even trite; nevertheless, they reinforce the novellas' thematic concern with political repression and their demand for resistance and dissent. In making a polemic call for dissent – emotional and explicit in *The Girl* and implied in *Sofia Petrovna* – both writers faced potentially dire consequences: imprisonment, exile, or death for Chukovskaya, writing in opposition to Stalin at the time of the Great Purges; and, less extreme but nonetheless painful, a gradual silencing for Le Sueur, writing at the time of America's Great Depression. Indeed, the rejection of her manuscript in 1939 foreshadowed for Le Sueur a period of silencing as she was blacklisted for being a member of the Communist Party and a radical writer. Nevertheless, she continued to write, though her manuscripts, like those of many Soviet dissidents, remained sequestered and unseen.[31]

Chukovskaya's manuscript, dangerously self-incriminating, was from its inception destined to be hidden. The friends who saved the manuscript,

Chukovskaya later wrote, "perished" in the siege of Leningrad (now once again St. Petersburg), while her little exercise book "miraculously" survived. During the "thaw," when Khrushchev himself officially approved the publication of Solzhenitsyn's *One Day in the Life of Ivan Denisovich,* Chukovskaya almost succeeded in having *Sofia Petrovna* published, but "new party decisions" reinstituted a suppression of "ideologically inadequate" novels.[32] Chukovskaya's extraordinary legal suit for payment for her unpublished manuscript elicited charges that both she and Solzhenitsyn had distorted the past in their writings. To Chukovskaya, this was a bizarre obversion in which state officials accused her of their own impugnable acts. Writing about a society that she said was "poisoned by lies," Chukovskaya insisted upon the truth of her novella and upon her role as historic "witness" to the persecutions of her times – to the arrests and imprisonment of loyal Soviet citizens, among them Solzhenitsyn, her own husband, who died in an arctic prison camp, and the son of the famous Russian poet Anna Akhmatova, upon whose fate she based the story of *Sofia Petrovna*'s son Kolya.[33] Like Le Sueur, who wanted to bear testimony to the lives of America's forgotten men and women, Chukovskaya wanted to keep alive the memory of the countless women who had stood in endless lines seeking word of their vanished loved ones, anonymous women, as well as women whose well-known names, like Akhmatova's, could be officially expunged from historical memory. For Akhmatova, being remembered had meant immortality as an artist.[34] "Only let my memory last, /Only don't take away my memory," Akhmatova wrote early in her career, pleading for her preservation as a poet. Echoing these words in another time and place, the American writer Le Sueur transformed the plea into a desperate political outcry. "Memory is all we got," Le Sueur has her nameless Girl cry out in protest against history's deletions; "we got to remember. We got to remember everything" (p. 142). Le Sueur called her book a "memorial" to the "heroic women of the depression" whose "struggle to be alive and human" survived in the stories told to each other and retold by Le Sueur in *The Girl.*[35] Chukovskaya also exulted in the publication of her long-repressed novella. She called *Sofia Petrovna* her "beloved book" because it had managed to survive the terrible historic moment it memorialized: "To this day (1974)," she wrote, "I know of no volume of prose about 1937 written in *this* country and at *that* time."[36]

The seemingly self-congratulatory afterwords of both writers testify to a struggle for artistic expression in societies that seem antithetical: a democratic society in which freedom of speech is a constitutional right and a totalitarian society in which repression and censorship were normative. Despite irreconcilable differences in the cultural contexts of the novellas – in the conditions under which they were produced and the cultural settings they reproduce – their similar publishing histories might evoke a critique of both American and Soviet cultures as inherently the same in their repressiveness. If a collapse of difference into sameness is one possible outcome of comparison, another is reaffirmation of difference – in this instance, differences between a flawed democracy that some-times abrogates the writer's freedom and a totalitarian state that always pre-scribes, censors, and punishes. While the significance of the novellas' parallel publishing histories may remain uncertain, a matter open to interpretation and dispute, their salient formal parallels can be traced, indisputably I would think, to genre. Both *Sofia Petrovna* and *The Girl* are stories of development.[37] Both de-fine a pattern of initiation in which a naive and innocent woman achieves ex-perience. Though Sofia Petrovna is mature, educated, and well-positioned, and the Girl young, unlettered, and underprivileged, both characters are initially ig-norant of the state, political and personal, in which they have been permitted to exist. That permission has tacitly been given by some inscrutable power becomes clear as the women's situations grow increasingly precarious. The Girl is grabbed by the police, assaulted, and incarcerated, though (as far as the authorities know) she is guilty only of being poor, unmarried, and pregnant. Her friend Clara is seized and subjected to electric shock treatments that kill her after having de-stroyed her memory – a technique of repression, the novella implies, that reveals a totalitarian aspect of the state. Like the Girl, Sofia Petrovna sees her friend Natasha ruined, ostensibly because she mistyped a single word, *Ret* for *Red,* though she is accused (wrongly) of having typed *Rat* as "an obvious act of class hostility." Clara's death impassions the Girl and rouses her to resist the forces si-lencing women. Natasha's suicide accelerates Sofia Petrovna's capitulation to fear. She is afraid she will be seized and imprisoned, like her innocent son, like the hundreds of ordinary people who have disappeared.[38]

This is a fate Sofia Petrovna could never have imagined even a few months ago when life brought her contentment as the mother of an exemplary son and as a respected Soviet worker. A senior typist in a Leningrad publishing house, she assigns documents to other typists in the work pool, a task that calls for con-stant and exact reckonings. In the course of a day, Sofia Petrovna "counts pages and lines" of manuscripts, distributes "accounts, plans, reports," and figures the number of minutes required for a typing task – "exactly twenty-five minutes, no sooner (p. 4). As collector of union dues at the office and apartment representa-tive at home, she makes additional calculations, submitted to her superiors in "impeccable accounts." Keeping account of words, time, and money, Sofia Petrovna establishes her value as a Soviet citizen; but with a sudden change in the object of her reckoning – in its purpose and substance – this value sharply declines and then disappears. Like Shukov, Sofia Petrovna precipitously be-comes a nonentity whose name is traded for a number. This loss of personal identity is entailed in a switch that requires Sofia Petrovna to count people rather than pages, though she still reckons up time with exactitude. "Five months, three weeks and four days, and five days, and six days . . . " (p. 62, original el-lipsis) – these figures describe a period of anxious waiting for word of her beloved son Kolya. Like countless other women, Sofia Petrovna has become a number in reckonings over which she has no control but into which she must enter as the mother of a son mysteriously arrested for crimes committed against the state. Like Shukov, she stands in line with multitudes of bereft and helpless people, waiting for a word from elusive state officials. Unlike these people, however, she refuses to acknowledge that she has become a member of a community of dispossessed people. She shuns other mothers standing on line with her because she believes their sons and husbands guilty of crimes against the state, while her Kolya is innocent. This belief both sustains and destroys her integrity, as does her now incessant counting. For as she counts the number of women in line before her, she maintains hope of reaching the bureaucrat who can give her news of her son and, perhaps, grant him freedom. But the constant need to count diminishes her sense of her self and demonstrates her helplessness. The more she counts, as time passes, the greater the sum of her losses.

Both *Sofia Petrovna* and *The Girl* trace a pattern of loss and attempted recovery. Because Sofia Petrovna has more than the Girl, she would have, arguably, more to lose. But the loss of an exemplary son cannot be reckoned against the loss of a feckless lover, nor the loss of status as senior typist against the loss of lowly job. Each novella judges its character's losses as immeasurable. In these reckonings, the novellas are similar; they differ in describing a pattern of recovery through which their dispossessed women try to get back what they have lost – not lost, actually, but had taken from them. In *The Girl,* women acquire language and engage in a collective act of writing that expresses their will to recover – to gather strength as a group and claim a place in society promised, ostensibly, to all Americans. As they set their demands on paper, they reenact Le Sueur's act of writing, and like her, they seek to place their words before the public. To be denied access to the public – or publication – is to be denied hope of recovery. Thus, almost uncannily, the theme of *The Girl* prefigures its publication history. In *Sofia Petrovna,* much of the action takes place in a Leningrad publishing house where Sofia Petrovna helps present the written word to the public. When she destroys what has been written, she expresses, as we shall see, the impossibility of recovering from the losses she has suffered, losses endemic to Soviet society. The characters in the two novellas inverse their relationship with the word as Sofia Petrovna loses the will to facilitate the flow of words, while the silent Girl becomes articulate and assertive. "Nobody can shut me up," she says in the final stage of her initiation to the ways of her world (p. 113). At this point, her pattern of development has diverged definitively from that of Sofia Petrovna, who becomes lost in an incapacitating silence the Girl has struggled to escape.

The rites of passage from innocence to experience, or ignorance to knowledge, cross rather than converge for the characters as the Girl embraces knowledge because she believes its truth is empowering, while Sofia Petrovna turns to lies because she fears the truth will be utterly destructive. The Girl develops hope, though her situation seems hopeless. Sofia Petrovna sinks into inanition, lying to herself and others as she tries to avoid the hopelessness of her plight.

Each is an emblematic character evoking meanings larger than her self. The nameless Girl becomes an eternal Kore, reenacting within depression America the mythic ritual of descent and resurrection of the raped Persephone. Sofia Petrovna stands as a fearful symbol of the Soviet state, a "poor, mad woman" (Chukovskaya's words) representative of the madness of Stalin's regime. Madness is induced in part by newspapers that Chukovskaya impugns as a pathogenic influence used by the Soviet state to "school" Sofia Petrovna "to believe newspapers and officials more than herself" ("Afterword," p. 112). Unchallenged and unresisted – resistance might be fatal – the schooling proves invidious. The Girl, on the other hand, has a benign if bizarre schooling as she is guided by a community of women experienced in suffering who teach her to distinguish between words she should reject and those she should appropriate. At the end of *The Girl*, the women are inscribing their words in leaflets to be distributed on their protest march. Surrounded by poor, dispossessed, women, some of them mad, the Girl comes to believe, rightly or not, that she gains strength from her sex, which has the power to produce life itself. Motherhood marks a final and climactic stage in the Girl's initiation to womanhood and brings Le Sueur's novella to a resounding if ambiguously triumphant resolution. *The Girl* ends with the birth of the Girl's baby. In contrast, Chukovskaya's novella ends with the spiritual death of Sofia Petrovna as a mother so depleted and destitute that she abandons her only son.[39]

Ironically, Sofia Petrovna's son had been praised on the front page of *Pravda* as an "Industrial enthusiast, [and] Komsomol member" who developed a method of industrial manufacture noteworthy as news (p. 24). This is a happy reference to newspaper reports which become increasingly ominous. Initially, newspapers had entertained Sofia Petrovna with their trivia, "local news . . . editorials and news dispatches" she browsed through until they put her to sleep (pp. 17–18). Neither the "international news" nor domestic affairs held her interest until the appearance of stories of spies and subversion that followed the assassination of Kirov – a signal of the onset of Stalin's Great Purges. As shocking accounts of political atrocities preempt the pages of *Pravda*, Sofia Petrovna begins to read the daily newspaper as she would a marvelous tale of suspense, betrayal, and unbelievable villainy. "Who would have thought it?," she says in endless wonder, never doubting the veracity of reports she finds unbelievable (p. 34).[40] She seems to regress to childhood as she listens to her friend Natasha read the day's thrilling story of terrorism and espionage, of "fascist spies" detected, pursued, and thwarted in their nefarious schemes. The daily atrocities reported in the newspapers thrill and shock the women, who become "indignant," vituperative, and, on occasion, witless: "She and Natasha had such a vivid picture of heaps of mutilated bodies with arms and legs torn off that Sofia Petrovna was afraid to spend the night alone and Natasha was afraid to walk home through the streets. That night Natasha spend the night with her, sleeping on the couch" (p. 34). This susceptibility to tabloid propaganda might be comic if were not destructive, contributing to Natasha's suicide and Sofia Petrovna's madness. Natasha insists upon the truth of each day's horrendous news stories, reading them aloud to Sofia Petrovna as examples of political treachery that she applies to people they know who are being seized as spies. Under Natasha's well-intentioned misguidance, Sofia Petrovna becomes an avid but old-fashioned reader of factual accounts that demand belief; *texts* that require interpretation are beyond her understanding. To Sofia Petrovna the printed word is a transparent medium that mirrors social reality, and newspapers are a direct reflection of her country's moral inviolability. "Nothing can happen to an honest man in our country," she says piously – except a "mistake."[41] When her son Kolya is accused of being "an enemy of the people" and forced to confess to crimes he did not commit (like Shukov in *One Day in the Life of Ivan Denisovich*), she considers his arrest a unique and correctable miscarriage of justice. Everyone else in prison must be guilty, she says, because "In our country innocent people aren't held" (p. 59). Nevertheless, she comes to dread the daily accounts of spies, traitors, arrests, confessions, and punishments. Finally, as though she were incorporating in her own body the terror spreading throughout the Soviet Union, she finds that "newspapers fill her with a vague terror." Terror translates into a myriad of specific fears: "She was afraid of the janitor . . . afraid of the house manager . . . mortally afraid of the wife of the accountant . . . afraid of Valya . . . afraid to walk by the publishing house . . . afraid to look at the table in her room: perhaps a summons from the police would be lying there . . . afraid of every ring of the bell: perhaps they'd come to confiscate all her belongings" (p. 92).

Fear isolates Sofia Petrovna. Like the Girl, who suffers a series of losses, of lover, father, and friend, Sofia Petrovna loses her husband, her son, her much-admired director, and her only friend; but unlike the Girl, she refuses to join with those who share her losses – the multitude of women and men whose family members have disappeared in the purge. While the Girl learns that she belongs within the community of her class and sex, Sofia Petrovna loses touch with everyone. Her alienation, the product of terror, betrays the ideal of social solidarity espoused by the Soviet Union and the mystique of nurturing Russian motherhood – a betrayal that leaves Sofia Petrovna devastated and dooms her son.[42] Kolya is destroyed by lies, those told by the student who informed against him, by himself in his false confession, by his mother, and by the bureaucratic voices of the Soviet state whose propaganda he has believed. In raising her own voice, Chukovskaya challenged these lies by telling the truth as she knew it through her own experience, describing in her novella an involuted pattern of transformation that changes an honest woman into a liar. Sofia Petrovna's lies are self-protective, a way of saving herself from detention as the mother of a spy and from the pain of facing her powerlessness to save her son. After months of fantasying Kolya's return, she might have come to believe he was on his way home, but she knows she is lying when she blatantly announces his imminent release. And when she destroys the letter Kolya has managed to have smuggled out of prison, she knows she is destroying the only evidence of the truth. Kolya has been arrested, beaten, forced to confess, and fated to die unless someone – his mother – comes to his rescue. Sofia Petrovna burns the letter and stamps on the flame, her brief final action, with which the novella ends, mimicking that of the prison guards who had deafened Kolya by stamping upon his head. Thus, a mother's symbolic violence against the son she cannot save reproduces the violence committed by the Soviet state against its citizens. Whatever her motives, however mad or expediently sensible her act, Sofia Petrovna destroys words that refer to reality and collaborates in her own subornation by internalizing the official word of the state.

In Meridel Le Sueur's novel *The Girl,* the union organizer Amelia tells the Girl "not to believe what was in the papers" (p. 135).[43] After the bank robbery in which her lover is killed, the Girl is "afraid to read the papers" because they might reveal her role as driver of the getaway car. But the newspaper has omitted certain facts about the robbery and given others that are "wrong." After reading this inaccurate account (elided from the text), the Girl gives her own version of what had happened, so that the distortions of the newspaper provide an occasion for the "truth" to be told as, and through, the Girl's story of her lover Butch's death and her escape. Having told her story, the Girl puts the newspaper to her own use by fitting it into the sole of her wornout shoe (pp. 108–9). Thus, it becomes a sign in a semiotic system of improvisations devised by the poor in their attempts to survive. Like the characters in *Sofia Petrovna* and *One Day in the Life of Ivan Denisovich,* the dispossessed women and men in *The Girl* are trying to survive circumstances in which they feel trapped: joblessness, poverty, social neglect, and abuse. In a vague and nebulous way, they see the state as their adversary since its bureaucracy supports the capitalistic system that the novella indicts. The state participates in class warfare by protecting scabs against striking workers. State agencies deny poor women welfare and refuse pregnant women milk; government agents follow women in the streets, seize them, incarcerate them, randomly sterilize them, "treat" them with electric shock, and destroy their memories – a human record of the past that Le Sueur seeks to recover. As a dissident writer of the thirties, Le Sueur dramatized the usurpation of economic power and wealth within a capitalistic system that she believed, according to classic Marxist theory, despoiled the working class. At the end of *The Girl,* "hundreds" of working women form a "big line" to march in a protest demonstration. As in *Sofia Petrovna,* the line grows longer, but the increasing number of women signifies strength rather than, as in the Russian novella, despair. The line remains "steady," moving first in protest, then in mourning over the dead Clara, and then in celebration of the Girl's newborn baby. Ultimately, the line of women becomes transformed into written lines as a process of writing begins. "Take it down," Amelia directs the insurgent women, telling them, as ethnographers of a culture of poverty, to write an account of their deprivation and need (p. 146). Their grievances become the text of *The Girl,* a syncretic text combining cultural description, social criticism, and art. In its account of hard times, it endorses the demand of its characters for social accountability. Like Amelia, it calls for "Attention" and (like Wilhelm) for a day of reckoning when "judgment" will be passed on those who denied poor women milk and "got rich on the labor of others" (p. 146). Amelia's clichéd political rhetoric suggests the radical tenor of the text, but not its lyricism and touching sense of love. The love is both personal, profoundly sexual between women and men, and impersonal, a feeling of oneness and communion with humankind. Love, like birthing, is never separate from pain. At the end of the novella, the Girl is counting her birth pains until she "didn't need to count" any longer because she was beyond pain. And the newspaper is completely subverted from its political purposes as it becomes an object used at the command of women: "Amelia said, Give me a newspaper to put the afterbirth in" (p. 148).[44]

With the birth of her daughter, the Girl affirms her love of life, and Le Sueur her hope for the future. Celebrating her ninetieth birthday in 1990, Le Sueur has lived to see the future realized in the present, as has Chukovskaya. One wonders whether Meridel Le Sueur looking at the homeless in the United States today would reaffirm the hope inscribed in *The Girl,* and whether Lydia Chukovskaya in a Soviet Union roiling with change would see possibilities beyond the hopelessness that prevails in *Sofia Petrovna.* In a later novel, *Going Under,* Chukovskaya depicted a Soviet woman who, unlike Sofia Petrovna, recognized and resisted the terror of Stalin's regime, a writer like herself, who refuse to submit though she saw others, respected friends and citizens, "going under." Her heroine in this novel, like Le Sueur's dispossessed women characters on the march, demands change in the world in which she lives. Unlike Bellow and Solzhenitsyn, neither Le Sueur nor Chukovskaya envisions an escape from the world through a transcendence achieved by the human spirit, which in their own ways they celebrate. To struggle here and now against inordinate and perhaps unvanquishable repressive powers constitutes their spiritual victory, and to set their own words as witnesses against those of the newspapers that are part of their daily lives expresses their will to convert texts into attestations.[45] Unknown to each other (as far as I know), both women have dramatized in their own lives a similar pattern of political activism and survival that reflects, by the sheer contingency of contrast in this essay, upon the passivity of the fictional characters portrayed in the first panel. Both have been unswerving in their commitment to change, daring commitments for their time and place – their place as women and their place in American and Soviet history. How the particularities of their political commitments reflect or comment upon each other I leave for later discussion, once again deferring judgment in order to move on to the next panel, which presents modern American and Russian women successful in marriage and careers.

A Missing Dress-Hook: Baranskaya and Heyman

the hooks in my belt fall into the wrong eyelets, one of which is missing

—the hook! I still haven't sewed it on

"A Week Like Any Other"

Within the different cultural settings portrayed in the novellas of this panel – "A Week Like Any Other" by Natalya Baranskaya and Arlene Heyman's "Artifact" – two modern, well-educated women characters, one Russian and the other American, lead strikingly similar daily lives.[46] Both women are research scientists, wives, and mothers; both have successful careers and happy marriages. Both commute between the city and its outskirts, one by bus to Moscow and the other by car to upper Manhattan. Olga Nikolaevitch Voronkova – Olya, for short – the narrator in "A Week Like Any Other," experiments with "a new plastiglass" by testing its "hygroscopicity, humidity resistance, heat resistance, cold resistance, fire resistance."[47] Her work engages her in a continuous process of reckoning that comes to include, in the course of a week, more than her physiochemical data – in effect, her self as a modern Soviet woman. Like Olya, Lottie Hart in "Artifact" seeks to account for her life as she would for the results of her experiments on rat salivary glands.[48] Her professional problem in writing a report of her findings parallels her personal difficulty in creating a coherent story of who she is.

Not surprisingly, differences in the heroines' daily lives and in their consciousness filiate from their different relationships to the state as a political entity, an immediate and demanding presence to Olya, but to Lottie of so little note that it is notable only as an absence. The Soviet state intervenes directly in Olya's life with an official questionnaire inquiring into women's personal affairs, in particular, the precise way they spend their time during a typical week. "What exactly are they after?," Olya asks, positing the state as an *other* with designs of its own – a *they* that would impress its collective public will upon her private life. Her friend Lusya explains that "they . . . want to know . . . why women don't want to have babies" (pp. 7–8); "our workforce is too small" (p. 10). Olya understands that an ideal Soviet woman would fulfill the needs of the Soviet state by adapting her role to the requirements of her historical moment. In a highly respected co-worker Maria Matveyevna, Olya sees the living representation of the Soviet ideal, an "exemplary" woman who has served her country heroically in the past and now devotes herself to "work, production figures, and the Party" (p. 12). With the authority of experience, the older woman praises Olya as "a good mother and a good worker . . . a real Soviet woman" (p. 12). "What is a 'real Soviet woman' anyway?," Olya asks herself (p. 12), posing a question raised by critics of contemporary Soviet culture, many of whom answer by pointing to Olya. For they find Olya's account of her week describing a typical consumption of a Soviet working mother's time – and her life – so graphically that they have appropriated her diary as their source material, as if "A Week Like Any Other" were not a literary text, but an ethnographer's field notes.[49]

In contrast to Olya, Heyman's Lottie in "Artifact" lives in a strangely uncircumstanced world – or rather, in the world of her own consciousness in which public events are either absent because they are irrelevant to her private concerns or else swept into her personal story. Of her many responsibilities as a scientist and professor, none is defined for Lottie by the state; she does not have to attend work-group seminars or answer official questionnaires. The questions raised in "Artifact" are her own and revolve around the enigma of her individual identity. Lottie never asks, "What is a real American woman?" Rather she seeks to know the real Lottie, as though she were someone distinctively different from other women (and, without question, from men). For an educated and self-aware modern American woman, she remains strangely oblivious to the stereotypical roles she has played at various stages in her life, assuming and dropping one after the other: the infatuated high school girl dreaming of the football hero; the wife and mother ensconced in the feminine mystique; the footloose divorcée looking for Mr. Goodbar; and now, married to Mr. Right, the wicked stepmother. These stereotypes place Lottie's story within a misogynist tradition that "Artifact" seems designed to subvert through a heroine who is a research scientist, a university professor, a writer of scholarly articles published in prestigious journals – and a wife and mother. In none of her roles does Lottie recognize herself as a type, let alone a stereotype. However, her sense of individuality, perhaps her most stereotypical American trait, cannot be separated from her feelings of alienation, explicable feelings for a modern American woman who seems to "have it all" – marriage, motherhood, and career.

If a successful combination of marriage and career represents an ideal for a modern woman, Russian or American, then the two women protagonists in this panel have realized this ideal in their daily lives. Baranskaya's novella focuses directly upon dailiness as its heroine gives an hour-by-hour, day-by-day account of her week – a typical week, she sums it up, one like any other. Occasionally, as though to convince herself of her own happiness, Olya counts her blessings: "a flat in a new estate, . . . wonderful children, . . . Dima [her husband] and I love each other . . . an interesting job" (p. 16).[50] Still, something is missing, a necessity as miniscule, perhaps, as her missing dress-hook, a single hook that makes all the other hooks fall into the wrong eyelets. Like the hooks, all the items on Olya's list – home, husband, children, work – fail to fall properly into place. They should all make her happy, but she is often on the verge of panic or hysteria, always hurrying but never catching up with whatever she has to do, usually tired and tense, sometimes collapsing into helpless tears or uncontrollable laughter. "Stop rushing like a madwoman," Olya's husband Dima tells her as they part in the morning after having dressed two small, sleepy, and sporadically shrieking children for day-care. But as she looks at the time, five past seven, she says "I, of course, must run" (p. 17). Running has become a matter of course.

She runs for the morning bus. She *runs, rushes, hurries, dashes, pushes, leaps,* and *jumps* throughout the day. She runs for the evening bus. Then she runs home. Once there, a new rush begins as she cooks, cleans, washes, mends, and irons clothes, cares for husband and children until, finally, she drops into an exhausted sleep. The day, like the week, reveals no gap in which she can find momentary relief from the frenetic rush that leaves her breathlessly behind schedule. Olya ends her account of the week, and brings the novella to an end, with the ringing of the alarm clock that will awaken her to another Monday that will start another week in which the missing dress-hook will not be sewn into place and in which something – time – will always be missing.

Where does time go? This is the question baldly asked in the official questionnaire that the women scientists, Olya, Shura, and the two Lusyas, can hardly spare time to answer.[51] For much of their time is preempted by officially designated duties, like their compulsory participation in group seminars held after work. When Olya rushes home late one evening after attending a seminar, she finds her angry husband reading the newspaper while the children stuff themselves with canned eggplant that gives them diarrhea. Though Dima is a loving husband and father, he limits his cooperation in the home, expecting his wife to meet a woman's traditional domestic duties; as he tells her, "You are the housewife." *We* usually yields to *I* as presumably shared household duties shift to Olya: "We undress our son. . . . We put away the children's clothes together. Then I tidy up the kitchen . . . [the bathroom] . . . and . . . wash and rinse clothes" (p. 43). Olya seldom complains about this shift. She complains, instead, of lack of time in which to do what is expected of her as a worker and housewife. For Olya has implicitly accepted the duties assigned her by the Soviet state, which granted women work opportunities that add to, rather than modify, their domestic obligations.[52] If modern feminism, in any of its variant forms, assumes that household chores traditionally assigned to women will be equally shared by men, then neither Olya, nor the novella, nor the Soviet state as portrayed in the text expresses a feminist position – or at least, so numerous critics and sociologists have argued.[53] "I want to read," Olya's husband says when called to help with the children, and, the distraught Olya notes, "he really is sitting and reading" (p. 53). Meanwhile, she has chores she *must* do: "I must get to grips with the kitchen, wash the stove and clean the gas rings, tidy up the cupboards . . . and wipe the floor. Then I must wash my hair, wash . . . [and] iron the children's clothes . . . wash myself, mend my tights, and I *must* sew the hook back on my belt" (p. 52, original emphasis). The missing dress-hook haunts Olya. She dreams it is miraculously sewn into place; she remembers, on the last night of the week, that it is not: " – the hook! I still haven't sewn it into place. Damn it!" (p. 62). "Damn, damn, damn everything!," she had cursed earlier (p. 15), displaying a rebellious anger that made her question what was wrong with her, rather than with her life as constituted. "What is the matter with me?," Olya asks as she drifts to sleep, only to say, poignantly, she does not know (p. 62).

A facile answer might be that nothing is the matter with Olya but that something is missing in her life that the missing dress-hook, insignificant in itself, represents – something her circumstances hardly allow her to hope for and that a modern American woman might take for granted. In Arlene Heyman's "Artifact," Lottie comes home from the laboratory to discover, as Olya would, a kitchen in disarray: on the table, children's crayons, dirty dishes, milk, and margarine; on the floor, a smashed Oreo cookie and scattered marbles. The disorder irritates Lottie. She looks at the "chart" taped to the refrigerator to see who is charge of dishes this day, assuming obviously that it is someone other than herself. For, household duties have been divided between Lottie and her husband – unequally, actually, since in the time of the text he shops and cares for the children more than she. When Lottie discovers that on this day *she* was to be charge of cleaning up, she is annoyed rather than chagrined. As though forgiving and yet blaming her family for not doing her chores, she sorts out her feelings: "She didn't mind the disarray so much as she felt irritated at the food left out."[54] Lottie's reaction to the disorder familiar to many housewives, American and Russian, shows her somehow distanced from the daily, necessary, and repetitive demands of a home. Clearly, she feels none of the compulsion expressed by Olya's obsessive repetition of *I must*. Unlike Olya, who whirls frenetically through a series of chores, Lottie occasionally wipes the kitchen table, squeezes oranges for juice, or bathes her children. Her home does not sap her energies or demand all her time. Rather, it provides a stage for the interesting daily drama of her life: petty conflicts with her stepdaughter, encounters with her husband – they talk, argue over children and money, make love – and potential tragedy with her young sons. Lottie has warned her sons not to touch the test tubes of chemical reagents she has brought home from the laboratory. "Not cautious by nature," as she describes herself, she has behaved carelessly as a mother, expecting the children to be careful. As with all the exigencies that arise in the novella, her son's accidental exposure to dangerous chemicals has no dire consequence. "Artifact" ends with Lottie and her family walking through a cool marshland and gazing at a star-drenched sky that makes them wonder about distance, time, and identity. In "A Week Like Any Other," Olya's family had also taken a Sunday walk and, for a brief happy time, gone sledding on the newly fallen snow of an irridescent city.

Such idyllic family interludes contrast with the usual state of the homes described in the novellas of this panel, not unhappy homes, but not havens of peace and order (an ideal seldom realized, perhaps, in literature or life). In Lottie's home, distribution of household chores (which would have made Olya ecstatic) fails to produce order or reduce family squabbling. It fails to bring contentment. For Lottie feels disconsolately that something is missing in her life, something that, unlike Olya, she cannot account for and that the novella cannot (or does not) represent through a concrete detail, a small but significant detail, like a missing dress-hook. Indeed, the *missing* missing-hook in "Artifact" raises for me the most interesting question about the novella's cultural import. What is missing in Lottie's life? What vital need is left so unsatisfied by marriage, motherhood, and career that Lottie ends up overcome by "a dreadful feeling . . . of disconnectedness," as if she were "some strange taped-together creature, the likes of which had never been seen before" (p. 49).

Common as a sense of estrangement is in American fiction, Lottie's alienation seems uncircumstanced and unattributable. Time, the missing element in "A Week Like Any Other," does not figure centrally in Lottie's mental reckonings, for while Lottie is as busy as Olya, she somehow remains at leisure. Having her own car (a sloppy affair, like Wilhelm's) gives her time that Olya lacks, but time does not give her peace of mind.[55] Ironically, time and privacy allow her to concentrate upon the uncertainties of who she is and why she feels alone and estranged. Unlike Olya, who may feel overwhelmed but not unreal or unconnected, Lottie seems haunted by a sense of self-alienation. She remembers herself as a child "overwhelmed" or "suffused" by a "swell of loneliness." Now feelings of self-alienation extend the "awful loneliness" experienced in the past as separation from others. Her parents, particularly her mother, are described as remote figures; her brother and sisters quickly dismissed with a summary of their defections, one sister pregnant, another drunk, and a brother caught cheating at school. Her first husband remains a mystery, the reasons for his alienation from her still unfathomable. But though dismayed by memories of loneliness, Lottie now seeks and enjoys solitude. The novella begins with her alone on a weekend night in the laboratory: "She liked being alone in her lab in the hushed city" (p. 11). She likes being alone on her long drive home, an occasion for her to think uninterruptedly about herself, the central enigmatic subject of her stream of consciousness. At a moment of recognition, she confronts a woman she is surprised to see: "a very substantial figure, responsible, solid, a matron. Who, me, Lottie?" (p. 13). This quizzical, even congratulatory, self-questioning soon turns into dismay. The novella ends with everything falling into place for Lottie, except the answer to her haunting questions about her identity. Lottie's uncertainties leave the reader with an enigma lacking a context of circumstances that can point either to its origin or its resolution.

Thus, while Olya keeps running, Lottie wonders. Aside from *wondered, thought, remembered,* her operative verbs are *liked* and *took pleasure,* though she also *hated, cursed,* and *felt like punching.* She is at once more angry than Olya and more aware of immediate pleasure, more sexually demanding, as she shall see, and always more subjectively oriented, *wondering* about her self. One question she does not ask in her constant self-questioning is why she must *wonder* about herself rather than simply *be* herself. Nor does she ask why she has created no significant relationships with other women. She recalls briefly two "women friends" of the past, now thousands of miles away but, she adds, "alive in her mind" – as though her consciousness confers upon them a reality they need not achieve on their own or in the text.

In contrast, Olya's women friends are clear and identifiable individuals, as well as representative figures. For the gallery of women co-workers who are Olya's friends represents various types of Soviet working mothers: the single mother; the unmarried mother; the wife whose husband wants her to quit work and have another child. These women relate to each other in ways that reflect upon Lottie's isolation from her sex. Indeed, Olya's life would be radically different, almost like Lottie's, without the friendships she has created with the women in her laboratory, scientists and mothers who share her research and her life. The women pool their chores as well as their feelings, each telling the other her secret anxieties, each consoling and cajoling the other so that they laugh and cry together. Olya makes the bond among them actual by describing them linked together by their shopping bags: "We put Shura in the middle and carry four bags between the three of us. . . . I feel happy because it's a sunny day, . . . because there are three of us ./ Because I'm not alone" (p. 48).[56] Her words echo those of the dispossessed women in Le Sueur's novel *The Girl,* women linked by class and sex. They are words that Lottie, regretting loneliness and yet seeking solitude, does not utter, though they might have told her what, at least in part, she is missing.

In the past, when Lottie felt lonely, she sought out men; sex appealed to her, not friendship. As a sexual woman, Lottie is forthright and demanding, the partner who initiates sex with her husband and, when between husbands, pursues it promiscuously with men she meets in her wanderings. Heyman describes Lottie's sexual relationships with each of her husbands briefly but graphically, showing a woman confident and knowledgeable, almost greedy, about her desires. As a daughter, Lottie remembers the thumpings of her parents in the bedroom and hints of her father's adulteries. As a mother, she notes the signs of sexual blossoming in her daughter, and when the girl's date arrives, Lottie gallantly resists looking at his crotch (p. 6). With a reticence considered typical of Soviet fiction, Baranskaya delicately suggests a sexual overture through Olya's stretching her hand to her husband as they lie in bed. Usually, sheer lack of time precludes sex during the frenetic week.[57] On Sunday morning, Olya refers obliquely to the night before by worrying whether she is pregnant or taking too many pills. Then she adds, "Or perhaps I don't need this kind of love any more?" (p. 57). Though the thought saddens her, Olya can contemplate a love separated from sexual desire because she has a sense of her own identity that loss of desire would not impair, perhaps because the social construction of Russian womanhood has not included sexuality as a crucial element. Neither sex nor love makes Lottie feel complete. In the novella's final scene, surrounded by a husband and children she loves, she experiences her most devastating sense of nonidentity.

What, if anything, one wonders, could produce the sense of community that Olya feels; that the imprisoned Shukov feels; that the Girl, poor, pursued, seemingly powerless, feels through her bond with the oppressed; that even the stripped and rejected Wilhelm feels as an oceanic sense of oneness with humankind? For Sofia Petrovna, withdrawal from others completes a process of

disconnection initiated by the Soviet state, which systematically separated people from each other, taking husbands from wives, and sons from mothers. Sofia
Petrovna's experience, like Shukov's and the Girl's, has profound and inextri-
cably political meaning. Lottie's sense of disconnectedness emanates from an undefinable discontent, as though she had been promised something she cannot
name that still has not materialized. In her fear that she may be an artifactual
rather than real person, a product of random happenings, she circles around a
missing element that, I believe, may be a sense of lack of control. She discovers
randomness where she wants to see design and will, her own will. Like Olya's
hook and eye, which do not come together, Lottie's past and present identities
seem to her unconnected because she does not see a causal link between her will
and her self. Something other than her own design has put together the dis-
jointed person she perceives herself to be, though others would see a successful
American woman. In her narcissism, Lottie resembles Tommy Wilhelm in *Seize
the Day,* though she lacks his comic sense of self-deprecation and his impersonal
if bizarre concern with the meaning of human life. Lottie want to know what
her own life means – whether it has been constituted by her actions or by
chance, whether she is "the real thing," to use her phrase, or an artifact.

"All one ever deals with is artifact," Lottie had said in justifying her scientific
methods (p. 11) – an observation pertinent to Lottie (as well as to Baranskaya's
Olya) as a fictional character and emblematic modern woman. Lottie believes
that "the conditions under which a given artifact is produced provide information about the actual nature of a particular organism which cannot be analyzed
in its natural form" (p. 11). Writing about biological organisms, Lottie assumes
the existence of an "actual nature" that particular scientific techniques extrapo-
late from its "natural form." This belief – which distinguishes between fact and
artifact – has been assailed by postmodern theorists of "laboratory life."[58] They
question the concept of "actual nature" or pristine scientific truth, arguing that
all "scientific facts" are artifacts, products of a process of social construction. This
process comes to completion with the act of writing, a stage in her work that
Lottie attends to so carelessly that her manuscript is returned for extensive revision. Almost perversely, she prides herself on presenting her conclusions "in a
matter-of-fact way," telling herself that she produced "the real thing" in her
hastily written articles, while those who lingered over their writing were cos-
meticians or interior decorators, not scientists (p. 8). Nevertheless, if she wants
to publish, she must rewrite, and she does. She assumes that rewriting, which
makes her article acceptable for publication, leaves her facts unaltered, still the
same essential "real thing." Lottie – and perhaps Heyman – wants to insist upon
a difference between artifacts and an "actual nature" or truth, as well as upon
the truth-value of artifacts. For artifacts will reveal (at least) an aspect of "actual
nature" that a particular scientific technique brings to light.

If, as Lottie argues, particular techniques produce particular artifacts, then
characters like Lottie and Olya, artifacts of literary creation, cannot be separated
from the writers' narrative strategies. This is to say that if Heyman had chosen

to create her heroine through a first-person narration in the form of a diary that contains specific answers to a questionnaire, she might have produced an American woman secure in her own identity, a woman like the Russian Olya. Olya's autobiographical form requires her to construct an "I" through whom she speaks.[59] This coherent and clearly identifiable "I" may be an artifact produced by the literary method that Olya – and Baranskaya – have chosen. By the same token, Lottie's sense of incoherence as a person may reflect her mode of self-reflection, a stream of consciousness that is free flowing and uncommitted to any form but its flow. This flow does have form, for Lottie remembers the past in segments: thoughts of her mother introduce a block of memories about her family; thoughts of her high school sweetheart recall her courtship, marriage, and divorce. The past that emerges seems more coherent than that brought to Wilhelm's mind through "involuntary memory." Nevertheless, Lottie sees her memories as segments that have remained discrete and that have diffused, rather than fused into, the self she desires to call her own. When she examines the disparate images of herself as child, young wife, and mature woman, she sees disconnectedness rather than development. Ironically, for a scientist who engages constantly in the process of "fixing" – tissues and, she believes, scientific truth – she cannot fix her own identity. She has turned her own subjectivity into an object of study only to encounter "the uncertainty principle" that she believes figures in scientific observation. Her troubling uncertainty about who is may be, however, an artifact produced by her method of self-examination. Having situated reality within her consciousness where memories and associations flow with the freedom of randomness, she feels herself a random creature, unvalidated by subjective choices and necessities that, she believes, would have made her real. Even her sense of her own artifactuality appears to be an artifact. By her own inordinate self-consciousness, Lottie has maintained, if not indeed constructed, a self divided between the "I" who wonders and an elusive "She." One may wonder (to assume Lottie's mode) whether this unexamined habit of self-examination has made Lottie seem unreal to herself; or whether she feels that she is an artifact because she has conformed, without realizing it, to factitious female stereotypes common in American literature and life. As for Baranskaya's Olya, does she seem real to the reader and to herself because she has a cultural model that encourages her to become "a real Soviet woman"? Or does she seem real because she writes down what she does, day by day, objectifying herself in and through her diary as a coherent and identifiable "I"?

Such questions suggest that a cross-cultural critique of literary texts needs to consider transcultural generic links which may influence the construction of character. "A Week Like Any Other" provides a modern and moving example of social realism, the genre of Soviet literature traditionally prescribed by the Soviet state. Written as though in response to a sociologist's questionnaire, it describes a "problem" in the life of a modern Soviet working wife which might be solved by rearrangements in her schedule that would introduce what has been missing. Just as a missing dress-hook can be sewn into place, the missing element of time can, conceivably, be found, and Olya might, conceivably, be less in a rush.[60] By placing its heroine within a clearly circumstanced context that allows her to define her problem, "A Week Like Any Other" differs significantly from "Artifact." For Olya writes down answers, while Lottie continues to ask questions. The answers imply the possibility of solving Olya's problems – sometime, if not now; Lottie's lack of answers suspends her in uncertainties that seem ontological, that may be cultural, or that are, perhaps inexplicably, personal. As Olya writes down answers to her questionnaire, she figures out precisely where her time goes, and if she wished, she could graph the hours of her day against her responsibilities as mother, housewife, and worker in the same way that she graphs physiochemical data. The pressure of one factor upon the other – never enough time to meet responsibilities – makes Olya's life harried. However, the account of her life is orderly, proceeding sequentially hour by hour, day by day, with brief flashbacks.

In contrast with the forward-moving account of "A Week Like Any Other," the movement of "Artifact" is unpredictable in its shuttling back and forth from present to past to present. Following the free associations that flow through Lottie's mind, the narrative line wanders arbitrarily, driven by jostling memories called forth by heroine's questions about her self. Descriptions of scientific techniques interpolated among Lottie's musings hardly deflect her from a steady concentration upon the mystery of her being. She may be attracted, as she notes parenthetically, to the "idea of a larger perspective" (p. 33), but political events meld into her musings only as they pertain to her personally. Olya refers to Vietnam and French politics, but Lottie, for all her freedom to move in space, lives in a claustrophobic world that offers no large perspective. She remembers a "coup" that "occurred in a small central African country" only because she had inherited her research project from an African graduate student killed in its violence (p. 9). The country, the coup, and the slain student come to mind as she tries to make the pieces of her past fall together and reveal a design in her life.

The stream-of-consciousness technique in "Artifact" affords the novella a narrative freedom that seems mimetic of the freedom of its American heroine, a woman with a strong sense of entitlement and expectation. Sadly for Lottie, expectation – strangely nebulous in what it promises – has become inseparable from disappointment and dismay. For in a society that values the "self-made" person, a modern American woman may have the freedom to make and remake herself, but her own self-fashioning may cause her to consider herself factitious rather than "real." Moreover, she may feel perpetually deprived of a happiness to which she believes herself entitled by the possibilities for seemingly limitless personal happiness promised in a constantly renewed contract between the individual and American society – the contract by which America constituted itself as the artifact of a text still being read and subjected to interpretation.[61]

This essay began with a question often posed by postmodern theorists: Do the social systems described in cultural critiques exist in actuality or do they come into being as artifacts produced by the process of writing? *Artifact* emerges as a key word in the essay's final panel, which re-poses the question raised in the introduction only to leave it, fittingly I believe, unresolved in the conclusion. Reckoning with the uncertainties of texts as literary and cultural artifacts, one may find their truth uncertain, obscured as well as illuminated by art. If the essay is by definition "a report of qualified findings,"[62] then it might end, like the reckonings of Bellow's Wilhelm, with an equivocation – a final judgment of the portrayal of Russian and American cultures in the triptych's novellas as True and False.[63] True need not imply truth, however, if truth, as Wilhelm believes, represents "Something" separate from and transcending ordinary, perceivable social actualities. As realistic fictions, the novellas of this triptych represent perceivable actualities as they might be encountered in the time and place depicted – actual places, real buildings, like New York's Hotel Ansonia, Moscow's Donskoy bus stop and Lenin Library, Leningrad's Liteynyi bridge, the Neva, the prison on Shpalernaya Street, empty windswept steppes with prison watchtowers.[64] Physical settings within the texts that can be located in real space, and events that have reality as historical happenings (like the Kirov trial in *Sofia Petrovna*), give credibility to the novellas' characters and plots. Yet as realistic as the novellas are, or seem, their references to historical actualities are few and fleeting, or as vague as Lottie's reference to an unnamed country somewhere in Africa where some kind of a coup occurred.

A sparcity of historical references may be irrelevant, however, either to the realism of the novellas or to their truth. For history inscribes change, while the essence of truth is immutability. Differences in the actual, immediate circumstances of the Girl and Lottie, or Sofia Petrovna and Olya, register the social changes that have taken place in historical time. But characters who seek truth, like Wilhelm in his quest for eternalities and Lottie pursuing the secrets of identity and of science, ignore (and seem ignorant of) history. They want to know what lies beyond ephemeral appearances, and they believe they can actually see an ultimate reality as the object of their gaze. So Wilhelm stands "gazing at the face of the dead" (p. 116), and Lottie, at the cells of a dead rat's salivary gland. The gaze reifies truth and delivers it to the discourse of religion or science – or of commonplace knowledge. Wilhelm's gaze leaves him convulsed, but his epiphanic realization that time flies and death is inevitable merely collapses truth into truisms. To suggest that *Seize the Day* ends with truisms rather than transcendence reveals how discrepant critical interpretations can be and how evocative of argument. For critics will argue over a diminished view of Wilhelm's passion and of the ending of *Seize the Day,* just as they have argued over the political implications of prison competence in Solzhenitsyn's *One Day in the Life of Ivan Denisovich.* Argument implies questions as well as conviction, for in challenging one interpretation of the novellas with another, the cross-cultural critic may legitimately be asked about the basis for hermeneutical decisions – asked to tell by what interpretive means, on what theoretical groundings, one can seek to explain how or why time, death, and love are construed as they are in Bellow's novella and how and why they are construed differently, through different tropes – or perhaps the same – in a Russian novella similar in form and theme. How does cultural context, perhaps nationality itself, figure in literary interpretation?[65]

Since theories about text and context abound and proliferate – to the point that distinctions between them have been blurred[66] – even so simple a matter as what a hat may mean can generate argument. Wilhelm views his hat as protection against the penetrating gaze of others rather than wind or cold, but the hat fails to conceal as he wishes and, instead, both deceives and reveals in unforeseen ways, as though it had a will of its own – as a hat might have in a fiction. To Shukov, his hat represents resistance against the cold and a penal code that would reduce him to a cipher in a system where the individual does not count. Within the texts, the characters' view of their hats is clear and explicit. To interpret the cultural implications of these views, the critic needs to provide a context within which to conceptualize meanings, as well as a theoretic ground for choosing, or constructing, this context.[67] In this essay, theory and contexts are submerged in the footnotes, so that the novellas, rather than critics, can engage in dialogue. This intertextual dialogue has allowed the novellas to interrogate each other and to ask what they can claim as common and as unique – as cultural, generic, gender or class-inscribed, and as inexplicably individual. To sustain this dialogue I have focused upon the texts themselves, and to keep the focus sharp I have concentrated upon small, inspectable details and short fictional forms that allow details high visibility. My purpose has been to try out – to essay – a practical method of criticism by moving from "local truths," with which this essay began, to cultural insights. At the same time, I have asked what critical or social ends this movement might serve. If answers are offered tentatively, equivocally, or in the form of possibilities still to be explored, that is because I wish to resist the modes of closure common to comparisons based upon binary oppositions. Since "cultural analysis" itself has been described as "intrinsically incomplete,"[68] a cross-cultural critique of literary texts can legitimately recognize its inchoateness along with its contingencies and temptations. Among the contingencies is a pairing of texts that is more arbitrary than might be acknowledged, since the critic, rather than the texts, calls for linkage and comparing. Among the temptations of its binary comparisons is the ease with which the critic can emphasize differences by defining them as polarities; or minimize differences by collapsing them into sameness; or deconstruct cultural stereotypes by showing them chiasmically crossed. A cross-cultural critique of any single set of texts may illustrate any or all of these possibilities, while a triptych, by mediating between the autonomy and the connectedness of its panels, may reveal other possibilities worth exploring.

In the triangulated paintings to which his essay is analogous, the central panel is usually dominant and the two side panels thematically, narratively, or pictorially subordinate, their secondariness sometimes indicated by their smaller size. But the triptych can also be nonhierarchical, each of its panels given equal valence, so that its form eschews authority – an effect that seems to me fitting if final judgment is to be deferred. As the triptych disrupts the narrative continuity it seems to be initiating, it fragments what promised to be a unifying and controlling – or totalizing – scheme. Its separations and juxtapositions accommodate difference, dialogue, and the drama of conflict. Separation also creates an illusion of sequence or the passing of time. Thus discrete actions held in arrest in individual panels acquire narrative momentum within the context of an encompassing frame that maintains a continuous tension between autonomous elements and an incorporating whole. For though the triptych isolates and individualizes moments by assigning them to separate panels, it also connects them by proximity, repetition, analogy, and cross-reference. This complexity opens possibilities for interpretations, so that the triptych will enact the hermeneutical purposes to which it can be put. In its own conflicted form, it can carry on, analogously, the continuous debate that constitutes literary criticism.

In works of art, an expanded form of the triptych is the polyptych, which can assume various shapes and designs through its multifaceted structure. The triptych expands into a polpytych in a number of ways, most simply by an addition of panels, and more complexly by including within the boundaries of an individual panel other, self-contained panels. Alternatively, or in addition, a series of smaller panels can transverse the length of the entire triptych, bordering top or bottom margins, or both, with subsidiary sequences.[69] Thus the narrative, historical, and interpretative possibilities of the form open and increase. This open-endedness would appeal to the literary critic who wants to move beyond the boundaries set by binary opposition, to multiply cross-references, and to look upon texts from the various perspectives required by cross-cultural criticism.

Looked at one way, the novellas within each panel of this triptych sustain the cultural stereotypes that an ordinary, unalienated American reader might expect to find: the American fictional characters, whatever their particular complaints, are free, and the Soviets are constrained and oppressed, if not actually imprisoned. This difference prevails over differences of class, gender, and historic moment. Despite Wilhelm's mawkish bemoaning in *Seize the Day* that he is not free, that a man in his "position," neither poor nor rich, can never be free (p. 490), he has the freedom to go where he wishes in the city and across the continent, to take or quit a job, to marry or leave a woman, to save or waste his money, to follow a hat vagariously through his day. Shukov is free to take his hat off at the dining table, but he cannot erase the number inscribed upon it which identifies him, irrefragably, as a prisoner of the state. Similarly, the Girl may be poor and oppressed, but she is free to speak, organize with others in her class, and march in open protest against political powers she can hope to transform. Sofia Petrovna has been isolated and silenced, and deprived of hope. Freedom may feel like an existential burden to Lottie in "Artifact," but nevertheless, she is free, like Wilhelm, to wander where she chooses and to choose as she wishes while Olya, her Soviet counterpart, feels impelled to follow a relentless schedule imposed upon her by society and the state and introjected as duty and daily necessity. Unlike Olya, Lottie could find or make time to sew a missing dress-hook in place, but she would choose not to sew.

From another point of view, however, one can discover a chiasmic crossing between texts as Shukov demonstrates an inner freedom, even by so minute a gesture as taking off his cap, while Wilhelm remains "a slave," whether to his own misshapen self, reified in his "misshapen hat," or to a social system that demands blood money (p. 40). Harried as Olya is throughout her day and week, she achieves a sense of self and of consoling solidarity with her family, her co-workers, her women friends. In ways that cultural critiques of Soviet women would not lead one to expect, she expresses a strong feminist sensibility that Lottie, unexpectedly, lacks as a modern American woman. Olya may need to insist that her husband acknowledge an equality that Lottie can take for granted, the equality of her education with his, of her right to work, and her right to satisfaction in work. Though work imposes upon her the Soviet woman's typical "double burden," it also realizes a feminist ideal: it creates a community of women that connects her with others and reinforces her sense of self.[70] Both self and others elude Lottie, who remains locked within her own consciousness; if she suffers from any definable cause, it is her quintessentially American individualism, her bourgeois markings, to give a class name to her status and state of mind. As for the Girl, her hope for a better tomorrow may be as futile as Sofia Petrovna's delusion that her son will come home. Indeed, as one text is set against the other, this delusion functions subversively, for Chukovskaya's account of a dismembered social body implicitly discounts Le Sueur's vision of a society based upon an ideal of social solidarity that is shown in *Sofia Petrovna* as corruptible and already, at the very time Le Sueur was writing, corrupted in the Soviet Union. This last comparison suggests the possibilities for collapsing differences between the novellas in each panel into sameness, as those in the second impugn both societies they depict as an inhumane and oppressive, while those in the first panel describe comparable struggles for survival, and those in the third, a comparable incompletion in women's lives.

Seen as a sequence rather than separately, the panels offer possibilities for viewing historical change. In the Russian novellas, political conditions improve over time; given the Great Terrors of the Stalin decades, they could hardly have gotten worse.[71] Olya is oppressed by time and the demands placed upon women by society and the state, but she is not depleted and driven to madness by sorrow and fear. Her physical circumstances are, as she catalogues them, comfortable; her children, her home, her friends – all unlike Sofia Petrovna's – secure, unthreatened by coercions by a state that exercises power barbarously and arbitrarily. Similarly, historical change has given Lottie opportunities for self-advancement denied the Girl as a woman and all the novella's working people as a class. This is not to say that the novellas show that historical change has brought women characters the happiness they seek nor the certainty of where and how to pursue their desires. In some ways, social class gives them their direction and marks their differences. Class differentiates the Girl and Lottie, for example, not only in their economic circumstances, but also in their sensibilities. Different as their day-to-day lives are, as one has money (not enough, Lottie thinks) and the other has nothing, their sense of themselves is even more radically polarized. As a working-class woman, the Girl learns to think of union – of actual organization and of emotional affinity with others like herself. Lottie's almost obsessive absorption in herself has already been discussed as reflecting a bourgeois mentality that she finds mysterious, and that another self-absorbed American character, Bellow's Tommy Wilhelm, considers a transcendent human quality. To Wilhelm, his single-minded concern with himself signifies a universal need for a man (a generic term by which he excludes woman) to "know why he exists" (p. 39). This "visionary" aspect of his being does not interfere with his obsession with money, which Wilhelm equates with survival. Money may be a universal concern that transcends cultural, temporal, and sexual boundaries. Wilhelm quarrels passionately with his wife over money, and so do other couples: Lottie and her husband, Olya and her husband, the Girl and Butch. All the characters, including the "saintly" Shukov, count money, however else their reckonings may differ. And the process of reckoning itself remains constant while historical, cultural, and personal circumstances in the novellas change.

Thus, a series of subsidiary panels depicting individuals in acts of reckoning could be interposed across the triptych, transforming it into a polyptych that reveals different moments and kinds of reckoning along with its incessance. Some of the reckonings are gender-inscribed. As Olya fills out her questionnaire, she reckons up the "frightening" amount of time that she has spent as a mother with her children (p. 6), for she, and never her husband, has stayed home with them when they were sick. Nevertheless, she loves and has wanted her children, even when she knew another baby would make her complicated life as harried as it has. Perhaps motherhood is a socially constructed role, but all of the women characters in these novellas, however different or contrasting their circumstances, not only accept but desire it, resisting pressures to denial. Both Olya and the Girl, in their radically different situations, first agree and then refuse to have the abortion insisted upon by the men in their lives. Their decisions throw into relief thematic ambivalences toward motherhood in both novellas, but also affirm its joys. Extrapolated from the texts, the relationships of fathers to their children seem rescindable. Dr. Adler can willfully banish his son for his failures, Wilhelm leaves his sons when he leaves his wife, and Shukov replaces a dead son

with a stranger, but the loss of her son, banished by the state, drives Sofia Petrovna mad. Cross-references thicken, as do possibilities of leaping from particulars and details to generalizations about class, gender, and cultures that may, or
may not, turn out to be (or said to be) artifacts created in and by the critic's act
of writing.

What can be said unequivocally? Certain words denoting commonplace, recognizable objects like a dress-hook, a man's hat, a daily newspaper appear and
reappear in the novellas. Certain other words state, as explicitly as words can,
the characters' reactions to these objects: Sofia Petrovna's *frissons* as she reads
Pravda, for instance, or Olya's frustration over the missing hook, Wilhelm's mistaken faith in a gaudy straw hat. Each of the objects exists within a context or
within several contexts simultaneously – and at this point, equivocation sets in,
for the definition of context can quickly become a matter of theoretical dispute,
including arguments, already noted, over its independence from text and its integrity as a concept.[72] The arguments multiply as *context* becomes modified by
cultural, and as literary critics appropriate the conflation. Indeed, the more fash-
ionable a term like *cultural context* becomes in literary critical theory (providing,
after all, the basis for schools of criticism, like the New Historicism), the more
subject it becomes to scrutiny and dispute, perhaps also, ultimately, to dismissal.
One soon arrives at the aporias of cultural criticism with which this essay began
by posing questions about the apprehensibility of truth that the novellas themselves have raised and evoked. Rather than offering answers, the essay has engaged in a process of reckoning or weighing interpretations against each other.
For this triptych is an essay in the etymological sense of the term: a trial effort
and an *exagium* or weighing. If one way of weighing the truth of a text is by historical documentation – by referring to events that actually and indisputably occurred – then the novellas of this triptych can be judged, in accordance with the
wishes of Solzhenitsyn, Chukovskaya, and Le Sueur, as witnesses to the truth of
their time and place. This judgment, however, need not be – and I would argue, should not be – final or the last.

In The Last Judgment, two books are weighed against each other. The books
have been compiled by two guardian angels who recorded the sins and the virtues
of the person under judgment. The angels have, in effect, each written – or constructed – a story of the person's life. The truth of the stories is not subjected to
judgment. Only the weight of the books enters into the final reckoning, and one
must prevail over the other. Though I have placed two books together for critical analysis, I have tried to avoid this kind of absolute final judgment. In its stead,
I offer not the reckonings of relativism, but the tensions and abreactions of a multifaceted form that has, in its realizations in the visual arts, transcended time and
place. Assuming protean forms over the centuries, the triptych has accommo-
dated to multifarious subjects and styles. It has ranged from traditional representation of Christian myths and iconography – including The Last Judgment, in a
sixteenth-century triptych by Lucas de Leyde – to the tumultuous black-and-

white abstraction by Jackson Pollock, the great black Rothko murals at Houston, and Rauschenberg's multi-imaged representation of the American flag. In adapting its triangulated form to the essay, I see the triptych not as a solution to critical problems, but as a recognition of their persistence and the arguments they will continue to evoke. For the triptych is a permissively open form that can accommodate interpolation, revision, and exception, and add suppleness and surprise to the stringent binaries of cross-cultural literary criticism.

Notes

1   Saul Bellow, *Seize the Day* (New York: Viking, 1956), pp. 117–18. Subsequent references are given in the text.

2   In his influential essay, "Thick Description," Clifford Geertz asserts that "culture is not a power, something to which social events, behaviors, institutions, or processes can be causally attributed; it is a context, something within which they can be . . . described" (*The Interpretation of Cultures: Selected Essays* [New York: Basic Books, 1973], p. 14). Though Geertz may seek to separate culture from power, and power from social causality, other critics (New Historicists, for example), search out the sources of power, individual and institutionalized, within the cultures that they describe contextualizing the texts they interpret. Needless to say, Michel Foucault's manifold discussions of power have focused much of postmodern criticism upon its ubiquitous historical influence and its expression and exercise through discourse. Culture may serve as a site for description, as Geertz claims, but that is not to say that description will not, perhaps invariably, locate sites of power. Since I am not proposing to offer a New Historicist critique, I do not focus primarily upon power, though I discuss the way its presence and pressures seem inscribed in the texts.

3   While critics may differ in their definitions of *postmodern,* they generally agree that the term implies a fundamental questioning, if not outright dismissal, of the grounds upon which belief in truth has traditionally been established. This dismissal would invalidate claims, however circumstanced, for the absoluteness or universality of human values, for essentialism, and for the possibility of transcendence. In a definition he considers simplified to the extreme, Jean-François Lyotard describes *postmodern,* the subject of his "report," as incredulity toward metanarratives," the most "grand" of which is truth (*The Postmodern Condition: A Report on Knowledge,* trs. Geoff Bennington and Brian Massumi [Minneapolis: University of Minnesota Press, 1984], p. xxiv). Postmodern theorists in a wide and diverse range of disciplines argue that their subject of study – whether literature, history, anthropology, law, and science, or more specifically, human victimization, to mention only a few examples – has been socially constructed (Kaplan, White, Geertz, LaFree, Latour, Woolgar, Bumiller cited below). Thus they reject a traditional view that social realities (if such an expression can still have cogency) exist as facts. Rather they discover in their stead historically produced artifacts. As is well known (too well known to require documentation here), a concept of gender as socially constructed underlies contemporary feminist theories, which much as they may differ will agree that gender, as a social construction, is distinguishable from sex as a biological fact. Another "construction," with a history too complicated to recapitulate, is the reader – or more precisely,

"the implied reader," described by Wolfgang Iser as "a construct and in no way to be identified with any real reader" (*The Act of Reading: A Theory of Aesthetic Response* [Baltimore: The Johns Hopkins University Press, 1978], p. 34). Since constructs come into existence through a dialectic relationship with something hypothesized as other, as reality or truth, truth remains to be reckoned with even as it is being set aside. Iser implicitly brackets the truth of his theory of constructs, or of any theory, as he asserts that "any theory is bound to be in the nature of a construct" (p. x). I cannot tell what "in the nature of" is meant to equivocate here. The final judgment – to use a key term of this essay – on truth is, of course, not in, and a critic like Eagleton, who argues, on his own grounds, for the use of a term like *truth* should be taken into account. Quarreling with poststructuralists who he believes commonly denounce those who "employ words like 'truth,' 'certainty' and the 'real,' " Eagleton makes a pragmatic point: "To say there are no absolute grounds for the use of such terms as truth, certainty, reality, and so on is not to say that these words lack meaning or are ineffectual." It is to make us "prisoners of our own discourse" (*Literary Theory: An Introduction* [Minneapolis: University of Minnesota Press, 1983] p. 144). (That a discourse intended to show that "man's soul" knows – and has always known – absolute Truth can become a morass of self-subverting metaphors seems to me patently demonstrated by Allan Bloom's language in *The Closing of the American Mind*. For an analysis of this language, the medium Bloom shares with postmodernists he attacks, see Blanche H. Gelfant, "Allan Bloom's Battle for Man's Soul: Metaphor as Revelation," *New England Review and Bread Loaf Quarterly* 12, no. 1 [Autumn 1989]: pp. 93–7.)

4 This is not to deny that pictures and other particularly representational forms (or forms of action, like dance) can describe and interpret. However, this essay is concerned with written interpretations, such as those created by literary and cultural critics. In attempting to sort out philosophically the meanings of fact, fiction, and truth – while arguing for the "factitiousness of fact" – Nelson Goodman discusses similarities and differences in the ways that the visual arts, music, literature, as well as science, "make" the world they depict or express. See *Ways of Worldmaking* (Indianapolis: Hackett, 1976), esp. pp. 91–107; and *Languages of Art: An Approach to a Theory of Symbols* (Indianapolis: Hackett, 1976) esp. pp. 177–221). Goodman translates "ineffability" into "density" (*Languages of Art,* p. 252).

5 In this statement (Geertz, "Thick Description," p. 19), "it" refers to formulations that, apparently, exist prior to and independent of inscription – the act of writing that Clifford considers "central to what anthropologists do in the field and thereafter" (Geertz, Introduction to *Writing Culture: The Poetic and Politics of Ethnography,* ed. James Clifford and George E. Marcus [Berkeley: University of California Press, 1986], p. 2). In his introduction to *Writing Culture,* Clifford notes that "the essays of this volume do not claim ethnography is 'only literature.' They do insist it is always writing" (p. 26).

6 In the essays of *The Interpretation of Cultures,* Geertz alleges that "cultural forms can be treated as texts, as imaginative works built out of social materials" ("Notes on the Balinese Cockfight," p. 449); and that the "concept of culture [he] espouse[s] is essentially a semiotic one . . . not an experimental science in search of law but an interpretive one in search of meaning" ("Thick Descriptions," p. 5). For a definition and critique of "interpretive anthropology," see George E. Marcus and Michael M. J. Fisher, *Anthropology as Cultural Critique: An Experimental Moment in the Human Sciences* (Chicago: University of

Chicago Press, 1986), pp. 25–40). As Barbara Herrnstein Smith has said (in discussing poetry "as fiction"), "The meanings of 'interpretation' are no less multiple than the meaning of 'meaning' " (*On the Margins of Discourse: The Relation of Literature to Language*
[Chicago: University of Chicago Press, 1978], p. 39). Some meanings are "historical and
determinant," subject, one would assume, to a cultural critique. Others, "historically indeterminate," pertain to the "fictiveness" of poetic utterance. To place a literary work of
art, of which a poem is paradigmatic, within an historical context in order to "interpret"
its cultural meanings deprives it of the aesthetic qualities that define it as art – at least, so
John Mort Ellis argues in a work to which Smith refers favorably. If cultural criticism implies (re)placing a text within the context in which it was produced, then in Ellis's view
its status as a literary text is jeopardized, if not destroyed: "The one thing that is different
about literary texts . . . is that they are *not* to be taken as part of the contexts of their origin; and to take them this way is to *annihilate* the thing that makes then literary texts . . .
they are not just literature misused, they are no longer literature" (Ellis, *The Theory of Literary Criticism: A Logical Analysis*) [Berkeley: University of California Press, 1974],
pp. 112–13, emphasis added). One might conclude from this argument that cultural criticism converts a text into a document.

7. Critics who deal with practical issues like diversifying traditional literary canons usually elide such questions, since they assume that words refer to an understandable social
world and not unremittingly to other words (as Derridean postmodern theories contend).
Thus, in arguing for the inclusion of "noncanonical texts" within academic curricula,
Paul Lauter offers a straightforward answer to the question why read texts within the context of other texts: because, he says, they "*teach us* how to view experience through the
prisms of gender, race, nationality, and other forms of marginalization" (*Canons and Contexts* [New York: Oxford University Press, 1991], p. 161, [original emphasis]). By *us*,
Lauter means, presumably, nonmarginalized readers. Those on the margins of American
society would learn from reading literary texts "a vital way to gain power in a literature
society" (p. 161). In an early essay, I proposed some other reasons for including American ethnic fiction in academic curricula (see "Mingling and Sharing in American Literature: Teaching Ethnic Fiction," *College English* 43 [1981]: pp. 763–72).

8 Geertz, *Interpretation of Cultures*, pp. 19–20.

9 This essay was in process before I read Michael Riffaterre's *Fictional Truth*, (Baltimore:
The Johns Hopkins University Press, 1990), which provides a sophisticated and esoteric
terminology for a process of textual analysis I describe here in ordinary terms. Marcus and
Fischer consider a "hunkering down on detail" (p. 118) common not only among anthropologists, but also among "the social and historical sciences" and "generalist cultural
critics" (like David Riesman).

10 Their countings and calculations are too various and incessant for this essay to reckon
with them all. In addition to money and units of time – minutes, hours, days, and years
(Wilhelm looking ahead to eternity) – characters count people, possessions, manuscript
pages, the number of typewritten lines on a page; meals and dishes; microscopic salivary
gland cells; chemical properties of polymer plastics – among other items.

11 Georg Lukács, *Solzhenitsyn* (Cambridge, Mass.: MIT Press, 1971), p. 15. Limitation
of space as well as purpose prevents me from discussing the considerable body of works
that Bellow and Solzhenitsyn have produced. Just as the writers concentrate upon one
day as emblematic, I would concentrate upon one novella. The choice may be supported
by Lukács's arguments that Solzhenitsyn's novella represents an initial or preliminary

working out of motifs and materials developed in his monumental novels. Kathryn Feuer admits that (unlike Lukács) she "was not among those who recognized Solzhenitsyn's potential greatness in *Ivan Denisovich*," but she now sees it presenting many "essential clues" to the later works. See Feuer, ed., *Solzhenitsyn: A Collection of Critical Essays* (Englewood Cliffs, N.J.: Prentice-Hall, 1976), p. 15. For a discussion of these clues, see pp. 15–18.

12 In his review of *Seize the Day*, Alfred Kazin declared Wilhelm's situation representative of "the world we really live in each day" – the "we" referring, presumably, to normative middle-class Americans ("In Search of Light: Review of *Seize the Day*," *New York Times Book Review*, November 18, 1956, pp. 5 and 36). In contrast, however, an English reviewer found Wilhelm's failure "arbitrary" because it fails to reflect "the society that has produced him and . . . condemned him" (Francis Wydham, "Review," *London Magazine* 5 [1957]: p. 66). The many reviews of *One Day in the Life of Ivan Denisovich* share a strongly expressed opinion that the novella reveals, as one reviewer put it, the "truth" of Soviet life and that Shukov represents "the Russian national character" (Alexei Kondratovich, "In the Name of Truth," *Soviet Literature* 4 [1963]: pp. 169–71]. Lukács described "Solzhenitsyn's achievement" as the "transformation of an uneventful day" into a "symbol of everyday life under Stalin" and of "a typical camp" into a symbol of Soviet society (*Solzhenitsyn*, p. 13).

13 On the subtle religious overtones of *One Day*, see Andre Kodjak, *Alexander Solzhenitsyn* (Boston: G. K. Hall, 1978), pp. 37–8 and 43–7; and on Solzhenitsyn's use of "several lexical categories," particularly of *skaz*, see Christopher Moody, *Solzhenitsyn* (New York: Harper & Row, 1973), pp. 50–68. An (embattled) American translator of Solzhenitsyn notes that his conversational style was typically "Soviet Russian, robust, staccato, with a modern vernacular . . . an ancient folk proverb from the depths of rural Russian, and occasional prison camp terms" (Olga Carlisle, *Solzhenitsyn and the Secret Circle* [New York: Holt, Rinehart and Winston, 1978], p. 16). Reading texts in translation inevitably involves a loss that can modulate meaning – a loss that becomes particularly heavy for the critic engaged in a cross-cultural study of literary texts. Reviewers of *One Day in the Life of Ivan Denisovich* disagreed categorically about the quality of the two translations into English that appeared simultaneously. See, for example, the reviews of Marc Slonim, "The Challenge Was the Need to Stay Alive," *New York Times Book Review*, April 7, 1963, pp. 4 and 34; Andrew Field, "A Soviet 'Eastern,' " *Partisan Review* 30 (1963): pp. 297–9; and Sidney Monas,"Ehrenburg's Day, Solzhenitsyn's Day," *Hudson Review* 16 (1964): pp. 112–21. For an "evaluation of the major English translations of Solzhenitsyn's fiction," by Alexis Klimoff see *Alexsandr Solzhenitsyn: Critical Essays and Documentary Materials*, ed. John B. Dunlop et al. (Belmont, Mass.: Norland, 1973), pp. 533–42. As language has become crucial to theories of textuality, and textuality central to self-reflective revisionist anthropology, the issue of translation should be salient, I would think, to cross-cultural critics. It was a concern to one of the founders of modern anthropology, Bronislaw Malinowski. In his diary of 1914–15, Malinowski "noted two defects in his approach – he did not observe the people enough, and he did not speak their language" (*A Diary in the Strict Sense of the Term*, tr. Norbert Guterman [New York: Harcourt, Brace and World, 1967], p. xiv). Mindful of my language deficiency, I have consulted with the distinguished translator of Slavic and Germanic literature, Professor Walter Arndt. I wish to thank Professor Arndt for commenting on passages of the English editions of Solzhenitsyn and Chukovskaya referred to in this essay. Exactness of translation seemed to me crucial to an interpretation of the ending of *Sofia Petrovna*, in which the words *trampled*

and *stamped* appear in proximity. Professor Arndt translated the words of the Russian text as *stamped* (implying action that takes place more than once) and *stamped out* – a seemingly slight difference from the translation in the available English text (which was *trampled* rather than *stamped*), but one that connotes a similarity of actions I find significant to an understanding of the end of the novella.

14 Wilhelm's qualifications are as dizzying as his nonsequiturs. "So at least he thought" supersedes "was"; "a certain amount of evidence" suggests an unusual cautious reckoning; "no, not quite," Wilhelm admits, deferring to truth rather than perpetuating the lie with which he has been living. Looking back at his life, Wilhelm defines the past as a "story" that has had "several versions," all concocted out of "lies." Now, on this day of reckoning, he gives the "true events"; finally, he tells "the truth" (p. 15).

15 As fool, failure, and survivor, Wilhelm conforms to the classic Jewish character of the *schlemiel*. See Sanford Pinsker, *The Schlemiel as Metaphor: Studies in the Yiddish and American Jewish Novel* (Carbondale: Southern Illinois University Press, 1971), pp. 125–57 on Bellow's "psychological schlemiels" and on Wilhelm in particular (pp. 148–51). All of the characteristics of the schlemiel as a literary figure that Ruth Wisse describes apply to Wilhelm, included comic perversity and an irradicable ambivalence (Ruth Wisse, *The Schlemiel as Modern Hero* [Chicago: University of Chicago Press, 1971]). Wisse relates the schlemiel's failure to his "refusal to be defined by others" (p. x) and his survival to a willingness to sacrifice "possessions and reputation to protect the inner self" (p. 16). See Wisse on Bellow's schlemiel, Herzog, as "liberal humanist" (pp. 92–107) and on the schlemiel as an historic figure (as Jew) and literary character (passim). Though he is a comic figure, Wilhelm resembles Arthur Miller's famous salesman, Willie Loman (low man), also a failure who wants to be loved, and also a character critics discuss as an American cultural icon.

16 Alexandr Solzhenitsyn, *One Day in the Life of Ivan Denisovich,* tr. Ralph Parker (New York: Signet, 1963), pp. 108 and 114. Subsequent references to the text are to this edition.

17 Describing Solzhenitsyn's use of detail, Lukács notes that "every detail presents an alternative between survival and succumbing, every object is a trigger of a salutary or destructive fate" (Lukács, *Solzhenitsyn,* p. 20). Kodjak claims that in Shukov's "well-formulated strategy for survival . . . eating becomes almost a sacrament" (*Alexander Solzhenitsyn,* p. 29). Terence Des Pres describes Shukov enjoying his soup as though he were receiving "the fullest beneficence of God" ("The Heroism of Survival," in *Alexsandr Solzhenitsyn,* ed. Dunlop et al., p. 50). Des Pres argues that Shukov "transcended his situation," living his day "on the edge of happiness" and achieving a desirable form of freedom (p. 51). Clearly, the views expressed by critics who see Solzhenitsyn sharing their own commitments to Soviet socialism or to Christianity need to be contextualized, though the task of judging a judgment of Solzhenitsyn seems inordinately difficult. See, for example, Dunlop on Solzhenitsyn's reception in the United States (in *Solzhenitsyn in Exile: Critical Essays and Documentary Materials,* ed. Dunlop et al. [Stanford, Calif.: Hoover Institution, 1985], pp. 24–55), and for critical responses in other countries, see pp. 2–23 and 56–142. See also Irving Howe on Lukács on Solzhenitsyn in *Alexsandr Solzhenitsyn,* ed. Dunlop et al., pp. 147–55.

18 Moody, *Solzhenitsyn,* p. 42. Though he undercuts his own generalization, Shukov connects individual character with nationality or ethnicity. He says, for example, that he had never found any "bad eggs" among Estonians (p. 56). The novella gives a synoptic view of Soviet ethnic and social diversity. As Moody points out, the inmates in Shukov's camp "represent something of a cross-section of Soviet people, the workers, peasants, intellectuals and nationalities . . . [and] the successive wave of prisoners who were sent to the camps throughout the 1930s and 1940s" (pp. 36–7). A discussion of ethnic diversity in *One Day* and its absence in the other novellas is beyond the scope of this essay.

19 Like Shukov and Tiurin, the old *zek* observes a self-imposed decorum when he eats, placing his food on a much-washed white napkin. In contrast, Wilhelm's slovenly eating habits disgust his father as they breakfast together in the hotel (p. 36). Mealtime offers another perspective on individual values and cultural patterns.

20 Kodjak sees Kuziomin as a "prophet" and his sermon on survival as biblical, sounding "like the word of God" (*Alexander Solzhenitsyn*, p. 38). Alexander Schmemann emphasizes "the Christian inspiration" of Solzhenitsyn's writing: "the most important, the most joyful news of the 'miracle' of Solzhenitsyn was that the first national writer of the Soviet period of Russian literature [Schmemann's claim for Solzhenitsyn] was at the same time a Christian writer" ("On Solzhenitsyn," in *Alexsandr Solzhenitsyn*, ed. Dunlop et al., pp. 38–9). Rosette Lamont says that in *One Day*, "the physical realm" – like "a bowl of soup" – "is vested with spirituality," so that a "man of the people" – like Shukov – becomes "his own church" (in *Alexsandr Solzhenitsyn*, ed. Dunlop et al., pp. 112–13). See Tolstoya, cited below, on the "cultural taboos" in Russia that "forbid" judgment of its peasants.

21 Bellow represents the break in a graphic image of vandalism: the breaking of the stone bench that had linked the graves of Wilhelm's mother and grandmother.

22 In describing the genesis of his character, Solzhenitsyn refers to the "real Shukov," to *gulag* prisoners he knew, and to "an autobiographical element": "I could not have described him [Shukov] if I hadn't served as a simple bricklayer in the camp" ("An Interview with Nikita Struve" in *Solzhenitsyn in Exile*, p. 308). Solzhenitsyn attributed his "real understanding" of the work of a bricklayer to his own experience as a camp prisoner, indicating that Shukov's fictional *how-to* instructions are actual. Though critics have assumed that the fidelity of such details to fact contributes to, or indeed constitutes, the truth of a text, underlying questions about "fictional truth" nevertheless persist. Another persistent question pertains to Shukov's competence at his assigned work; does it signify a prisoner's will to survive or a victim's complicity with his oppressions? Viewing the *victim* as a social construction, Kristin Bumiller (following Bettelheim) discusses the "rationalizations" that permit oppressed people, like Shukov, to tolerate and, implicitly, help maintain their intolerable conditions (*The Civil Rights Society: The Social Construction of Victims* [Baltimore: The Johns Hopkins University Press, 1988], p. 36). Shukov works so happily that he hardly notices the time and, in fact, he works overtime to finish a job, though his lateness places him in jeopardy. Commitment to work, which would make him an admirable Soviet citizen, may reveal him as a complicit victim. See below for references to critical dispute over how to interpret Shukov's exemplary behavior as a prisoner.

23 For a discussion of Bellow's eschatological vision in *Mr. Sammler's Planet*, see my short essay "In Terror of the Sublime: Mr. Sammler and Odin," *Modern Fiction Notes* 11 (1978): item 25. For a detailed study of "the Russian view of the *eskhaton*" and its bearing on the form of Russian fiction from Dostoyevsky to Pasternak, see David Bethea, *The Shape of the Apocalypse in Modern Russian Fiction* (Princeton, N.J.: Princeton University Press, 1989). As Bethea points out, reactions in Russia to the Chernobyl nuclear plant disaster reveal the persistence of "the Russian myth" of inevitable apocalypse. Bethea discusses briefly the relation of this myth to Solzhenitsyn's novella, "Matryona's Homestead" (pp. 272–3).

24 Solzhenitsyn himself has linked Ivan Denisovich's fate with the fate of Russia. See, for example, his comments in a 1967 interview in *Solzhenitsyn: A Documentary Record,* ed. Leopold Labedz (Bloomington: Indiana University Press, 1973). Since Lukács viewed Solzhenitsyn's novella as both preserving Soviet socialism and prefiguring social change – change that would restore original socialist ideals – its tragic "slice of life" constitutes for him "not an end but a social prelude to the future" (*Solzhenitsyn,* pp. 22–3).

25 Solzhenitsyn, "Novel Lecture," tr. Alexis Klimoff, in *Solzhenitsyn in Exile,* p. 497 (original emphasis).

26 For a discussion of both the illiteracy prevalent among prisoners and of prison writings, see Ioan Davies, *Writers in Prison* (Cambridge, Mass.: Basil Blackwell, 1990). Davies notes that though Solzhenitsyn, among others, claimed that prisons shared "a common culture," there were no universal characteristics defining either "the contexts within which prisons were located or the backgrounds from which prisoners came." Rather than writing about a universal prison community he may believe exists, Solzhenitsyn "knows that he is only writing about the Gulags – indeed, that he cannot write about anything else" (pp. 50–1). H. Bruce Franklin (*Prison Literature in America: The Victim as Criminal and Artist* [New York: Oxford University Press, 1989]) considers "American prison literature . . . very much part of American culture"; he sees a "radical" difference in "outlook" among prison writers of different times and different nationalities. At the same time, he admits that imprisonment has "common features" that transcend boundaries of time and place (pp. 235–6). Both Davis and Franklin describe inmates achieving literacy and even rhetorical eloquence while in prison, and committing themselves to political ideas that empower them in the world to which they return.

27 Kodjak concludes that "we may wonder whether Solzhenitsyn's characters strive for freedom" (*Alexander Solzhenitsyn,* p. 157) or whether they "seek a new authority . . . [that] they can trust, and perhaps worship again" (p. 158). Des Pres argues, on the other hand, that as a "survivor," Shukov becomes by his mere existence "a reproach to the system"; "like the saint . . . [he] is invested with a power that moves other men to thought and inspiration" ("The Heroism of Survival," p. 49). Thus, Shukov would influence political change through his influence upon his readers. However, Bruno Bettelheim disagrees with Des Pres, pointing out in his study of survivors that "what the prisoner can do . . . is insignificant compared to the need to defeat politically or militarily those who maintain the camps – something that the prisoners, of course, cannot do" (*Surviving and Other Essays* [New York: Knopf, 1979], p. 289).

28 See, for example, the "Questions" concerning Solzhenitsyn raised by Czeslaw Milosz, specifically, the question, "Is Solzhenitsyn a conservative?" – to which the answer (as Bellow's Wilhelm might have it) is yes and no, depending upon the definition of the term (in *Alexsandr Solzhenitsyn,* ed. Dunlop et al, pp. 450–1). The explicit question points to a well-known controversy still being carried on over Solzhenitsyn's political views. Common charges are that Solzhenitsyn cannot understand American democracy and that Americans cannot understand Solzhenitsyn's deeply rooted Russian character. For a biased but not unique view of Solzhenitsyn the man, see Carlisle (*Solzhenitsyn and the Secret Circle*), who describes him turning into "an authoritarian figure who thought nothing of attacking those who had helped him, none more virulently than those in the West" (p. 179). Now that Solzhenitsyn plans to return to his native country (and by now has returned), Russians are raising new questions about the sacrifices entailed in his exile. The questions ask what sacrifices he suffered during the years he lived in comfort and ease in his lovely Vermont home, and what sacrifices he faces when he returns to live in the fine house he is building for himself in Russia. In presenting his revisionist view of anthropology, Clifford Geertz finds that "it becomes profoundly unclear how individuals enclosed in one culture are able to penetrate the thought of individuals enclosed in another" ("The Way We Think Now: Ethnography of Modern Thought," in *Local Knowledge: Further Essays in Interpretive Anthropology* [New York: Basic Books, 1983], p. 149). The questions raised by Solzhenitsyn's countrymen, however, imply that they believe they can, perhaps, penetrate the mind of an individual, even an extraordinary as a great writer, who comes from the same cultural background.

29 Milosz, "Questions," p. 455.

30 As an idiomatic expression, to tell or "tell on" someone means to reveal and incriminate. Both writers have defined themselves as story*tellers* who reveal a truth about the past that has deliberately been hidden and, in doing so, incriminate those responsible for the past and its misrepresentation. In an afterword to *Sofia Petrovna* (tr. Aline Worth [1967; rept. Evanston, Ill.: Northwestern University Press, 1988]), Chukovskaya declares her wish to reinstate "the true history" of Soviet life under Stalin, one that had been "replaced by fictitious history," the state's self-serving version of events (p. 112). For an elaboration on writing as a form of "telling" in *The Girl* – which uses the equivalent slang word *stooling* – see my essay " 'Everybody Steals': Language as Theft in Meridel Le Sueur's *The Girl*," in *Tradition and the Talents of Women,* ed. Florence Howe (Urbana: University of Illinois Press, 1991), pp. 183–210). Le Sueur tells how working people are opposed and repressed in her pieces of reportage, well known in their time. See *Salute to Spring* [1940; rept. New York: International, 1966] and *Song for My Time: Stories of the Period of Repression* [Minneapolis: West End Press, 1977]. In *North Star Country,* she recapitulates past oppressions of Native Americans, midwest farmers, and small-town workers. She tells also of a rich and beautiful land that was despoiled (see Blanche H. Gelfant, Forward to *North Star Country* [Lincoln: University of Nebraska Press, 1984], pp. vi–xvii).

31 An active literary and political figure in the 1930s and 1940s, Le Sueur had gained recognition as a writer of realistic stories intensified in their power by mythic and lyric overtones, and as a journalist deeply empathetic with the struggling people about whom she wrote – strikers, impoverished farmers in the Midwest, hungry women on breadlines. In the dark time of the blacklisting, when Le Sueur was followed by FBI agents and, presumably through their intervention, fired from the meager jobs she could get, Le Sueur actively resisted silencing by continuing to write, publishing as best she could in radical or communist journals and presses. As with dissident Soviet writers, many of her manuscripts remained unpublished and sequestered. For an account of Le Sueur's political radicalism, see Linda Ray Pratt, "Woman Writer in the CP: The Case of Meridel Le Sueur," *Women's Studies* 14 (1988): pp. 247–64. For recently gathered oral accounts of political harassment and blacklisting, personal stories that contextualize Le Sueur's experience, see Bud Schultz and Ruth Schultz, *It Did Happen Here: Recollections of Political Repression in America* (Berkeley: University of California Press, 1989).

32 Chukovskaya relates the publishing history of her novella in a prefatory Note and an Afterword to *Sophia Petrovna* (pp. 1–2 and 111–20). According to Chukovskaya, when a promise of publication was broken, she sued for damages and won her suit. She stated in her argument "that if they stopped publishing Solzhenitsyn it would be a great shame for the country." In answer to the publisher's defense "that after the publication of *One Day in the Life of Ivan Denisovich* the publishing house had been swamped by a torrent of prison camp books," Chukovskaya said, "my *Sofia Petrovna* and his *Ivan Denisovich* were novellas written at different times, about different times, and on different themes; his was about the camps, mine, about 'ordinary life' " (Afterword, p. 117). The Afterword to *Sofia Petrovna* is an excerpt from Chukovskaya's book *The Process of Expulsion*, published in 1979, a time when Chukovskaya was still waiting, she wrote, for "just one thing": "to see my book published in the Soviet Union./In my own country. In Sofia Petrovna's country./I have been waiting patiently for thirty-four years" (Afterword, p. 119). In 1988, *Sof'ia Petrovna* was published in Moscow, and Chukovskaya's long wait was finally over.

33   According to Carlisle, Chuvoskaya had been "the most eloquent spokesman for Alexander Solzhenitsyn in the USSR," playing "a crucial part in his survival" (*Solzhenitsyn and the Secret Circle*, p. 134 fn.). For Chukovskaya's remembrance of meetings with Solzhenitsyn at the house of her father, the celebrated critic, translator, and writer Kornei Ivanovich Chukovskii, see the excerpt "Solzhenitsyn at Peredlkino," taken from Chukovskaya's account of her 1974 expulsion from the Soviet Writer's Union, *The Process of Expulsion* (in *Solzhenitsyn in Exile*, pp. 287–97).

34   In time, Akhmatova would entitle a sequence of poems "Requiem" (1935–1940) in remembrance of those who disappeared or died during the Great Purges. In one of the poems of the sequence, a line that describes Akhmatova's destitution as a woman "alone" specifies Sofia Petrovna's losses and those of countless Soviet women: "Husband in the grave, son in prison" (*The Complete Poems of Anna Akhmatova*, ed. Roberta Reede, tr. Judith Hemschemever [Somerville, Mass.: Zephyr, 1990], Vol. 1, p. 101). In another poem, Akhmatova has become, as would Sofia Petrovna, a cipher in a crowd of women whose loved ones have disappeared in the Great Purges, a multitude in which she is "three-hundredth in line" (Vol. 1, p. 101). As Akhmatova's translator has noted, while the sequence refers to the poet's own experience in Leningrad during the time her son was imprisoned, the "you" it evokes "becomes all Russians imprisoned and tortured by their own government" (Vol. 1, p. 4). Chukovskaya has published two volumes of memoirs of her meetings with Akhmatova during the 1930s as her way of preserving the life of the poet. I might add parenthetically that Theodore Dreiser, who figures significantly in the essay that follows, had reported on the sudden disappearance of men accused in secret conspiracies against the state, disappearances that took place several years before the notorious Stalin purges (*Dreiser Looks at Russia* [New York: Horace Liveright, 1928], pp. 125–9). As a former newspaper man, Dreiser was particularly appalled at the secrecy of the trials and death sentences that followed upon the disappearances: men were on "trial for their lives! Yet no word in any of the papers – not a word" (p. 126). That word was withheld from the public evoked in Dreiser, and in time it would evoke in the world, a sense of "terror."

35   Le Sueur, "Afterwords," in *The Girl* (Minneapolis: West End Press, 1978), np.

36   Chukovskaya, "Afterword," in *Sofia Petrovna*, p. 111 (original emphasis).

37   I realize that "development is a relative concept colored by many interrelated factors, including class, history, and gender" and that "distinctive female paradigms" give the *Bildungsroman* a multivalence that traditional generic definitions, based upon male patterns, have overlooked (Elizabeth Abel et al., eds., *The Voyage In: Fictions of Female De-*

velopment [Hanover, N.H.: University Press of New England, 1983], pp. 4 and 19). I discuss the significance of gender in the essay " 'Everybody Steals': Language as Theft in Meridel Le Sueur's *The Girl*," and its relation to Le Sueur's appropriation of Native American cultural forms of expression in "Meridel Le Sueur's 'Indian Poetry' and the Question of Feminine Form," in *Women Writing in America: Voices in Collage* (Hanover, N.H.: University Press of New England, 1984), pp. 72–91.

38 Also seized and spirited away to unnamed prison camps are her son's best friend, Alik, accused of terrorism; an "esteemed doctor," friend of Sofia Petrovna's dead husband; "an old friend" of Sofia Petrovna who "taught French . . . and lived just like everybody else"; Sofia Petrovna's much-beloved director and his secretary; the new director who had betrayed the old; and relatives of the countless women with whom Sofia Petrovna lines up every day in front of the prosecutor's office.

39 Neither ending is unambiguous, and both are troubling, since, as the Girl knows, winter will soon come, a season of death in which daughters, like the mythic Persephone with whom she is identified in the text, cannot remain on earth. On the "confusion" of myth, feminism, and Marxim, see Gelfant, " 'Everybody Steals.' "

40 Given its daily publication of official lies, that the word *pravda* means *truth* is bitterly ironic. However, as Vera Sandomirsky Dunlap explains, modulations of meanings in the word suggest that it may portend violence: "The Russian word *pravda* . . . is not altogether synonymous with . . . the western word *'truth.'* It connects rather with *rectus, dexter, justus,* and has a strong undercurrent of justice and due process before God. The ancient moral meaning was revolutionized by nascent bolshevism into aggression. And truth as retaliatory social justice held the entire bolshevik ideological framework together. But that which was participatory or corporate in this principle began to ring hollow under Stalin's rule" (see *In Stalin's Time: Middleclass Values in Soviet Fiction* [Cambridge: Cambridge University Press, 1976], p. 74.). Sofia Petrovna's way of reading *Pravda* blurs the distinction that Pierre Bourdieu has made between the "sensational" and the "informative" press in *Distinction: A Social Critique of the Judgement of Taste,* tr. Richard Nice (Cambridge, Mass.: Harvard University Press, 1984), pp. 440–51. Sofia Petrovna finds the newspaper's political (mis)information highly sensational, and other material soporific. A comparison between what Sofia Petrovna and the Girl reads does not show the "class distribution of newspaper reading" that Bourdieu finds in his study of cultural taste (p. 21). Both characters read what has been made available to them, so that a study of the production and distribution of newspapers might be more edifying about the novellas' cultural contexts than a consideration of consumption habits. Foucault pursues this line of inquiry in "The Discourse on Language" (in *The Archaeology of Knowledge & The Discourse on Language,* tr. A. M. Sheridan Smith [New York: Pantheon, 1972]), hypothesizing that "in every society the production of discourse is . . . controlled, selected, organized, and redistributed" (p. 216). (Incidentally, in Solzhenitsyn's story, "For the Good of the Cause," a seemingly sophisticated student upholds the credibility of Soviet newspapers when he asserts, like Sofia Petrovna, that "Newspapers don't make mistakes." See *Stories and Prose Poems,* tr. Michael Glenny (New York: Farrar, Straus and Giroux, 1971), p. 72.

41 For other references to mistakes, see pp. 72, 75, and 77. Sofia Petrovna argues with her son's friend Alik, soon to be seized, that "Kolya was arrested through a misunderstanding" (p. 60). She tells the wife of her imprisoned director that her son "was arrested by mistake," to which the wife replies angrily, "Here, you know, everything's by mistake" (p. 75).

42 See a carefully documented and important historical account of the mystique of motherhood in Joanna Hubbs, *Mother Russia: The Feminine Myth in Russian Culture* (Bloomington: Indiana University Press, 1988).

43 Earlier, the Girl learns how crooked politicians stage a phony raid on the speakeasy where she works so that there will be "something to print in the paper" (p. 20). A persistent complaint in American history has been that while "the news" purports to be objective or true to the events it reports, it is biased and manipulative – a view succinctly summarized by Edward Said, who defined "the news" as "a euphemism for ideological images of the world that determine political reality for a vast majority of the world's population" ("Opponents, Audiences, Constituencies, and Community," in *The Politics of Interpretation,* ed. W. J. T. Mitchell [Chicago: University of Chicago Press, 1983], pp. 7–32 and 31–2). In his sketch of Soviet life, Dreiser had complained about the strict censorship imposed upon Russian newspaper, specifically, the official state newspapers *Izvestia* and *Pravda* (*Dreiser Looks at Russia,* pp. 94–9). He "took a particular interest," Dreiser wrote, "in the Communists' repeated declaration that in Russia there was absolute freedom for the press to think and say what it chose," but he noted that "no news from within or without Russia may appear which does not tend to glorify the principles of Marx and Lenin" (p. 96). Then with an equivocation that signified his attempt at fairmindedness, Dreiser asked whether the Catholic Church had done any "better" in allowing criticism.

44 Newspaper had also been used to wrap the aborted fetus of the Girl's friend Belle (pp. 54 and 75), thus figuring in the novella's vision of both the impossibility, as well as the possibility, of new life for its dispossessed women. (In Joan Didion's novel *Play It as It Lays,* mothers similarly connect newspapers with the life and the death of children – as an improvised blanket to protect them and as a wrapping for the protagonist's aborted baby.) In noting that the Girl's lover Butch sold newspapers when he was a boy, the text evokes an almost folkloric role of newspapers in American culture as a stepping-stone to success. Newspapers also provide mindless entertainment. When the Girl is incarcerated in a women's hospital-jail she reads newspaper "funnies" (p. 132) donated by charity ladies. Newspapers serve various incidental purposes in the novellas. Shukov makes himself a cigarette by rolling his tobacco in a piece of newspaper. Lottie rolls a newspaper into "truncheon" that she intends to throw at her stepdaughter and then, in a typical self-refereeing and self-dramatizing action, unrolls the paper, rips it into confettilike pieces, and wafts the pieces through the air.

45 Both writers attest also to the political and moral integrity of their parents, uncompromising figures who remained faithful to social ideals that placed their lives in jeopardy. Both paid tribute to their parents in books that preserve their memory (see Le Sueur's *Crusade* [New York: Blue Heron, 1955] and Chukovskaya's *To the Memory of Childhood,* tr. Eliza Kellogg Klose [Evanston, Ill.: Northwestern University Press, 1988]). In her memoir of her father, a famous writer, Chukovskaya connects writing, historical memory, and culture: "What's written by the pen can't be cut out by the axe. Culture is the trail of the noble impulses of the human spirit, hardened and set, the tracks intersect, cross and lay down new roads to the future. Fearless memory preserves these tracks, defends them . . . sometimes from atrocity . . . even the tracks of atrocity must be preserved. (Otherwise people will not know that culture is not simply work, it is *battle.*)" (p. 144, emphasis added). For an account of Chukovskaya's relationship to her father, the most important formative figure in her life, see Beth Holmgren, *Women's Works in Stalin's Time: On Lidiia Chukovskaia and Nadezhda Mandelstam* (Bloomington: Indiana University Press, 1993), pp. 29–43. Holmgren's book, which appeared after my account of Chukovskaya was in press, should impress American readers with Chukovskaya's importance as an historical and literary figure, and as a woman (pp. 29–94). Holmgren sets the texts she discusses, *Sofia Petrovna*, *Going Under*, and *Notes on Anna Akhmatova* (to which my references are necessarily brief), within an historical context that affirms the factuality – a term less mooted than truth – of Chukovskaya's writings.

46 I wish to thank Professor Darra Goldstein of Williams College for her exceedingly helpful recommendation of a number of books pertaining to modern Russian literature and life, among them, Baranskaya's "A Week Like Any Other."

47 Natalya Baranskaya, "A Week Like Any Other," in *A Week Like Any Other: Novellas and Stories*, tr. Pieta Monks (Seattle: Seal, 1989), p. 13. Further references are given in the text. "A Week" was originally published in the USSR in *Novy Mir* in 1969.

48 According to two of my colleagues, each kind enough to read a novella and evaluate the research project and procedures of its protagonist, the experiments of both women scientists are equally respectable; both engage in calculations that are standard, neither groundbreaking nor outmoded. My thanks to Charles L. Braun, Professor of Chemistry of Dartmouth College, and to Edward M. Berger, Professor of Biology, for graciously taking time to comment on the scientific aspects of the texts. To gauge the position that Baranskaya's heroine holds in her laboratory, as well as the scientific roles of the other women characters, see Norton T. Dodge, "Women in the Professions," in *Women in Russia*, ed. Dorothy Atkinson et al. (Stanford, Calif.: Stanford University Press, 197), pp. 205–24.

49 In her important study *Women in Soviet Society* (Berkeley: University of California Press, 1978), Gail Warshofsky Lapidus absorbs Baranskaya's novella into a cultural analysis of modern Soviet life by noting that it gives "direct expression" to the "findings of innumerable time-budget studies" of modern Soviet women in the "work-force" (p. 281). Olya's situation as a working wife and mother serves to illustrate and confirm cultural studies of women in Soviet society, and Baranskaya's portrayal is, in turn, validated as "true" and representative by these studies. In a similar way, Helena Goscilo notes that Olya's "dilemmas . . . [as] an educated working family woman" represent "the concrete application of . . . socialist theory" and confirm, and are confirmed by, "a recent survey" of Russian homelife (Goscilo, ed., *Russia and Polish Women's Fiction* [Knoxville: University of Tennessee Press, 1985], p. 22). For her success in managing (p. 57), Olya might be viewed as as a modern example of "the strong woman," a stereotype discussed in an influential essay by Vera Dunlap. Having documented the persistence of a type in "The Strong-Woman Motif," Dunlap describes historical changes in the fictional representaton of women in "The Changing Image of Women in Soviet Literature," in Donald Brown, ed., *The Role and Status of Women in the Soviet Union* (New York: Teachers College Press, 1968), pp. 60–97. In an essay entitled "On Happiness in Recent Soviet Fiction" (*Russian Literature Triquarterly* 9 [1974]: pp. 473–85), Xenia Gasiorowska discusses Olya within the context of *byt*, an elusive term that refers to the complex of customs that constitutes everyday life and determines woman's place within her culture. As Gasiorowska points out elsewhere, Soviet fiction often describes a struggle between old *byt* and the new as women seek to break out of their traditional genderized roles (*Women in Soviet Fiction: 1917–1964* [Madison: University of Wisconsin Press, 1968]). See also Barbara Heldt, *Terrible Perfection: Women and Russian Literature* (Bloomington: Indiana University Press, 1987), for a literary and historical contex within which "A Week Like Any Other" can be (in Geertz's sense of term) described.

50 As American readers, we may not appreciate the importance of Olya's new flat, the first item on her list, a primary matter. (Since I wrote this note, news reports have given shocking accounts of the murders and crimes committed over housing. Apparently, the current housing shortage in Russia has led to widespread financial swindles and violence.) A mock-heroic epic, *The Ivankiad* (1976) describes a monumental, comic (and not so comic) battle over an apartment, and the desire for a place to live figures in a marriage of expediency and violence in Anna Maas's story, "Lubya's Wedding," *Russian Literature Triquarterly* 9 1974), pp. 145–59. The division of her apartment into subflats turns out to have serious consequences for Sofia Petrovna once her son is arrested. Subdivided flats, new apartments, hotels, deserted warehouses (refuge for the dispossessed women of *The Girl*), a trailer, an old country house – the highly specified places where characters live provide "inspectable" details other than those of this essay for the "thick description" of a cultural critique.

51 For an example of a time-budget questionnaire of the 1960s, see Michael Sacks, *Women's Work in Soviet Russia: Continuity in the Midst of Change* (New York: Praeger, 1976), pp. 183–7; and for examples of time-budget tables drawn from such a questionnaire, see pp. 188–94. On the "methodological advantages" of time-allocation analyses, see Lapidus, *Women in Soviet Society*, p. 269. In a recent study of American women's housework, many detailed questions were asked directly in carefully patterned interviews. For the "interview schedule," see Kathleen Gerson, *Hard Choices: How Women Decide about Work, Career, and Motherhood* (Berkeley: University of California Press, 1985), pp. 259–85.

52 As Lapidus points out in her introduction to her study of women in Soviet society, "new economic and political obligations were superimposed [by Soviet policy] on traditional feminine roles, creating for women a palpable 'double burden' in daily life" (*Women in Soviet Society*, p. 6). For a detailed discussion of recent Soviet policy that attempts to respond to the "contradictions in women's dual roles," see esp. pp. 287–309. Almost all accounts of modern Soviet working women agree that they carry a "double burden." Indeed, Mark Field, in an essay entitled "Workers (and Mothers): Soviet Women Today," in Brown, ed., *The Role and Status of Women in the Soviet Union*, alleges that women who "work side by side with men, while at the same time carrying the burden of domestic duties and the bearing and care of children . . . in essence, [carry] a double, if not *triple,* load" (p. 8, emphasis added). See also Atkinson et al, *Women in Russia,* particularly on "Women's Double Burden and Professional Productivity," pp. 223–4; Goscilo, *Women's Fiction,* pp. 22–3; and Richard Stites, *The Women's Liberation Movement in Russia: Feminism, Nihilism and Bolshevism, 1860–1930* (Princeton, N.J. :Princeton University Press, 1978), pp. 317–45. In her recent account of Soviet women, Francine du Plessix Gray shows the "double burden" unrelieved. As one woman whom Gray had interviewed says: "Soviet women are *not* neglecting their domestic duties . . . we want to write our theses but we also feel we should be making *pirozhki.* . . . We've been brainwashed with the notion that our state had done everything for us to reconcile the two roles, but the state hasn't begun to provide for us" (*Soviet Women: Walking the Tightrope* [New York: Doubleday, 1990], p. 90, original emphasis). The subtitle to Gray's book provides a metaphor for the precarious position of modern Soviet women who are trying to balance their various roles – an attempt given preeminence in the title of Goscilo's anthology, *Balancing Acts: Contemporary Stories by Russian Women* (Bloomington: Indiana University Press, 1989). The title is inspired by a story of Anna Maas in which the narrator, a women field-anthropologist and a wife and mother, describes herself living "two dissimilar lives . . . proceeding along parallel lines" between which she sometimes threw a bridge that enabled her to cross over from one life to the other – a "swaying" bridge on which she had to perform a "balancing act" ("A Business Trip Home," pp. 37–8). On the other hand, a self-styled "cross-cultural" study of the modern woman concludes happily that her household tasks are "few and manageable," child-rearing is neither heavy nor restricting, and apartments require "little housekeeping" (Constantina Safilios-Rothschild, "A Cross-Cultural Examination of Women's Marital, Educational and Occupational Options," *Acta. Soc.* 14, nos. 1-2 [1970]: pp. 96–114 and p. 100). All of this would be news to Olya.

53   Goscilo notes a general indifference among "Slavists" to feminist theories and literature (*Balancing Acts,* p. ix). She questions "simplistic assumptions about Baranskaia's feminism" (p. xi) and quotes Chukovskaya's dismissive attitude toward the concept of "women's literature" (p. xxiii). (I tend to differ with Goscilo in her interpretation of Baranskaya's story "The Kiss," since I do not see the protagonist's decision to help her daughter rather keep a date with a man as contrary to feminist values.) According to du Plessix Gray, a dismissive attitude toward feminism is shared by Tatyana Tolstaya, perhaps the most renowned woman writer on the contemporary Soviet scene. Tolstaya is quoted as equating feminism with goals Soviet woman wish to avoid and, with lesbianism, which she finds highly aversive. Gray considers Tolstaya's views typical of "the overwhelming majority of even the most progressive Soviet intellectuals" (*Soviet Women,* pp. 177–9 and 201–2). (For Tolstaya's view on Stalin's Great Terror as a continuation of the "Little Terror" that she believes constitutes Russian history, see her review of Robert Conquest's *The Great Terror: A Reassessment,* "In Cannibalistic Times," *New York Review of Books,* April 11, 1991, pp. 3–6). Lapidus believes that "if no feminist movement exists today [1978] in the USSR, it is because the women question is viewed as solved" (p. 4), presumably by Soviet decree. For interesting insights into the views of contemporary British women on Soviet interpretations of "the woman question," see Barbara Holland, *Soviet Sisterhood* (Bloomington: Indiana University Press, 1985), particularly pp. 24–53; and for a British perspective on Russian feminist movements in pre-Revolution decades, see Linda Edmondson, *Feminism in Russia, 1900–17* (Stanford, Calif.: Stanford University Press, 1984). On the efforts of Soviet feminists to voice their views and the repressive official reactions to these efforts, see *Women and Russia,* edited by a leading Soviet feminist, Tatyana Mamonova (Boston: Beacon, 1984).

54   Arlene Heyman, "Artifact," in *Epoch* 39 (1990): pp. 6–49. Subsequent page references are to this publication. Heyman received the Hathaway Prize for "Artifact" in 1990.

55   The differences in the way the women commute may influence – and in turn reflect – the way they feel about themselves. Lottie cultivates a feeling of aloneness in her car that becomes indistinguishable, finally, from self-alienation; Olya's daily contacts on the bus, where people help her jump on or hang on to her shopping bags, give her a daily sense of recognized presence. In his well-known study *The Country and the City* (New York: Oxford University Press, 1973), Raymond Williams suggests a relationship between the feeling that modern city dwellers have of being "at once central and marginal" to their lives (Lottie's confused sense of herself) and the feelings evoked by their typical means of transportation, the automobile. To Williams, a peculiarly alienating urban "mode of relationship [is] embodied in the modern car: private, enclosed, an individual vehicle in a pressing and merely aggregated common flow" (p. 296). In *Seize the Day,* Wilhelm's car and his perversely careless way of driving project the willful disarray of his

self as well as a typical urban sense, shared by Lottie, of being alone and isolated while in the midst of others.

56   Olya's words, as she expresses her closeness to others of her sex and class, echo those of Amelia in *The Girl*: "You are not alone," she tells the pregnant Girl; "You'll never be alone." Motherhood, in Le Sueur's novel, constitutes both the sign and reality of woman's relationship to others, a bond that links the Girl, as a symbol of all girls who mature to womanhood, to her child, her sex, and her class. As I noted in " 'Everybody Steals,' " Le Sueur's overt celebration of motherhood does not mean her views are either unambivalent or simple, or that she considers "mothering" an activity exclusive to women.

57   Olya's haircut, hurried into during her lunch hour, inspires a subtly suggested sexual desire in her husband, who sees her as the young slim woman with whom he fell in love. Hair plays a significant symbolic role in the busy life of a middle-aged professional woman in I. Grekova's story "Ladies' Hairdresser" (1963) in Grekova, *Russia Women: Two Stories* (New York: Harcourt Brace Jovanovich, 1983). The director of a Moscow computer institute and a single parent, Marya Vladimirovna Kovaleva finds no time to carry on her research, as an inner reckoning shows: "If you count in absolute, astronomic time, then I guess I'm not so terribly busy. I could grab two hours or so for research. But it doesn't work. A research problem requires total concentration, and I've got to pay attention to a thousand little trifles. I'm all over the place" (p. 24).

58   A study of scientists at work, conducted by a French philosopher and an English sociologist, concludes that scientific facts are artifacts produced by the politics of laboratory life and by the process of writing (Bruno Latour and Steve Woolgar, *Laboratory Life: the Social Construction of Scientific Facts* [Beverly Hills, Calif.: Sage Library of Social Research, 1979]). In a modern self-reflective mode, the authors explain that they call their project "an anthropology of science" and that, as "anthropologists," they observed "the culture of the laboratory" and the processes by which the laboratory scientists produced their cultural "objects," their so-called hard facts and their various documents. The end product of laboratory life turned out to be "literary" – also the end-product, one might add, of an anthropology of science. Since this study focuses upon "the process of construction" that goes on in the laboratory, it displaces truth and falsity with a continuum of references to "the conditions of construction" and places facts and artifacts, both neither true nor false, in a relative positions within this continuum (see, for example, p. 176).

59   Various critics have argued that the act of writing creates, rather than records, the "I" of autobiography. See, for example, Louis A. Renza, "The Veto of the Imagination: A Theory of Autobiography," *New Literary History* 9 (1977–78): pp. 1–26.

60   In defining a difference in function between literary texts and sociological documents, Stephen Dunn and Ethel Dunn note that "under Soviet conditions, specifically literary material serves to alert the general public to the existence of problems, and to prepare the public psychologically for action to solve them" (*The Study of the Soviet Family in the U.S.S.R. and in the West: Slavic Studies Working Paper*, no. 1 [Columbus: American Association for the Advancement of Slavic Studies, 1977], p. 50). This may not seem a distinction to postmodern critics, but rather an erasure of difference that turns a text into a document.

61   For discussions of the American Constitution as a "literary text" (rather than a document), see Robert Ferguson, "We Do Ordain and Establish: The Constitution as Literary Text," *William and Mary Law Review* 29 (1987): pp. 3–25; and Richard Weisberg, "Text into Theory: A Literary Approach to the Constitution," *Georgia Law Review* 20 (1986): pp. 934–94.

62 "An essay is a trial effort, a tentative exploration, . . . a report of qualified findings," Arthur Danto notes in a review that ends with a reference to Abelard's *Sic et non*, quoted in a contemporary book of essays that, Danto writes approvingly, is filled with "qualification, extenuation, and exception" (see Danto, "Are We Cracking under the Strain?: A Review of Modernity on Endless Trial, by Leszek Kolakowski," *New York Times Book Review*, December 23, 1990, pp. 1 and 22).

63 Distinctions between these categories – the true and the false – have also been construed as social constructions. See, for instance, Foucault, "The Discourse on Language," pp. 219–20 and passim.

64 As the essay notes, Bellow transmogrifies the Hotel Ansonia into surreal images that change with the weather (and with Wilhelm's premonitions of drowning). In contrast to a real hotel that turns surreal, the Hotel Gloriana, where Wilhelm is spending his last day, refers to the phantasmagoric place of Spencer's *Fairie Queene*. As the essay has also noted, the novella and its befuddled salesman, both unmistakably American in their circumstances, draw upon English literature so heavily that the matrix of literary allusions could provide grounds for a cultural analysis. Wilhelm's literary education in New York schools has steeped him in English poetic tradition, a matter that may strike the contemporary reader as quizzical. One could approach a cross-cultural study by considering literary influences that transcend boundaries of time and place, such as those of genre (mentioned in the second panel) and those of one writer upon another. Bellow has expressed his admiration for the great Russian novelists of the nineteenth century and, clearly, patterned his first novel, *Dangling Man*, upon Dostoyevsky's *Notes from Underground*. Solzhenitsyn has declared his indebtedness to, and difference from, the American writer, John Dos Passos ("An Interview with Nikita Struve" in *Solzhenitsyn in Exile*, pp. 314–16). Solzhenitsyn notes that he "got to know his [Dos Passos's] writing in a rather original setting – the Lubianka prison" (p. 314).

65 The introduction (if only in a footnote) of nationality as a context or a concept relevant to this essay sets *artifact* within yet another discourse. In *Imagined Communities: Reflections on the Origin and Spread of Nationalism* (London: Verso, 1989), Benedict Anderson describes nationality and nation-ness as "cultural artefacts" produced by "discrete historical forces" and preserved by a "variety of political and ideological constellations" (pp. 13–14). Anderson's analogy between a nation as an "imagined community" and the world of a novel or of a newspaper (pp. 31, 37 and passim) creates a context for a critical discussion of the novellas in the second panel and of realistic novels written in and about different countries.

66 In *Rethinking Intellectual History: Texts, Contexts, Language* (Ithaca, N.Y.: Cornell University Press, 1983), Dominick LaCapra asks, "What is meant by the term 'text'?" (p. 26), a question that raises for him issues of how properly to read and interpret texts and how to avoid an hypostatization of *context*. Arguing that a text is "the scene of an interplay between different forces," he adds that "context itself would have to been seen as a text of sorts" – a view that leads him to propose a reversed intertextual reading in which the "text itself" would provide a "model for the reconstruction of the 'large context' " (pp. 116–17).

67 Bizarrely enough, Nancy Reagan's hat (an imagined hat) has been used to introduce a detailed review of "feminist thinking about representation" and the "collapse of a feminist consensus" in Catharine Stimpson, "Nancy Reagan Wears a Hat: Feminism and Its Cultural Consensus (1987)," in *Where the Meanings Are: Feminism and Cultural Spaces* (New York: Routledge, 1988), pp. 179–96. (One needs to question whether there ever was a contemporary feminist consensus to collapse.) Nancy Reagan's imagined hat, like Shukov's and Wilhelm's, has no existence as a "real" object that can be contextualized within actual historical circumstances. However, there is a real hat that has "in fact" exerted significant historical influence, contributing to the formulation of fundamental American constitutional rights. For a man's "right to wear his hat if he pleased" was an important issue in debates over the precise wording of the First Amendment. The hat and the issues it entailed recalled to members of the newly formed U.S. legislature the 1670 trial of William Penn in England's Old Bailey. In this trial, considered a notorious example of "judicial tyranny," Penn had been held in contempt for wearing a hat he was told to put on after he had taken it off to show proper respect in court. The main charge against Penn had been unlawful and tumultuous assembly, a charge brought to prevent Penn from preaching Quaker doctrine, that is, to limit speech. In opposing a move to exclude from the First Amendment a clause explicitly granting Americans the right of assembly, Congressman John Page of Virginia refuted claims that the clause was "trivial . . . no more essential than whether a man has a right to wear his hat or not." Page argued that just as "a man [Penn] had been obliged to pull off his hat when he appeared before the face of authority; [so] people have also been prevented from assembling together on their lawful occasions." For a detailed account of how William Penn's hat figured significantly in the framing of American constitutional rights, see Irving Brant, *The Bill of Rights: Its Origin and Meaning* (New York: Bobbs-Merrill, 1965), pp. 54–61. Hats came to the mind of a famous American writer traveling through the Soviet Union in the late 1920s in order to gather impressions of the new state which he could report to his American readers. In *Dreiser Looks at Russia* (cited above), the American writer had used hats to illustrate the practical methods for teaching children that he observed in Soviet schools. The child is given an object, Dreiser notes, "His hat, say. Well, what is the thing he has in his hand?" It is a hat. What is a hat? What is it like? What is it made of? Has it color . . . a shape? . . . Suppose we lay a lot of hats in a row. How many hats are there?" By engaging in such questions, Dreiser says, wearing the hat of cultural critic, "you bite into life anywhere," and biting into life constitutes an admirably "intelligent approach toward . . . education" (p. 18).

68 Geertz, "Thick Descriptions," p. 29.

69 In effect, this critical tritypch has been transformed into a polyptych by blocks of notes which, like the subordinate panels that traverse the lower margin of a triptych's panels, narrate subsidiary stories.

70 I can only suggest differences in the gender relationships that Baranskaya and Heyman have dramatized in their novellas. Such relationships would provide yet another context for a cross-cultural critique of literary texts. In an analysis of the intertwining of gender and work in American households, Sarah Fenstermaker Berk provides a conceptual framework for comparing characters in American and Russian texts, such as those in the third panel (*The Gender Factory: The Apportionment of Work in American Households* [New York: Plenum, 1985). While household work imposes a double burden on Olya, a drawback of work without marriage and home is the emptiness a woman may ultimately face, as Baranskaya suggests in her story, "The Retirement Party," tr. Anatole Forostenko, *Russian Literature Triquarterly* 9 (1974): pp. 136–59.

71 Even this point can be – and has been – disputed. In an interview published in 1976, Michel Foucault responded to the interviewer's claim that "there has been a certain amount of change in the Soviet Union" by arguing that an abatement of "the reign of terror" was inherent in the Soviet system and signified its continuity rather than its dis-integration ("The Politics of Crime," tr. Mollie Horwitz, *Partisan Review* 43 [1976]: pp. 453–59, here p. 458). In the same interview, Foucault disintegrated the boundaries between bourgeois and Soviet "forms of social control," including imprisonment: "the mechanisms of power in the Soviet Union – systems of control, surveillance, punish-ment – are versions of those used . . . by the bourgeoisie as it struggled to consolidate its power" (pp. 455 and 459).

72 Taking issue with Geertz, LaCapra argues, for example, for the categorization of cul-ture into various cultures: "official culture, high or elite culture, mass culture, and pop-ular culture" (*Soundings in Critical Theory* [Ithaca, N.Y.: Cornell University Press, 1989], p. 135), to which can be added "political culture." Following this classification, one could discuss the newspapers that Sofia Petrovna reads within the context of official or state cul-ture, and the newspaper "funnies" that the Girl reads within the context of mass culture. The distinction is apropos, though it may merely reformulate obvious structural differ-ences between American and Soviet Russian society. Underlying arguments over the proper definition(s) of culture are questions about representation, its legitimacy and lim-its, complex questions that emerge, change, and elicit different responses with the pas-sage of historical time. Writing in the 1980s, James Clifford concludes in *Writing Culture: The Poetics and Politics of Ethnography* (Berkeley: University of California Press, 1986), that the "criteria for judging a good account [of a culture] has never been settled and are changing" (p. 9). He traces change and lack of consensus to a proliferation of theories re-volving around "the limits of representation itself" (p. 10).

Panel II: On Transgressions

Je suis moy-mesmes la matiere de mon livre.

Montaigne

I cannot explain how Theodore Dreiser's *Sister Carrie* insinuated itself into an essay on American women's autobiography – except to say that I have always loved the novel and often found (or made) it relevant to what I was writing. I cannot explain how Emma Goldman's *Living My Life* insinuated herself into my writing – except to say that I have always admired daringly radical women. The two texts, *Sister Carrie* and *Living My Life*, suddenly jumped into juxtaposition when I was asked to write an essay on American women's autobiography. This was a project I was reluctant to begin because I thought I might end by subsuming differences within gender and nationality under a generic rubric. I knew that generic studies of American women's autobiography usually called attention to the reticence or silence imposed upon women. This seemed to me a worthy polemic theme, but I thought it minimized unhelpfully women's power to speak. On significant occasions in the past, women had not been silent, or private and confined, or domesticated. They had come out of the home onto a public stage in order, as they said, to speak their own piece. Some feminist critics have maintained that outspoken women, like Emma Goldman, were silenced even as they spoke, but I believed that arguments centered upon female victimization allowed for exceptions. This was, at least, a possibility I wanted to try out in an essay on the autobiographies of radically public American women.

My original intention was to describe a subgenre of women's autobiography, but as in life, so in the essay, Emma Goldman came to command special attention. And my own fascination with particular texts – with *Living My Life* as a unique if examplary confessional – began to subvert an intent to write in generalities, that is, about a genre. I convinced myself that the way to genre was through example, and the way to a theory of genre was through practical criticism. Soon a seemingly fixed assignment to define American women's autobiography led to questions concerning the fixity of generic definitions and of the images of women projected by feminist theories of victimization. When confronted by Emma Goldman, the theories, I thought, did not hold. Nor did received definitions of women's autobiography. The genre seemed to fall apart in *Living My Life* – or more precisely, Goldman's text effected so many criss-crossings of different genres, ideologies, and national identities that it collapsed the boundaries between American women's autobiography and other forms of discourse.

Goldman's transgressive fusions of various discursive modes became the focus of the essay, which described Goldman as a transgressing figure who crossed cultural boundaries. Her life took shape as a mediation between Russian and American influences, and her life story mediated between fiction and history, drawing upon the vast repertoire of books she had read and the dramatic historical events she had witnessed or created. Her commitment to her *Ideal* – the principle of anarchy, which she equated with freedom – involved her in almost every social, economic, and political struggle of historical significance, and involved her so prominently and persistently that she became Red Emma, the bane of the American government. Finally exiled by a federal law passed to provide a legal ground for getting rid of her, she became the bane of Soviet Russia's rulers. They also sought relief from her criticism by getting her out of the country.

Homeless and homesick for America, Goldman lived a peripatetic life, settling long enough to write her autobiography. She presented her book as profoundly personal, consubstantial with herself. "Ainsi, lecteur, je suis moy-mesmes la matiere de mon livre" – this was Montaigne's introduction to his collected *essais*, and it could stand as the epigraph to Goldman's *Living My Life*. Goldman wanted her readers to encounter a woman whose ideals were always honorable and whose emotions were fallibly human. As this woman emerges in the autobiography as the artifact of its language, she turns out to be, I believe, an extraordinary historical figure and the figuration of a fiction constituted by competing and melding discursive modes and by a complex of cultural crossings. How these crossings are effected is the subject of "Speaking Her Own Piece." How *Sister Carrie* pertains to this subject I leave the essay to explain.[1]

Notes

1 I have by now spoken my own piece on *Sister Carrie* in an essay entitled What More Can Carrie Want? Naturalistic Ways of Consuming Women, forthcoming in *Prospects* and in the *Cambridge Companion to American Realism and Naturalism*.

Speaking Her Own Piece:
Emma Goldman and the
Discursive Skeins of
Autobiography

I was woven of many skeins, conflicting in shade and texture.
Emma Goldman

Oh, the tangle of human life!
Theodore Dreiser

They live harmoniously and cordially and quietly and happily and gayly and actively.
Nikolai Chernyshevsky

It was August 1889. A young woman boarded a train for Chicago. She was eighteen years old, full of the illusions of youth and hopeful, though she had only four dollars, a small trunk and cheap imitation alligator satchel, a purse, and a scrap of paper with an address. As the train clacked on its way, the threads that bound her to family and home were irretrievably broken.

It was August 1889. A young woman was arriving in New York, having boarded the cheapest train out of Rochester. She was twenty years old, eager to enter the strange and terrifying new world before her, though she had only five dollars, a small hand-bag, a sewing-machine, and three local addresses. As she set foot in the city, all that had happened to her was left behind – cast off like a worn-out garment.

On the train, the first young woman met a man who would alter the course of her life; and on her first day in the city, the other woman meets the man with whom her destiny, shaped in great part by their relationship, will be forever linked. Then, as August 1889 recedes into the past, resemblances between the two women begin to fade but not to disappear entirely. Both find themselves welcomed coldly by their relatives, a sister and an aunt. Both are told that times are hard and they must get a job to pay for their board. Both will leave their relatives, one more quickly than the other, and each will assume a relationship with the man she met on her first day in the big city. By that time, both will have worked in factories for less than five dollars a week and responded, each in her own way, to the immense disparities they saw between the mansions of the rich and the meager lives of the poor. Both will move from place to place, assuming new names in new situations. Meanwhile, however, their ways will separate and diverge. Carrie Meeber will become an actress, her electrified image emblazoning Broadway while she, the young woman, sits in her rocking chair, gazing out her window and wondering whether she will ever be happy. Emma Goldman will also assume the stage, but not to mouth the words of others that she had memorized. Rather, she would electrify audiences with her impassioned oratory as America's most famous and notorious anarchist.

Different as the destinies of these two will be, the stories of their lives as told in Theodore Dreiser's novel *Sister Carrie* and Emma Goldman's autobiography *Living My Life* resemble each other in ways that should not remain unremarked, for they are neither insignificant nor coincidental.[1] Nor are they, as might be thought, signs of intertextual influence or of a coalescence of fiction and autobiography as narrative forms.[2] Rather they represent a coalescence of the complex narrative designs of two subversive writers seeking to gain acceptance for their unacceptable social views.[3] Their strategy was one of rhetorical overdetermination. Both Dreiser and Goldman counted upon the confusion and profusion inherent in their literary forms to obscure and yet reveal their ideological alienation from established social norms. As writers, they could seem to be conforming, if only to the standards of literary genre, because these standards allowed for, and indeed demanded, deviation and variety, freedom of rhetorical choice. Thus, unexpected similarities in their texts emerge less from thematic agreement than from similarities between literary forms that contain inchoate and indeterminant elements. These overlapping elements blur the boundaries between the naturalistic novel and (women's) autobiography and between the discursive modes of either genre and those of history, journalism, philosophy, myth, melodrama, romance, apologias and confessions, and propaganda.[4] Instead of selecting a single predominant discourse, Dreiser and Goldman conflated the various modes available to them, as though hoping that rhetorical excess would make their unacceptably radical social criticism seem cogent, logical, and, as expressed in familiar literary conventions and clichés, acceptable.[5]

This strategy of overdetermination was at once defensive and aggressive, an attempt to prevent rejection and to overpower the reader with the sheer redundancy of a text's rhetorical assaults. Neither writer succeeded in lulling public suspicion. Dreiser's readers knew that his novel violated literary conventions as flagrantly as his heroine transgressed the bounds of conventional society. As even Carrie dimly perceived, transgressions were entangling as well as liberating; they could disorder a character's life. They could also produce disarray in a writer's style. Dreiser's style in *Sister Carrie* has been called confused, clumsy, and clichéd – a tangled web of discursive skeins that (in Goldman's words) conflicted "in shade and texture." Goldman's autobiographical style, a melee of incompatible styles, has been similarly criticized, as has the "clumsy and awkward" prose of an extraordinary novel to which Goldman explicitly refers: Nikolai Chernyshevsky's *What Is to Be Done?*[6]

The suggestion that *Living My Life* is an autobiographical redaction of *What Is to Be Done?* is supported by Goldman's claim that literature, and this novel in particular, shaped her life.[7] Goldman said she had patterned her self upon Chernyshevsky's feminist heroine, Vera Pavlovna, and she might have patterned her prose upon that of a writer whose revolutionary vision and rhetorical purposes she shared, one as didactic as she and as desirous of avoiding interdiction. However, Goldman believed she had to translate her anarchism, clearly traceable to foreign revolutionaries, into an American idiom, for she wanted her autobiography to establish her as a citizen worthy of readmission to the United States. As an exiled radical alien, she had much at stake in her style, which by discursive variety and profusion might accrete enough persuasive force to effect an ideological reconciliation with her American readers. She hoped her story, told in language modulating from didacticism to indictment, and sentimentality to passion, would represent a multifaceted woman admirable for her honesty and humane ideals. Goldman may have been an aging and unwanted exile, but through writing she could appropriate a traditional American role by beginning with a young girl's entry into the city of her dreams, a conventional novelistic beginning, used famously in *Sister Carrie*. Immediately, she would be typified as an American, a newcomer arriving at a new world. It was, of course, the world of perennial opportunity and freedom – and freedom was America's sign and Goldman's aspiration. Strategically, Goldman began the story of her life, as Dreiser began *Sister Carrie*, with a traditional scene that would appeal to American readers, whatever their political persuasion, because it epitomized a mythic American experience. A young innocent enters a great American city, her new world, and seeks in its lavish and alluring excess the fulfillment of a heart's desire. Carrie's vague but incremental desire was for happiness; Goldman dreamt of independence and freedom – and of revolution.

In 1928, when the fifty-eight-year-old Goldman was inscribing her hopeful, if hackneyed, opening scene, she had been living in exile for almost ten years. She was disillusioned with Soviet Russia, a refuge she had by now rejected as she rejected all coercive states (and to her all states were coercive). She was tired of wandering. She wanted to return to the United States, the country she considered home. Since she had been deported because of ideas the government considered politically dangerous, she needed to place her anarchism within a context that would demystify it without attenuating its social and moral urgency. She would not deny her revolutionary past – she could not, since she considered fidelity to the "Ideal" of anarchism the essence of her life. But she would try to dispel fears her anarchism aroused by contextualizing it within a historical process of conflict and change. Centering herself within this process, she described her actions as consistently furthering the cause of freedom. This was, she noted, a quintessentially American cause. It was also a universal dream, for all revolutionary ideas of liberty – including those of Thoreau and Emerson, whom she considered early American anarchists – flowed together, she believed, in a historic ideological stream coursing toward freedom.[8]

As Goldman faced the task of writing herself into history – while, conversely, personalizing history by writing it into her life story – she had to resolve problems other than those usually attributed to women autobiographers (and to women writers in general). She did not have to overcome a fear of speaking in her own voice or displaying herself upon a public stage. She had not lived a private, silenced, and covertly rebellious life. On the contrary, like other radical women of her time – Mother Jones, Elizabeth Gurley Flynn, Charlotte Perkins Gilman, and Margaret Sanger, all of whom wrote autobiographies – Goldman shattered the stereotype of woman as private, selfless, and submissively conforming to social expectations she sought secretly to subvert.[9] Goldman's rebellion was overt, her stage public, and her voice, heard by thousands, respected and feared. In 1917, when she was ordered by a U.S. marshal not to speak in public, she had an audience stomping and screaming as she appeared on stage with a handkerchief stuffed in her mouth. Even gagged, she could not be silenced. Nor could she be domesticated. Her autobiography recounts her lifelong resistance to men who wanted her to marry, bear children, and stay at home as wife and mother. She defied her father, whose physical violence and emotional abuse blighted her young years; and she refused her lovers, who wanted her to relinquish her political ideals and public persona. Though autobiography, one might think, was generically different from propaganda, Goldman would not mute or mutate her political discourse because she would not misrepresent the woman it had taken her a lifetime to create. On the other hand, simply to restate her ideology would have been redundant and inexpedient. Autobiography permitted her to recontextualize her much-rehearsed social criticism within the personal story of a woman's life, while at the same time, it allowed her to reidentify the woman with her ideas. "E. G. the woman and her ideas are inseparable," she wrote (I, p. 268).

Goldman realized that creating the autobiography implied an act of self-appropriation that placed her in a politically contentious position, for she was in effect challenging a public image of Red Emma, the notorious demagogue who could, presumably, persuade a naive listener to violence, even to assassination. Like other public women in American history, Elizabeth Cady Stanton and Charlotte Perkins Gilman, for instance, Goldman believed she had to confront a factitious image created by the public to serve interests often antithetical to her own. Like these women, she proposed to modify and correct, or erase, a portrait painted by admirers as well as adversaries. Autobiography would permit her to reclaim her image from the public and redefine herself.[10] She defined also her own recuperative strategies, different from those of other radical women. Stanton, for example, tried to modify a public perception of her as an extraordinary person by emphasizing her ordinary daily activities; the story of her private life as wife, housekeeper, and mother, she wrote, might "amuse" and "benefit" her readers.[11] Gilman, on the other hand, stressed her debilitation, calculating for her reader the productive years she might have enjoyed had she not been incapacitated by recurrent episodes of depression (pp. 97–104). At the same time that these women were disavowing their public images, they reiterated their ideological positions, so that their autobiographies reinscribed an impression that, ostensibly, they wished to revise. Even as they revealed their ordinariness or inadequacy (usually equated with conformity or debilitation), they emerged as extraordinary women, strong and contentious, and threatening to the established social order from which, for all their attempted reconciliations, they remained alienated.[12] Goldman's need for an ideological reconciliation with her readers was more urgent than that of Stanton and Gilman because her situation was more critical. And her motives were more conflicted than theirs, her discursive modes more diverse and entangled. She wanted to assert her Americanism, but she could not resist advertising her alienating (and alienated) political views. Her complicated and perhaps duplicitous design was to persuade her readers that alienation itself was an American strain – an indigenous tension and ideological identification. As an unregenerate revolutionary, she could be an American and a prodigal American daughter returning home.

Goldman's efforts to revise Red Emma's tabloid image tested her rhetorical powers as a writer. She knew she possessed the power of speech. Indeed, if she had been less persuasive as a speaker, less public and publicized and, of course, less sweepingly revolutionary, she might not have marshaled against her the full power of the U.S. government. Now she needed the power of the written word to create a self-portrait that would show everyone that E. G. and her ideas were benignly conceived and morally sound. As she knew, Red Emma personified two ideologies unacceptable to the American public: anarchism and radical feminism. Both were perceived, as she herself perceived them, as forces that would destroy society's founding institutions: marriage and the state. To Goldman, both were inherently oppressive. As a woman who had not only advocated but also acted out a woman's right to economic and sexual independence – and sought to subvert accepted views of family life, motherhood, and education – Goldman now faced formidable obstacles in creating a portrait of herself that would validate her politics and her person.

In an oblique way, Goldman outlined a strategy for creating such a portrait in her prefatory essay entitled "In Appreciation." These few pages suggest a theory of autobiography that implies a reciprocity between self and style, each revealing in the other conflicting elements that could coalesce to form a self inseparable from social history, and an autobiography thematically unified by interactions between society and the self. In this "appreciation," an acknowledgment of her indebtedness to others, Goldman wrote about writing her life as though, strangely, the life she was writing about was not her own. To begin with, she projected the desire to write upon anonymous others, describing herself as the passive recipient of suggestions that "came" to her uninvited. This self-effacement, uncharacteristic for Goldman, may represent a proleptic denial of the charge of egotism she anticipated as a woman autobiographer. It may also be a conciliatory gesture toward the convention that women writers should approach self-expression reluctantly, with an appropriate sense of modesty; and, indeed, Goldman had justifiable misgivings about self-exposure. Nevertheless, she produced a two-volume work in which (contrary to contemporary views that she hid her personal self) she revealed startling secrets that might never have been told.[13] The occasion for writing also "came" to her (through the unwelcome leisure of exile), its timing fortuitous, since she was old enough to have lived a life, but not so old that her powers of recall and recreation were impaired. Goldman felt hindered, however, by a lack of documentary materials she considered essential to the autobiographer as archivist of an historical past as well as a private life. Since all her private papers and files had been confiscated in a federal raid of her office, she had lost historical documents (including those she had created, like issues of *Mother Earth*) that could testify to the "truth" of her autobiography, its fidelity to fact. Fortunately, public documents were retrievable, but not documents of another kind needed to recreate the "personal atmosphere" of her past. How could she retrieve the hundreds of unduplicable love letters she had written under the sway of passions she intended to reveal? Her "appreciation" expresses her gratitude to friends and former lovers who found the documents she wanted and supported her "research" – an odd but pointed term that implies a claim to scientific objectivity. As Goldman added secretarial help, editorial assistance, and financial support to her list of prerequisites, she implicated many others in the making of her autobiography, so that *Living My Life* seems, finally, the artifactual product of a large cooperative effort. Even the title – in which the possessive pronoun declares her autonomy or, at least, her desire to resist appropriation – came from someone else, her lifelong friend and fellow anarchist, Alexander Berkman. Thus, in describing the genesis of her text, Goldman was already creating a woman she wanted the public to see as inspiring people to work together in voluntary cooperation. Such cooperation, she would show in the text, was the ideal end of anarchism. Goldman's introduction, appreciative of her friends, somehow impersonalized her relationship to this text. It set standards that seemed unsuited to autobiography as a genre: distance and detachment; historical exposition; objective documentation, even of personal feelings – an effect of impersonality. These are criteria that historians and biographers have established for their narratives and that novelists like Theodore Dreiser prescribed for the realistic novel.

Neither in her preface nor her text did Goldman express doubt that she had a self who existed prior to the act of writing about her and apart from the language that was creating an autobiographical "I."[14] Indeed, she believed that the documents she had retrieved – newspaper reports, proceedings of her court trials, issues of *Mother Earth* – proved the existence of this self. She admitted that this self was conflicted and complex – that she was a woman "woven of many skeins." She knew she was elusive as a woman, to others and, sometimes, to herself. But her admission that she had "never been able to unearth" the "real" Emma Goldman (II, p. 529), affirmed, rather than denied, the existence of a continuous and authentic identity. The problems she encountered in translating Emma Goldman or E. G. into an autobiographical "I" were rhetorical and emotional, rather than ontological; and she resolved them by casting Goldman the writer in a variety of authorial roles. Writing as a revisionist historian, she interjected long expository descriptions of the background for her political actions, authenticating her accounts of the past with verifiable dates, places, and names. Just as Dreiser had interpolated a passage on a Chicago department store ("established about 1884") in order to preserve "an interesting chapter in the commercial history of our nation" (p. 22), so Goldman devoted chapters to American labor history and, as a setting of her story changed, to the early years of the Russian revolution. In describing the Haymarket Affair that had converted her to anarchism, she recounted historical events she had heard reported; in writing about the Hempstead strike – which linked her destiny indissolubly with that of Alexander Berkman, the young anarchist she had met on her first day in New York – she revealed how her actions created history. Her historical excursus are appropriately framed about herself as central character of her story, just as Dreiser's were framed about his heroine. Carrie looks for a job in a Chicago department store; Goldman recalls her young, impressionable self listening to the socialist Johanna Greie tell of the 1886 riot in Haymarket Square (I, pp. 7–9).

In describing how the Haymarket Affair had converted her to anarchism, Goldman's narrative strategy was complexly involuted, as were her autobiographical designs – her intentions and her narrative form. Almost fifty years after the Haymarket riot, Goldman still wanted to assert the innocence of the convicted anarchists and to justify her commitment to their cause, a definitive, lifelong commitment that was to transform her from a young immigrant woman into the Red Emma of tabloid notoriety. Goldman recalls that Johanna Greie had beckoned the awed young Goldman to her and prophesied that some day she would make the Haymarket anarchists' cause her own (I, p. 9). The prophecy, the speech, and the "cause" are framed as the memory of a memory. Goldman begins by remembering her first night in New York. She is excited and sleepless, having just heard a stirring "denunciation of American conditions" by the anarchist orator Johann Most. Then as she tosses about, she once more "live[s] through the events of 1887" (I, p. 6) – events that had taken place in Rochester almost two years ago and that recapitulated still earlier events now an inviolate part of American history and Goldman's past. Thus Goldman links her past, as she is remembering herself remembering it, to the American scene, tracing her feelings as well as her future to a flashback of Johanna Greie's impassioned speech. This involuted chronology coalesces time and the historical times. It places historical events in the past, while it makes history immediate in the living narrator (Greie) present before Goldman; simultaneously, it foreshadows the future by prophesying the execution of the Haymarket anarchists and Goldman's conversion to their cause. As this framing suggests, Goldman was violating the chronology of events in order to rationalize her radicalism as a justifiable response to what she believed were acts of flagrant injustice. She was also giving her life an inherently dramatic structure by beginning her story at a climactic moment of conversion that decides her to set out for the city in quest of a new life. Then, through intermittent flashes of memory, she recovers her childhood and past.[15] Unlike the autobiographies of activist women that begin with the moment of birth – "I was born in the city of Cork, Ireland," writes Mother Jones, and Elizabeth Gurley Flynn begins, "By birth I am a New Englander" – Goldman's autobiography opens with a memory of herself at the age of twenty hopefully arriving in New York, a strange "new world."[16]

Goldman's fractured chronology allowed her to present historical events like the Haymarket Affair as self-contained and didactic passages of exposition and as crucial moments of self-revelation that expose the genesis of desire. Just as Dreiser's historical account of the department store served to explain the origin of Carrie's desire for the trinkets and clothes on display before her (each item "dainty," "delicately frilled," and "dazzling," making her feel its "claim" and "all touch[ing] her with individual desire"), so Goldman's recapitulation of historical events provided an origin for the desire that Goldman said determined the course of her life. Though Carrie made money and material things her object of desire, and Goldman, social revolution – radically different objects, each subversive of the other – both women are described as pursuing an elusive, ever-receding ideal.[17] Like Carrie, who was to find "neither surfeit nor content" (p. 369), Goldman would never realize her "great ideal," though it remained the only permanent element in her life (I, p. 343). Thus, her story thematized a contrast between aspiration and history, between the permanence of human desire and life's disappointing transitoriness. This contrast is reflected in Goldman's rhetorical vacillations as she moved from an inviolate and ideal "Cause" to the various causes into which she was thrust by the vicissitudes of history. While she depended upon the cogency of facts to assert the realistic necessity behind these causes, she represented human aspiration through a romantically elusive image – that of humanity reaching for the stars. The image became muddled in its spatial designations when Goldman's aspiration signified sexual, rather than political, desire; then it described her "soaring high" (toward the stars) in a desire to experience the "depths" of passion. As in time the object of Goldman's sexual passion changed, each lover receded into the past to become part of her history, but her yearning for sexual fulfillment (like Carrie's yearning for happiness) never abated. Personal love began to seem as elusive to Goldman as her political ideals, and as enduringly desirable. However, though the end of one affair after another led her to question whether a woman's public life inevitably destroys private happiness, she never questioned or abandoned her ideals in order to keep her lovers.

Though Goldman's revolutionary ideal remained as inviolably fixed as the stars, her views on violence as the means to an end underwent revision. The change is an integral part of her autobiography as it traces the conception and reconception of ideas with which she was associated. Although Goldman knew as she wrote that she would disavow a position she was presenting as tenable, if not irresistible, she offered no clue to her subsequent reversals. Her dramatic denunciation of her idolized mentor, Johann Most, for example, was unforeshadowed and startlingly violent: she beat him with a horsewhip in front of a huge audience. Years later, she reconsidered her action, which she had justified as a righteous reaction to Most's disavowal of Berkman's attempted assassination of Henry Clay Frick. Most's disaffection had infuriated her as a betrayal of the anarchist cause as well as of Berkman. Later, she would feel betrayed by Berkman when he repudiated Leon Czolgosz, McKinley's assassin, for the same reason Most had condemned him: that his action lacked "social necessity" (I, p. 324).[18] Most's condemnation had enraged her; Berkman's evoked despair. For his difference with her left her totally rejected and alone. She believed that she had lost more than her beloved Sasha – as, for his sake, she had lost Most, her "teacher" and "inspiration": she lost confidence in her ability to stand alone. Reviled by friends and foes because of her sympathy for Czolgosz, a young man she believed haplessly misguided, Goldman felt abandoned and beaten. She saw her faith in the transformative processes of history betrayed, and human endeavor turned into a "cruel, senseless farce" (I, p. 324).

Unusual in its revisions, in effect Goldman's admissions of the serious mistakes she had made, *Living My Life* is extraordinary in its revelation of Goldman's part in a plot to assassinate Henry Clay Frick, the chairman of Carnegie Steel Company. His "inhumanity" to workers he had locked out of the Homestead steel mills and evicted from company houses aroused Goldman's revolutionary passion – and Berkman's incendiary rhetoric. Berkman denounced Frick as "the symbol of wealth and power, of the injustice and wrong of the capitalistic class, as well as personally responsible for the shedding of the workers' blood." Accordingly, he and Goldman plotted a political assassination or *Attentat* that would stir an "aroused" country, "strike terror in the enemy's ranks and make them realize that the proletariat of America had its avengers" (I, pp. 85–8). In his autobiography, *Prison Memoirs of an Anarchist*, Berkman never mentioned Goldman by name, alluding to her only as "the Girl," and her role in the assassination plot remained unknown and unsuspected.[19] If autobiographies are somehow self-serving, then *Living My Life* served, among other functions, as the confession of a secret Goldman found too burdensome, too guilt-ridden, to protect. At the time of Berkman's fateful attempt on Frick's life, the call to violence had seemed to them, she recalled, unequivocal and commanding, "the psychological moment for an *Attentat.*" This was the moment for which the young Berkman had waited: "this sublime moment to serve the Cause, to give his life for the people" (I, p. 87). In melodramatically ringing tones, Berkman declared his intention "to die by my own hand" after he had killed Frick; he wanted "to live [only] long enough to justify his act . . . , so that the American people might know that he was not a criminal, but an idealist" (I, p. 87). Even an involutedly plotted melodrama would not have produced the ironies that ensued from the young anarchists' action. Frick lived; Berkman was convicted as a criminal; and the "great suffering people" for whom he was sacrificing his life denounced Berkman and the assassination. An aftermath, congruent with melodrama, was Goldman's guilty secret and a need to expiate her guilt that autobiographical confession may have at last satisfied. Convinced that "they" were going to kill Berkman, Goldman wanted to share his fate. Her desire seems coercive as she reiterates the word *must*: "I must pay the same price as he – I must stand the consequences – I must share the responsibility" (I, p. 96). She never did. Her participation in the assassination plot remained secret – until the autobiography.[20]

By confessing to violence, Goldman placed herself in a position to repudiate it as a legitimate means for an anarchist. As she watched while Berkman worked on the bomb he planned for Frick, Goldman questioned their right to endanger the lives of innocent people: "What if anything should go wrong – but, then, did not the end justify the means? Our end was the sacred cause of the oppressed and exploited people. . . . What if a few should have to perish? – the many would be free. . . . Yes, the end in this case justified the means" (I, p. 88). Goldman's questions were fundamental to her ideology, and the answers she gave at the time would later produce in her feelings of "paralyzing horror" (II, p. 536). She came to see violence as incompatible with her ideals, and both the confession and repudiation of her willingness to bomb and kill seemed to her essential to her autobiography. For underlying all her motives as autobiographer was a desire to educate. This desire took precedence over self-interest. If she had hoped the autobiography would help her return to the United States, then a confession of complicity in an infamous assassination plot would be self-defeating. However, if she wished to defend the principles of anarchism, then a confrontration with the issue of violence, equated with anarchism in the public mind, was essential.[21]

The Frick affair called forth Goldman's most flamboyant rhetoric. Goldman describes events leading to Berkman's departure for Pittsburgh in a series of dramatically heightened scenes: a horrifying moment when she reads of police shooting strikers' families; a sudden decision to rush to Homestead; a tense experiment with bomb making; Berkman's departure as assassin and human sacrifice; and, finally, Goldman standing alone at the railway station, her arms outstretched toward the receding train that is carrying away her lover. These rapidly moving cinematic scenes end abruptly in a tableau of loss: "I ran after the vanishing train, waving and calling to him: 'Sasha, Sashenka!' The steaming monster disappeared round the bend and I stood glued, straining after it, my arms outstretched for the precious life that was being snatched away from me" (I, p. 91). This was a moment Goldman would recall fifteen years later as she stood at another railroad station awaiting Berkman's return. Melodramatically, the figures before her grow faint and blurred, the past rises out of the depths, she stretches out her arms, crying frantically, "Sasha! Sasha!" – and then, in a cinematic flash, the present reappears as she hears her name called, "Emma! Emma! The train is in" (I, p. 383). The exclamations, tears, and confusion, the physical details signifying panic and desire as Goldman describes her numb feet, clutching hands, throbbing heart, and burning brain – not to mention Berkman's "deathly white" face, outstretched hand, and pathetic gaze – show Goldman appropriating the language of melodrama and sentiment to express the pathos of two idealists (and lovers) who are sacrificing all for a transcendent Cause.

The morning after Berkman's departure, Goldman awakened to feel the anguish of a fictional heroine who had been tormented by the need to save her loved ones. She could see this distraught character lying in her bed, her face turned to the wall, her shoulders twitching, and she "could almost feel the same way" (I, p. 91). Goldman had now melded into Dostoyevsky's Sonya Marmeladov, the self-abnegating prostitute of *Crime and Punishment* who saves Raskolnikov's soul. Indifferent to the absurdity of identifying herself, a Jewish atheist, with a saintly Christian, Goldman followed Sonya's example by deciding to sell her body for money she needed to join Berkman. Melodrama merges with farce as Goldman faintheartedly parades the streets and finally attracts a man. He surveys her with an experienced eye and declares: "You haven't got it, that's all there is to it" (I, p. 93). Goldman fails at prostitution, but farce blends into fantasy as the mysterious stranger gives her ten dollars and sends her home with honor unsullied. In recounting this incredible sequence of events, Goldman violates the secrecy she considered vital at the time. Always didactic, she had wanted to give the stranger an impromptu lecture on the economic causes of prostitution (which she would delineate in her essay "The Traffic in Women"), but she silenced herself to keep "a juicy story" from the press (I, p. 93). Now, however, she reveals the long-kept secret, ennobling her attempt at prostitution by identifying herself with a suffering and self-sacrificing woman – or, to be precise, with a fictional character created by a novelist who abhorred anarchism (and the Nihilist Chernyshevsky, Goldman's hero) with an intensity bordering on obsession.[22]

A coalescence of literature with life was one of Goldman's rhetorical strategies of self-ratification. When she described moments of heightened emotions, she typically merged her character with those of fictional heroines and often spoke her piece in the clichéd language of sentimental or romantic novels. The effect was self-subverting, since she simultaneously enhanced and diminished an image of herself as an exemplary woman of her times – enhanced by imbuing herself with the emotional intensity of self-sacrificing and self-aggrandizing heroines like Dostoyevsky's Sonya and Chernyshevsky's Vera Pavlovna, and diminished by equating her own reality with that of merely imagined or unreal women. She seemed untroubled by discrepancies between herself as a "real" person and literary characters, or between women characters created by writers whose ideologies were diametrically opposed. However, literary characters could create trouble between her and her lovers. She tells, for example, how Ben Reitman, to whom she felt passionately enslaved, abruptly left her after reading D. H. Lawrence's novel, *Sons and Lovers*; like Lawrence's hero, Reitman was obsessed with his mother and he projected his emotional conflicts upon a character torn between sexual and maternal love.[23] She lost another lover, Edward Brady, because of Nietzsche. Brady's denunciation of Goldman's intellectual idol seemed to her more than a philosophical disagreement; it signified, she said, an intolerable violation of her freedom, "more precious to [her] than life." Following their quarrel over Nietzsche, she accused Brady of "binding" her "body" and her "spirit" and (in ascending order of insult) of trying to "tear" her away from "the movement," her "friends," and "the books I love" (I, pp. 194–5).

Usually, however, a shared love of books mediated Goldman's relationship with men. *What Is to Be Done?* immediately established a rapport with Berkman, her lifelong companion. When Goldman first met the young anarchist, she confided to him her dream: "I wanted to have time for reading," she told him, "and later I hoped to realize my dream of a co-operative shop. 'Something like Vera's venture in *What's to Be Done?*.' " A brief quarrel ensued when Berkman could hardly believe that this young woman had read a prohibited Nihilist novel. Goldman resented having her word or independence of mind questioned: "I repeated angrily that I had read the forbidden book and other similar works, such as Turgeniev's *Fathers and Sons*, and *Obriv (The Precipice)* by Gontcharov," she said, citing her reading as proof of her political and personal liberation. The books she named created a bond between the two young anarchists.[24] They also recalled scenes of violence Goldman had seen as a girl in Russia and novels she had read (*Fathers and Sons* and *What Is to Be Done?*) that articulated her inchoate feelings of sympathy for Nihilists executed by the Tsar – sympathies later conferred upon the Haymarket anarchists (I, pp. 26–8).

As the autobiography reveals, men who gave Goldman books became her political idols and her sexual partners, the list of her readings expanding with that of her lovers: Jacob Kershner, her feckless husband, whose "interest in books . . . had first attracted her" (I, p. 20); the anarchist Johann Most, who supplied her "with a list of books" that grounded her in revolutionary theory (I, p. 35); Edward Brady, who introduced her "to the great classics of English and French literature," to Rousseau, Voltaire, Goethe, and Shakespeare (I, p. 115); Stefan Grossman, who taught her to admire "the new literature – Friedrich Nietzsche, Ibsen, Hauptmann, von Hoffmansthal" (I, p. 172); and Max Baginski, who engaged her in "exquisite" discussions of Gottfried Keller, Strindberg, Wedekind,

Gabriele Reuter, Knut Hamsun, and her philosophical idol, Nietzsche (I, p. 239).[25] Goldman's literary prototype in this discipleship was Chernyshevsky's heroine Vera Pavlovna, who entered the world of ideas through books given to her by her brother's tutor, subsequently her rescuer and husband.[26] Ironically, prison offered Goldman the luxury of time to read; she always carried a book with her when she thought she might be arrested (she mentions, for example, *A Portrait of the Artist as a Young Man*). One of the prison reforms she effected was to win library privileges for women inmates.

Among the books Goldman remembered reading as a schoolgirl were popular romances – especially those of the nineteenth-century German writer Eugenie Marlitt – that had made her "grow tearful over the unhappy heroines" (I, p. 116). These romances left an indelible impression. Years later she recalled their trite sentimental images as she wrote about her own love affairs, the "ecstasy" and unhappiness that, like their romantic heroines, she too experienced. Clearly, Goldman adjusted her discursive mode to her immediate subject, changing from the journalistic, or didactic, or caustic style that described historical events to a murkily melodramatic language for romance. From popular novels she appropriated the prose she considered suitable to sexual passions she believed herself politically obligated to reveal. As an anarchist and a feminist, she wanted to dramatize through her own life a woman's freedom to love as she desired. She advocated frankness as an ideological principle; and in her autobiography she would describe her erotic yearnings, her passionate responses, and her abjectness toward lovers she knew were not her equals, particularly Ben Reitman, with whom she had a ten-year liaison. After all, if she was going to humanize Red Emma, she needed to show that she had experienced weakness and humiliation, as well as fulfillment, in her relationships with men. She told how she endured Reitman's obsessive infidelities, his boorishness, desertions, demands, and even his dishonesties and betrayals – and she was honest enough to suggest ulterior motives. For as her manager, "traveling companion," and "helpmate," Reitman relieved her of the burdensome details of her lecture tours and significantly enlarged her audiences (I, p. 433). As her "lover," he caught her in a "torrent of elemental passion" and she "responded shamelessly to its primitive call" (I, p. 420). Goldman knew that Berkman and other friends deplored her dependence upon a man inferior to her in intellect and conscience, but she turned to Reitman because, she wrote, he satisfied her "great hunger for someone who could love the woman in me and yet who would also be able to share my work. I had never had anyone who could do both" (I, p. 432). He fulfilled also her fantasy of experiencing in life the passions she had felt vicariously through literature. Indeed, as she described Reitman's "primitive" sexual appeal, she recreated him as the "savage" male considered generic to the naturalistic novel.[27] The story of his chaotic life, as she recounts his telling it, drew her to him because he "came from a world so unlike mine": "I was enthralled by this living embodiment of the types I had only known through books, the types portrayed by Dostoyevsky and Gorki" (I, p. 420).[28] Later, she refers to him passingly as Raskolnikov because he was "always stealing back to the scene of his old crimes" (II, p. 650).

Given Goldman's explicitness about her love affairs, one would think the issue of frankness irrelevant to her autobiography. Nevertheless, critics have raised it by asking pointedly, "What did she want to hide?"[29] According to a recent study of her love letters to Reitman, she hid the profoundly erotic desires she allowed herself to express in the private coded language of her love letters.[30] Such language supports a commonsensical view of autobiography as a self-interested account of a life which, in the act of revealing, inevitably selects, omits, and conceals. Contemporary critics trace the omissions in Goldman's life story to women's socially conditioned reticence; but a demand that Goldman tell all, especially about her love life, is not only unrealistic but sexually discriminating, since as we know, elisions in men's autobiographies are commonplace and commonly considered generic.[31] Given the times and circumstances in which Goldman wrote and the purposes she hoped to achieve, her frankness, rather than her omissions, seems anomalous. To ask, as modern critics do, what she was hiding is to assume a total congruence between the living woman and the autobiographical "I" (a naive assumption for contemporary theorists) and to overlook all that Goldman did reveal: an enslaving passion for Reitman inappropriate to her as an independent woman; desire for younger men that she could satisfy only by risking humiliating rejections; and (highly damaging to her image of herself as a feminist), constant need for support – moral and intellectual backing, money, and admiration – that she sought and received from men. She did not hide the fact that men bought her beautiful clothes and that (like Dreiser's Carrie) she wore them with pleasure.

More significantly, she did not hide her doubts about the psychological motives underlying her political commitments. She repeatedly stated her suspicions that work may have represented an escape from the emptiness of her life, as though her work and her life were discrete and not, as she also stated, interwoven. She did not hide her fear of nihilism. She referred recurrently to a sense of inner void that she identified with her empty womb; and she wondered if her desire to care for humankind was a displaced expression of her desire for motherhood.[32] Her equation of personal feelings with socially conditioned views of woman as biologically determined – as influenced in temperament and desire by her womb – subverted her feminist declarations of freedom. Nevertheless, she did not hide her sense of subservience to biological forces. Nor did she hide her periods of depression. She admitted her violent temper, her irascibility, her weaknesses, and her sexual wildness. Given her hope that the autobiography might present her favorably enough to allow her readmission into the United States, she was remarkably candid about her private life and admirably loyal to her anarchist beliefs. She never disavowed her social and political principles or attenuated her revolutionary purposes. She never hid opinions she knew would alienate her fellow revolutionists. Late in life, she paid dearly for her criticism of

Soviet Russia, just as she had, years ago, for her expressions of sympathy for President McKinley's assassin.[33] But she considered herself morally obligated to criticize a regime that she believed subverted the principles and purposes of social revolution. She might have hidden views she knew were unpopular with radical audiences she depended upon for support, but instead she insisted upon advertising them, and she devoted almost half of the second volume of *Living My Life* to a chronicle of disillusioning discoveries about the revolution that had been her visionary ideal. She might have tried to protect this ideal by hiding the facts as she knew them, but though her secrecy would have been undetected, since few at the time had the access to Russian life that she did, she refused the safety of silence.[34]

Speaking out and speaking her own piece constituted her integrity and the identity Goldman created for herself in life and in her autobiography. She shared with other radical woman orators a claim to autonomy in speech that Elizabeth Gurley Flynn epitomized in her retort to David Belasco, the impresario who had offered her a part in a play: "I don't want to be an actress! I want to speak my own words and not say over and over again what somebody else has written. I'm in the labor movement and I speak my own piece!"[35] Apparently Flynn never wondered whether her freedom to speak her own piece might be constrained by the political movements to which she was successively committed, labor unionism, socialism, and communism, or by the structures of language itself. Nor did Goldman. She too insisted she would speak her own piece, and though she made her first public appearances as a disciple of the anarchist Johann Most, lecturing on subjects he had chosen in a style he rehearsed, she soon saw "the need of independent thought" (p. 47). In time, she condemned the "meaningless prattle" she had appropriated from Most: "I realized I was committing a crime against myself and the workers by serving as a parrot repeating Most's views" (p. 52). Margaret Sanger expressed the determination of all these activist women when she wrote in her autobiography: "I *would* be heard. No matter what it should cost. I *would be heard*" (p. 56, original emphasis).

As such declarations attest, the issue in autobiographies of radical public women was not only women's claim to their own voice, but also their insistence upon self-possession: upon the "I" reiterated in their statements – "I" four times in succession in Flynn's self-appropriating words and Goldman's emphatic "I," "I," and "myself." Their pronouns signified their opposition to others, women and men, who presented them with social scenarios, as though they were derivative speakers, merely actresses reciting someone else's piece. Set beside Goldman's self-appropriation, as she refused to speak another's lines, the capitulation of Dreiser's Carrie Meeber to the lure of the theater reveals that for her success entailed denying the possibility of her own speech. Dimly as Carrie understood the forces about her, she knew she could attain money and fame by commodifying herself – by making herself into a representation of what others desired and could buy with a theater ticket. On a Broadway stage at last, before a large, paying audience, Carrie pronounces herself a public property. Asked by the company's male star, "Well, who are you?," she answers with uncharacteristic pointedness, "I am yours truly" (p. 314). Her "I" has collapsed in the "your" that Goldman had resisted as the sign of society's appropriation of women.[36]

In 1906, speaking her own piece on the corner of Broadway and 38th Street, Elizabeth Gurley Flynn was arrested. As a result of this arrest, she writes in her autobiography, she met Theodore Dreiser, then managing editor of *Broadway Magazine*, the journal in which Dreiser would publish his sketch of Flynn as "An East Side Joan of Arc" (p. 54). "I am very proud to have had a fleeting glimpse of this great American in his youth," Flynn writes, approving his "many struggles for American democratic rights" and his enlistment in 1945 in the Communist Party (p. 55). Charlotte Perkins Gilman also records her encounter with Dreiser, now editor of the *Delineator*, from whom she sought advice on how to have her essays published. According to her account, Dreiser said "gloomily," "You should consider more what the editors want" (p. 304). But like Flynn and Goldman, Gilman wanted to speak her own piece, even though she knew that all of her "principal topics were in direct contravention of established views, beliefs and emotions" (p. 304). She sought to publish her views precisely because they were subversive; and she resisted, even resented, Dreiser's advice as pressuring her to the conformity and silence that, she implied, had driven her to madness in her first marriage. Unlike Gilman, Goldman placed Dreiser in a position of authority in her autobiography, implicitly sanctioning her right to tell the story of her life because of his words. Goldman reports Dreiser telling her to write the autobiography: "'You must write the story of your life, E. G.,' he urged; 'it is the richest of any woman's of our century. Why in the name of Mike don't you do it?'" (II, p. 986). For Goldman, as for other radical women autobiographers, the authorizing male writer of their times was Theodore Dreiser.[37]

Goldman's frequent references to supportive men, including those who encouraged her autobiography, attentuates her claim to independence – or more precisely, to a desire for independence sometimes thwarted by her complex needs as a woman "woven of many skeins." Early in the autobiography Goldman drew upon images of piecing and weaving (activities that contemporary feminists consider characteristically "feminine") to describe her difference from the men she considered her counterparts. "I knew that the personal would always play a dominant part in my life," she wrote; "I was not hewn of one piece, like Sasha [Alexander Berkman] or other heroic figures. . . . I was woven of many skeins, conflicting in shade and texture. To the end of my days I would be torn between the yearning for a personal life and the need of giving all to my ideal" (I, p. 153). The image of herself as "woven" while men are "hewn" suggests Goldman's susceptibility to metaphors that reinforce gender differences her autobiography was seeking to deny – and did. For Goldman's lifelong devotion to her "ideal" showed that she was as much hewn of one piece as Berkman or any other man she considered heroic. In describing how an anarchist leader like

Johann Most longed for, even wept for, love and marriage, she erased the differences by which she rationalized her sexual needs. Indeed, Berkman, Most, and every radical man she mentioned (as well as radical women like Voltairine de Cleyre) could be considered woven of conflicting skeins, if conflict implied desiring personal as well as public gratification, love as well as political power. Though she projected upon Berkman her desire for total commitment to a cause and idealized him as the personification of selflessness, she complained about his intransigent single-mindedness. At the same time she revealed that for him, too, life was complicated by inner conflicts he could not resolve.

As she teased out and studied the diverse strands of her personality, Goldman drew upon various discursive modes, weaving them together into a literary style as mixed and inchoate as the conflicting skeins she considered intrinsic to her self. Though each discourse, whether of politics, romance, or propaganda, brought to mind its own clichés, an overlapping occurred, so that a public lecture became, like love, an "ecstatic song" (I, pp. 51 and 120). Thus, discourses sometimes merged indiscriminately, and yet if samples of Goldman's variegated autobiographical style(s) were set side by side, they would seem the product of different sensibilities working at cross-purposes. In this respect, *Living My Life* seems as inchoaté and discursively tangled as *Sister Carrie*.

If Goldman's text may be considered exemplary of a subgenre of women's autobiography – of those written by influential vocal and radical public women – then one might conclude that women who announce a desire to speak their own piece and represent themselves as doing so in their autobiographies speak (as perhaps we all do) various pieces at the same time, gathering threads from different and incongruous skeins of discourse and weaving them together to create a pattern characterized by contrasts and contradictions. Of the radical women autobiographers of her time, Emma Goldman created the most synthetic and most original piece. Like Elizabeth Gurley Flynn, Mother Jones, Margaret Sanger, and Charlotte Perkins Gilman, she defended radical views she presented as her own even as she traced them to their sources in political thinkers, social movements, and contemporary events. She traced them also to books, particularly and perhaps surprisingly, to novels. Each source offered its own discursive mode, whether expository, polemic, reportorial, didactic, melodramatic, sentimental, or romantic. Her autobiography modulated from one to the other, and her readers selected one or the other to admire or criticize, just as today they select from among her various causes a particular social view to reinforce, by its historical precedence, one of their own.[38] Her most consistent theme was freedom, and when her beloved Berkman criticized her for dancing with "reckless abandon" at an anarchist party, she "grew furious" because she believed her freedom had been constrained and their "Cause" falsified – "a Cause which stood for a beautiful ideal, for anarchism, for release and freedom from conventions and prejudice" (I, p. 56). She declared her personal freedom as a woman emblematic of an ideal of freedom that included all humankind. As she said, "I want freedom, the right to self-expression, everybody's right to beautiful, radiant things" (I, p. 56). She aestheticized her politics by making "beautiful" an epithetic qualifier of "freedom," "ideal," and, even more elusively, all "things" to which she believed everyone entitled. As she described her quest for freedom, she implied that her life exemplified an historical process in which woman represented the future. This was Chernyshevsky's explicit claim for his heroine Vera Pavlovna, whose ringing words in *What Is to Be Done?* inspired Goldman. "I wish to be independent and live in my own fashion," Vera Pavlovna had cried; "I wish to act after my own fancy; let other do the same. I respect the liberty of others, as I wish them to respect mine" (p. 35).

Though she declared a desire for independence and implied that it foreshadowed sweeping revolutionary change, Goldman candidly revealed her dependence upon men who were her political mentors, financial supporters, managers and promoters, lawyers, disciples, and lovers. If as many modern theorists claim, language represents a legacy of patriarchal power, then she depended upon men, above all, for the very possibility of speaking her own piece. She did not attempt to create a language of her own, though she might not have lacked the ambition if she had lived at a time when the notion of such originality was current.[39] She conceived of her autobiographic writing as a weaving together of the different and conflicting skeins of her personality and her politics. Unlike Theodore Dreiser, who in his great first novel *Sister Carrie* also wove strands from various and incongruous discursive skeins, Goldman did not end her story with a vision of life as a tangle. "Oh, the tangle of human life!," Dreiser wrote at the end of *Sister Carrie*. Emma Goldman's life may have been knotted and tangled with diverse historical events, social and political ideas, and conflicting personal desires, but her vision remained clear and simple – and so wishful it seems dreamlike. It was a vision of a happy ending that would result from a revolution in consciousness and in society. It is expressed in its naiveté and hopefulness by a single sentence from Chernyshevsky's *What Is to Be Done?*: "They live harmoniously and cordially and quietly and happily and gayly and actively." Of all the discursive skeins in Emma Goldman's *Living My Life*, the most vulnerable to criticism is the idyllic and utopian. It is also the most enduringly appealing.

Notes

1 Theodore Dreiser, *Sister Carrie*, ed. Donald Pizer (New York: W. W. Norton & Company, 1970, published originally in 1900). This edition contains background and source material that shows a relationship between sections of the text and Dreiser's journalistic writings. Emma Goldman, *Living My Life* (New York: Dover, 1970, 2 vols., published originally in 1931).

2 Paul de Man makes the issue of generic coalescence moot by arguing that "the distinction between fiction and autobiography is not an either/or polarity; . . . it is undecidable," ("Autobiography as De-facement," *Modern Language Notes* 94 [1979]: p. 921). However, his essay is decisive in its view of autobiography as a "figure of reading" rather

than as a genre or a mode. "Empirically as well as theoretically," de Man writes, "auto-biography lends itself poorly to generic definition; each specific instance seems to be an exception to the norm; the works themselves always seem to shade off into neighboring or even incompatible genres" (p. 920). In referring to "*the* norm," de Man implies, one assumes, a generic definition based upon the practices of male autobiographers. While genre is at issue to de Man, gender, a concern of many contemporary critics, is absent from his considerations. The view that autobiography is generically "an instrument of reading, not primarily a formula for writing" is reiterated by Janet Varner Gunn (*Autobiography: Towards a Poetics of Experience* [Philadelphia: University of Pennsylvania Press, 1982], p. 21).

3 Apparently, Dreiser was not above hoodwinking his readers with prose that deliber-ately obfuscated the ideas it was espousing – at least, not when it came to writing about "the most important American woman of her time," Emma Goldman. Richard Linge-man reports that after Dreiser met and argued with Goldman – fittingly, in Greenwich Village at an Anarchists' Ball – he "commissioned a profile of her for *The Delineator*, in-structing the writer to pretend to denounce her while smuggling across her ideas" (*Theodore Dreiser, An American Journey*, 1908–1945 [New York: G. P. Putnam's Sons, 1990], p. 34).

4 In discussing the naturalistic novel as a genre – with *Sister Carrie* as "an exemplary case" – June Howard (*Form and History in America Literary Naturalism* [Chapel Hill: Uni-versity of North Carolina Press, 1985], p. 41) enumerates the different narrative strate-gies the genre deploys and the "different generic discourses" these strategies introduce into a single text: "Naturalist novels frequently incorporate conventional elements from popular literary genres like the adventure story and the domestic novel" (p. 142). In her discussion of *Sister Carrie*, Rachel Bowlby disagrees with Sandy Petrey's view of Dreiser's " 'two styles' – the simple narrative and the prosy moralizing which has [sic] earned him epithets like 'cloddish,' 'clumsy,' 'elephantine' " (*Just looking: Consumer Culture in Dreiser, Gissing, and Zola* [New York: Methuen, 1985], pp. 64–5).

5 The tenacity of clichés and, of course, the ease with which they come to mind also explain their frequency in the texts of the two writers, both of them more concerned with social ideas than with style, though clearly both were striving for a style that could evoke intense emotions as well as explain, argue, persuade, philosophize, and convert. Envisioning themselves as cultural critics, one more sweeping and radical than the other, both developed, I believe, similar strategies of rhetorical indifference – that is, both used all stylistic means they saw available and were indifferent to their generic origins. Gold-man's text gives little evidence, explicitly or formally, that she was writing in a literary tradition particular to women – or that she thought there was such a tradition for her to follow. Clearly, gender was central to many of Goldman's anarchist arguments, but if genre implies formal design, as distinct from thematics, then the relationship between gender and genre seems to me difficult to discern in her autobiography. This is not to deny that "there is a literary tradition in which women write autobiography that is dif-ferent from men" – Estelle Jelinek's conclusion (preface to *Women's Autobiography: Es-says in Criticism* [Bloomington: Indiana University Press, 1980], pp. xi – xii). Rather it is to suggest that Goldman's rhetorical strategies resemble those of her contemporary (male) novelists who held subversive views of society and of literary realism.

6 Nikolai Chernyshevsky's *What Is to Be Done?* (Boston: Benjamin R. Tucker, 1886) was written while the author was in prison, under a lifelong sentence, for his politically

subversive ideas. Its serial publication in 1863 in *The Contemporary* (a journal Cherny-shevsky had edited) has been attributed in part to its "turgid prose," which presumably the censors thought would "discredit Chernyshevsky among the young intelligentsia" (p. ix). This, at least, is what Kathryn Feuer reports in her introduction to a recent edition of the novel. A new and detailed study of the novel confirms that its style was consid-ered "atrocious" in its own time and still strikes the modern critic as "clumsy and awk-ward" (Irina Paperno, *Chernyshevsky and the Age of Realism: A Study in the Semiotics of Behavior* [Stanford, Calif.: Stanford University Press, 1988], p. 26). I have read the three English versions of the novel cited below. In a prefatory note to the Ardis edition, Feuer says there are "distortions, bordering on deceptions" in the Virago edition (*What Is to Be Done?*, tr. N. Dole and S. S. Skidelsky [Ann Arbor, Mich.: Ardis, 1986], p. xxxvi). Page references in this essay are to Tucker's 1886 edition. I might add that in a chapter enti-tled "Goldman as Rhetor," Martha Solomon describes Goldman's autobiographical style as "straightforward" and "dull" (*Emma Goldman* [Boston: Twayne Publishers, 1987], p. 143) and her prose in general as "clear and vivid" but "also heavy and graceless" and of-ten "turgid" (p. 145). Turgidity and vividness seem difficult to reconcile, and yet they appear together commonly, as is well known, in criticism of Dreiser's style, as well as in that of Chernyshevsky.

7   A work of considerable influence in Russian intellectual history, *What Is to Be Done?* provided Goldman with a theoretical basis for her revolutionary beliefs, and its famous feminist heroine, Vera Pavlovna (to whom Goldman explicitly refers), prefigured prac-tical ways for her to achieve independence. Like Pavlovna, Goldman starts a liberated new life with a sewing machine, and like her, she relies upon the tutelage and ideas of men while she pursues her ideal of woman's autonomy. Richard Drinnon has noted the importance of Chernyshevsky's novel in shaping Goldman's life as a revolutionary woman. Though Drinnon called the novel "artistically inferior" (a failing that apparently did not attenuate its influence upon contemporary readers), he pointed out that "a large part of her [Goldman's] later life was consciously patterned after Vera Pavlovna, the hero-ine of *What Is to Be Done?*" (*Rebel in Paradise: A Biography of Emma Goldman* [Chicago: University of Chicago Press, 1961], p. 10). Elsewhere, enumerating specific ways Gold-man emulated Vera Pavlovna, Drinnon stated (in language Goldman might have used): "Emma soaked in the ideas of Chernyshevsky as rain is soaked in by the desert sands" (p. 25). I find more parallels between Goldman and her fictional prototype than Drinnon, among them her triangular love affair with men who were best friends, her venture with them into a cooperative form of production, her marriage of convenience (made late in life), and her ambition, admittedly short-lived, to become a doctor. In her autobiogra-phy Goldman stressed her love of gaiety, parties, good food, and dancing, an enjoyment of life she shared, almost programmatically, with Chernyshevsky's heroine.

8   In defining what is American about American radicalism, David DeLeon has focused upon anarchism, an inveterate American "resistance to institutional authority" (the hall-mark of Goldman's anarchism), which he traces to indigenous cultural conditions and self-consciously native writers like Emerson and Thoreau. DeLeon points out that "American symbolism" was "prominent" in Goldman's social commentary (*The Ameri-can as Anarchist: Reflections on Indigenous Radicalism* [Baltimore: The Johns Hopkins Uni-versity Press, 1978], pp. 95–6). In her autobiography Goldman describes her encounters with American anarchists and her realization that Americans were capable of the ideal-

ism and sacrifices demanded of anarchists in their struggle for freedom (*Living My Life*, I, p. 155 and passim).

9 This view off women as writers, in particular as writers of their own life stories, is summarized and reiterated in the essays of Jelinek's *Women's Autobiography: Essays in Criticism*, cited above. Currently, feminist critics have begun to question or coalesce the polarities used to define differences between women and men as literary figures – specifically, polarities between private and public realms, between silence and speech, otherness or alterity and selfhood, emotionality and intellect, covertness and assertion, and, formally, between fragmentation and linearity, and openness and closure – in short, between feminine and masculine as culturally defined antinomies. See, for example, the theorizing about women's autobiography in Stanton ("Autogynography: Is The Subject Different?," in *The Female Autograph: Theory and Practice of Autography from the Tenth to the Twentieth Century*, ed. Domna C. Stanton [Chicago: University of Chicago Press, 1984]; in Sidonie Smith (*A Poetics of Women's Autobiography: Marginality and the Fictions of Self-Representation* [Bloomington: Indiana University Press, 1987), whose study begins by putting "into question its own terms" – private and self; and Julia Watson, who describes a collapse of the "Other" into the autobiographical "I" ("Shadowed Presence: Modern Women Writers' Autobiographies and the Other," in *Studies in Autobiography*, ed. James Olney [New York: Oxford University Press, 1988], pp. 180–9). A collapsing of these particular binaries is adumbrated in Louis A. Renza's essay, "The Veto of the Imagination: A Theory of Autobiography," *New Literary History* IX (1977–78); and in Elizabeth Bruss, *Autobiographical Acts: The Changing Situation of a Literary Genre* (Baltimore: The Johns Hopkins University Press, 1976). Bruss concludes that a common generic tendency was "toward discontinuous structures . . . with disrupted narrative sequences and competing foci of attention" – formal markers that Jelinek and others find characteristic of women's narrations. In a startling declaration that patriarchy is now extinct in the Western world, Elisabeth Badinter says "a different world order is coming into being" that will dispel the patriarchal forms of sexual "complementarity" which have, historically, related men and women in "a power system that places the One above the Other" (*The Unopposed Sex: The End of the Gender Battle*, tr. Barbara Wright [New York: Harper & Row, 1989], published originally in 1986 in France by Editions Odile Jacob as *L'un est l'autre*, pp. xi and xiv). Instead of inequality based upon claims of difference, she sees "democratic societies currently generating a completely new model: *the resemblance between the sexes*" (p. xiv, original emphasis). Though her prediction that "a cultural mutation" will equalize the sexes carries her far beyond issues of gender differences in literary genres, it is germane in suggesting a belief among some contemporary theorists that meaningful differences between women and men are erasable, or as Badinter would have it, have already been erased in the Western world.

10 Bruss points out that one deliberate (and legitimate) use of autobiography may be "to rebut" a writer's "public character" (*Autobiographical Acts*, p. 12).

11 Elizabeth Griffin speculates that Stanton may have chosen "to appear more commonplace in an effort to have more in common with her readers, to convert them by an ordinary example rather than to inspire them with extraordinary accomplishments. As she [Stanton] asserted in the preface, she was just a 'wife . . . housekeeper . . . and the mother of seven children' " (*In Her Own Right: The Life of Elizabeth Cady Stanton* [New York: Oxford University Press, 1984], pp. 207–8). Jelinek believes that Stanton's subject

in her autobiography was her "public career," her purpose to "convert" her reader to the women's suffragist movement, and her strategy "to omit anything that might case a negative light on her achievements" (*Women's Autobiography*, p. 74).

12   To cite an example from a later period, Eleanor Roosevelt – who believed, obviously, in ameliorative rather than revolutionary change – repudiated a common and comic public view of her as ubiquitously intrusive by claiming that her public life was the result of chance rather than her choices or competencies. Her autobiography would have value, she said, if others could learn from her mistakes: "perhaps my very foolishness may be helpful!" (*The Autobiography of Eleanor Roosevelt* [New York: Harper and Brothers, 1961, abbreviated edition], p. xvii).

13   What Goldman hid and whether hiding is a characteristic mark of gender in women's autobiography are issues discussed later in this essay.

14   In "The Veto of the Imagination," Renza states that "the autobiographer must come to terms with a unique pronominal crux: how can he [sic] keep using the first-person pronoun, his sense of self-reference, without its becoming – since it becomes, in the course of writing, something other than strictly his own self-referential sign – a de facto third-person pronoun?" (p. 9). After kindly reading this manuscript on *Living My Life*, Professor Renza asked me whether Goldman's reference to herself as "E. G." (quoted above) is a "trope of familiarity, of self-demystification . . . or of social resistance" – a shedding of the name by which society identifies the self? Since Goldman quotes Dreiser as referring to her, in her presence, as "E. G.," this third-person abbreviation might pose additional questions about the naming and the splitting of the self in autobiography. (I might add that occasionally Goldman refers to herself as "Emma Goldman.") In the context of her use of "E. G.," Goldman seems to me involved in self-repossession rather than self-demystification; she was appropriating her self from others (male financial benefactors) who are telling her how to behave. Dreiser's address may signify his appropriative attempt to familiarize (or diminish) Goldman so that *he* can tell her what she "must" do; he assumes authority as he directs a depersonalized (and degendered) "E. G." to write. I am grateful to Professor Renza for helping me "bleed out," as he put it, some of the tensions within my account of Goldman's self-representation.

15   *Sister Carrie* begins with Carrie as a young adult and refers briefly and barely to her past, almost as though she had no childhood. Like the trains that take Carrie first to Chicago and then to Montreal and New York, her life moves in one direction, inexorably forward toward a future that Dreiser envisions as an evolutionary unfolding. A recent attempt to reconstruct Carrie's past draws upon her brief memories of home and its deprivations to explain the "melancholic part" of her mind (Thomas P. Riggio, "Carrie's Blues," *New Essays on Sister Carrie*, ed. Donald Pizer [Cambridge: Cambridge University Press, 1991], pp. 23–41). Goldman's story of her life shuttles back and forth, from present to past, action to memory. The past, as personal and social history, is crucial to Goldman's rationalization or ratification of her life.

16   The discovery of "a new world" as a metaphor for conversion to a social cause, while particularly appropriate to Goldman as an immigrant, appears in the autobiographies of other public women. Margaret Sanger, for example, describes her decision to speak out for birth control as an "illumination" that reveals "a new day" and "a new world" (*My Fight for Birth Control* [New York: Farrar & Rinehart, 1931], p. 56).

17   Given the initial similarities between Carrie's story and Goldman's, the differences that ensue are diametric and irreconcilable. If modern interpretations of *Sister Carrie* are correct, then the novel (perhaps unintentionally) endorses capitalism and its values, while *Living My Life* is a testament to a revolutionary ideal that would demolish all capitalistic institutions. See, for example, June Howard, *Form and History in America Literary Naturalism* (Chapel Hill: University of North Carolina Press, 1985); Amy Kaplan, *The Social Construction of American Realism* (Chicago: University of Chicago Press, 1988), pp. 140–60; and Walter Benn Michaels, "*Sister Carrie's* Popular Economy," *The Gold Standard and the Logic of Naturalism* (Berkely: University of California Press, 1987), pp. 31–58. In his recent biography of Dreiser, Richard Lingeman notes in passing that "Carrie is a sister to a generation of remarkable women carving out a place in the world–Jane Addams, Emma Goldman, Margaret Sanger, Alice Hamilton, and others." But differences between Carrie and Goldman as "sisters" seem more salient than similarities, since Lingeman has just described Carrie as passive, materialistic, and uneducated, traits that clearly do not relate her to Goldman (*Theodore Dreiser: At the Gates of the City*, 1871–1907 [New York: G. P. Putnam's Sons, 1986], p. 256).

18 In a letter written to Alexander Berkman in 1928, more than a quarter century after the act, Goldman said she still could not forget or forgive Berkman's intractable rejection of Czolgosz's attack upon President McKinley, a response she found "as absurd now as I did then" (Richard and Anna Maria Drinnon, eds., *Nowhere At Home: Letters from Exile of Emma Goldman and Alexander Berkman* [New York: Schocken Books, 1975], p. 95).

19 For a full and emotional account of Berkman's belief at the time in the messianic meaning of revolution and political acts of assassination and in self-sacrifice or suicide, see his story in *Prison Memoirs of an Anarchist* (New York: Mother Earth Publishing Association, 1912).

20 Advised by an attorney friend to omit her involvement in the Frick affair because it might jeopardize her chances of readmission to the United States, Goldman replied that she "would rather never again have the opportunity of returning than to eliminate what represents the very essence of my book." Her "connection with Berkman's act" was, she said, "the pivot around which my story is written" (Drinnon and Drinnon, eds. *Nowhere At Home: Letters from Exile of Emma Goldman and Alexander Berkman*, pp. xix–xx).

21 Goldman tells of committing various acts of violence, all of them, like the horse-whipping of Most, melodramatic gestures of outrage. She threw a pitcher of water at a woman who insulted the Haymarket anarchists and a glass of water at a detective who suggested she spy for the police. She also threw a Bible at a prison matron, furiously swept a tray of jewelry to the floor, and attacked her lover with a chair. Ironically, Goldman describes other seeing her as pacific and benign. "I don't believe you could hurt a fly," she reports a prison doctor saying to her, "A fine inciter you would make!" (*Living My Life*, I, p. 187). Because of their public image as incendiary figures, radical women often surprised those they met in private (including each other) by their pleasant appearances– as Elizabeth Gurley Flynn, Mother Jones, and Margaret Sanger indicate in their autobiographies. See, for example, Flynn's reaction on first meeting the "fiery agitator" Emma Goldman (*I Speak My Own Piece: Autobiography of "The Rebel Girl"* [New York: New Masses and Mainstream, 1955], p. 39). Goldman mentions Flynn's imprisonment for expressing pacifist views during World War I (*Living My Life*, II, p. 640) and Mother Jones's "deportation" from the scene of a miners' strike (II, p. 521); she considers both women victims of society rather than threats. Writing about women anarchists from 1870–1920, Margaret Marsh points out that they were commonly accused of fomenting public violence, but Marsh denies that Goldman "incited her hearers to riot." Rather, she says,

"Goldman used the tactics of nonviolent confrontation to assert her right to speak." Nevertheless, the "fantasy" of anarchist violence persisted (*Anarchist Women: 1870–1920* [Philadelphia: Temple University Press, 1981], pp. 110–12).

22 Dostoyevsky created Lebeziatnikov of *Crime and Punishment* and the narrator of *Notes from Underground* as vitriolic parodies of Russian Nihilists (anarchists). His opposition to Chernyshevsky was specific and profound, as pointed out by Irina Paperno, who suggests that "Dostoevsky was trying to refute Chernyshevsky not just by attacking his initial premise and final conclusion, but also by attacking his pattern of reasoning itself: the logical sequence of cause and effect" (*Chernyshevsky and the Age of Realism: A Study in the Semiotics of Behavior* [Stanford, Calif.: Sanford University Press, 1988], p. 202). Paperno goes on to say that "Dostoevsky's objections to Chernyshevsky rested on ethical, epistemological, and psychological considerations," as well as on religious grounds (pp. 203–4) – which leaves little room for negotiation between the two.

23 On Ben Reitman's reading, see *Living My Life*, II, p. 518.

24 Like Goldman, the idealistic ideologue Alexander Berkman had seen his future projected in Chernyshevsky's characters, with whom he associated himself immediately in his own autobiography, *Prison Memoirs of an Anarchist* (pp. 6, 7, and 9). In the most portentous moment of his life, when he arrives in Pittsburgh to assassinate Frick and immolate himself as a revolutionary hero, Berkman registers in a hotel under the name Rakhmetov, man of the future and hero of *What Is to Be Done? Prison Memoirs* unintentionally introduces a comic note when it describes the police interrogation that follows Berkman's capture. A detective tells Berkman, "I know a good deal more about you than you think. We've got your friend Rak-metov" (p. 41). *Prison Memoirs* has been highly praised for its "masterful artistry"; and Berkman's "adroit handling of a variety of literary styles" has been compared in "caliber" to that "found only in the most finely wrought fiction" (Thomas P. Doherty, "American Autobiography and Ideology," in *The American Autobiography: A Collection of Critical Essays,* ed. Albert E. Stone [Englewood Cliffs, N.J.: Prentice-Hall, 1985], p. 99). Written to condemn a repressive state, Berkman's text – whether viewed as autobiography, self-serving apologia, or fiction – gives an account of daily prison life that invites comparison with Solzhenitsyn's novella, *One Day in the Life of Ivan Denisovich*, discussed at length in Days of Reckoning.

25 Throughout the autobiography, Goldman continues to add to her list of readings as friends, usually men, introduce her to books and writers she had not known. One friend, Alexander Harvey, gave her "several volumes of Greek plays in English translation" and, as a supreme compliment, compared her to Antigone. In an ironic reply, she asked him "to explain the existence of slavery in his beloved old [Greek] world" (II, p. 682). She always enlarged her reading when she traveled, at home and abroad, and when she was (comparatively briefly) in prison. She met many American and English writers of her time and established friendships with some of them, like Frank Harris, whose novel *The Bomb* she both praised and criticized, and Rebecca West, who tried to help her when she was being denounced for her anti-Soviet views.

26 In Theodore Dreiser's novel, Carrie begins to perceive the possibility of ideals beyond the dream of money and fashion when the exemplary male character Ames derides the popular books she enjoys. He recommends Balzac, and when last seen, Carrie is reading *Père Goriot*. I have described Carrie as a reader and the city as her text in an essay called "Sister to Faust: The City's 'Hungry Woman' as Heroine," *Novel: A Forum on Fiction* 15:1 (Fall 1981): pp. 23–38. Goldman could be considered a "hungry" woman reader, though I use the term to define a literary type.

27 Howard has described the "brute" or savage in the naturalistic novel as a generic character who embodies atavism. He represents also a process of proletarization or social decline that may produce a social victim, a criminal, or (particularly pertinent to Goldman's lover, Reitman) a tramp. Though Reitman was a doctor, he had taken up the life of a tramp and affiliated himself in his wanderings with criminals, prostitutes, and the poor, the underworld of American society. An intense and almost obsessive sexuality also characterized Reitman, as it does Howard's "brute" (*Form and History in America Literary Naturalism*, pp. 36–103).

28 Clearly, Goldman knows she is coalescing life and fiction and reversing their usual relationship by valuing a "real" living person because he resembles literary "types" (underworld types that seemed to her exotic because their marginality was different from hers as a radical woman immigrant). Goldman had studied Shakespeare's plays, and in describing her seduction through stories, she may having been casting herself, however inappropriately, as Desdemona listening to Othello's exotic tales.

29 Quoted from Karen Rosenberg, "An Autumnal Love of Emma Goldman, *Dissent* (Summer, 1983), 30:3, p. 380. Patricia Spacks relates "hiding" to gender in her essay "Selves in Hiding," in *Women's Autobiography: Essays in Criticism* (cited above). Spacks concedes that in the context she has hypothesized "Emma Goldman presents something of an anomaly" (p. 118); nevertheless, she tries to fit Goldman into the pattern of self-abnegation and reticence she considers typical of public women's autobiographies. Though Goldman described her slavish infatuation with Reitman (and included photographs of him in the autobiography), Jelinek declares that "Goldman excludes her ten-year relationship with Ben Reitman out of fear that her public image will be even more tainted or devalued by intimate disclosures" (*The Tradition of Women's Autobiography* [Boston: Twayne Publishers, 1986], p. 129). In fact, Goldman refused to listen to friends' advice that she omit her love affairs; she considered women's sexual freedom crucial to her anarchistic ideal, and she would not compromise this ideal by eliding her sexual passion and needs. Goldman's affairs did disturb some contemporary radical women, like the journalist Dorothy Day, who wrote in her autobiography that she was "revolted" by Goldman's "promiscuity" and would not read *Living My Life* "because I was offended in my sex" (*The Long Loneliness: The Autobiography of Dorothy Day* [New York: Harper and Brothers, 1952], p. 60). Day surrounds her comments on Goldman with expressions of doubt about her own commitment to the social causes she served (and with sexist remarks).

30 Candace Falk has described her extraordinary discovery of the love letters and reproduced many of them in *Love, Anarchy, and Emma Goldman* (New York: Holt, Rinehart and Winston, 1984).

31 As we know, Henry Adams omitted twenty years from his famous autobiography and mentioned his wife only once. Dreiser wrote several volumes recounting the story of his life, and omitted more than he revealed – understandably, when one sees what he might have told if he had transferred information (mainly on sex and money) from his private records to his autobiographies. Dreiser's private papers are in the Van Pelt Library of the University of Pennsylvania.

32 Goldman's views on motherhood were complex and contradictory. She considered herself deprived of the joys of motherhood, which she wanted the reader to believe she had sacrificed to her ideal. On the other hand, she described motherhood as "that blind, dumb force that brings forth life in travail, wasting woman's youth and strength, and leaving her in old age a burden to herself and to those to whom she has given birth" (I, p.

340). Contrary to critical views that women's autobiography reveals strong mother – daughter ties, Goldman's "life" describes estrangement between her and her mother. Her half-sister Helena acted as her surrogate mother, lavishing upon her the love denied by her parents.

33   Characteristically, Goldman refused to "be gagged on the question of Bolsheviki." "I had kept silent long enough," she writes, and she determined "to speak out" and to speak her own piece (II, p. 936). When her criticism of the Bolsheviks appeared in American newspapers, a political ally called for communist volunteers "to burn E. G., at least in effigy." Goldman's comment typifies her hyperbolic caustic style: "What a picture! The chairlady intoning the *International*, and the audience holding hands in an orgiastic dance round the flames licking Emma Goldman's body to the tune of the liberating song" (II, p. 38).

34   Dreiser reported his equivocal views on Soviet Russian life in his books *Dreiser Looks at Russia* (New York: Horace Liveright, 1928) – views gathered during the several months he toured the country as a guest of the government. He had been invited, along with other notable Americans, to celebrate the tenth anniversary of the Russian Revolution. While he found himself critical of many aspects of Soviet Russian life, among them the censorship of newspapers and art, he sympathized with the stated egalitarian goals of Soviet society. Sometimes he wrote as a discomforted American tourist as well as a presumably objective observer, so that his *look* turned inward and out, refocusing its attention from conflicting images he saw in the world to his own conflicted responses. Today, *Dreiser Looks at Russia* elicits little critical interest, though it was widely reviewed when it was appeared and much discussed, in part because of public charges that it had plagiarized passages from Dorothy Thompson's book on Russia. It merits rereading, I believe, for its relevance as a historical document, an autobiographical portrait of a complex and often perplexed American writer, and a straightforward reportorial cross-cultural critique. As a critique, it presents Soviet life from the limited perspective of an outsider whose relationship to the culture he examines is brief and mediated, and yet it exudes authority that its political insights legitimize (for some of these insights, see notes 35, 44, and 68 to Days of Reckoning). Dreiser's rambling style, bothersome to his reviewers, seems to me suited to – and, indeed, constitutive of – a subject that eluded closure, requiring space and latitude to reveal its historical aporias. "Mysticism? Thy name is Slav," Dreiser wrote (p. 31), and his mixed language of awe, criticism, and credulity sought to capture the strange mixture of mysticism and cruel expedience that, he believed, characterized Soviet Russian culture. He described repression, inequality, inefficiency, and sheer sordidness as inextricable from ideals that were, he thought, both remote and attainable. A decade earlier, Goldman had found her revolutionary *Ideal* already subverted. She had looked at Russia and condemned what she saw. Dreiser looked, equivocated, and ended up, like his unsettled Sister Carrie, rocking and dreaming of a happiness that is still to come.

35   Flynn reports this interview in *I Speak My Own Piece*, p. 53. Goldman was actually prepared to do an "act" in Oscar Hammerstein's theater, but once backstage she was appalled at the prospect and fled (II, p. 536).

36   If Dreiser appropriated Goldman for his portrait of "Ernita" in *A Gallery of Women*, Vol. I (New York: Horace Liveright, 1929), as Richard Lehan claims (*Theodore Dreiser: His World and His Novels* [Carbondale: Southern Illinois University Press, 1969], p. 172), he so thoroughly changed her that his representation distorts her life and politics. Unlike the exiled Goldman, "Ernita" moved voluntarily from America to the Soviet Union, and once there, her acceptance of the revolutionary regime, and in particular of Lenin (*A Gallery of Women*, Vol. I, p. 346), had little in common with Goldman's critical appraisal. Richard Lingeman gives evidence that "Ernita" was based upon the life of Ruth Kennell, who served Dreiser on his Soviet trip as his secretary, translator, companion, and "political conscience on Russia" (*An American Journey*, p. 311 and passim). Lingeman notes that Dreiser was "eager" to include a sketch on Goldman in *A Gallery of Women*, but he never did. Apparently he "was more interested in aiding Goldman than in writing about her" (p. 31). In an 1918 interview that contains "some near seditious thoughts," Dreiser called Goldman, now marked for deportation, " 'one of the noblest women who ever lived' " (interview quoted in Lingeman, *An American Journey*, p. 166).

37 Margaret Sanger included Dreiser in her list of "distinguished men" who supported the cause of birth control during "the dark early days of the movement" (*My Fight for Birth Control* [New York: Farrar & Rinehart, 1931], pp. 202–3). While Sanger named many men as her supporters, some of whom did little more than give her verbal assent, she carefully omitted Goldman's active role in the birth control movement. David Kennedy discusses the strategic usefulness of this omission to Sanger and the image of herself she wished to project in her autobiography (*Birth Control in America: The Career of Margaret Sanger* [New Haven, Conn.: Yale University Press, 1970], pp. 18–20). Goldman, on the other hand, was generous in assigning credit for the birth control movement in America to others. "Neither my birth-control discussion nor Margaret Sanger's efforts were pioneer work," she wrote; then she listed the men and women (comparatively unknown today) whom she considered the "pioneers and heroes of the battle for free motherhood" (*Living My Life*, II, p. 553).

38 An example is Alix Shulman's strong emphasis upon Goldman's feminism (*To The Barricades: The Anarchist Life of Emma Goldman* [New York: Thomas Y. Crowell, 1971]) and *Red Emma Speaks: An Emma Goldman Reader* [New York: Schocken Books, 1983]). In her autobiography Goldman confessed that she had difficulty maintaining friendships with women (particularly articulate and activist women like Voltairine de Cleyre), that she was drawn into divisive political rivalries with women who advocated the same cause (like Margaret Sanger), that she lacked sympathy for and belief in the suffragist movement, and that suffragists and other women reformers considered her a "man's woman." Like Goldman, the labor organizer Mother Jones expressed her belief that women did not need the vote in order to raise political "hell." In her autobiography Mother Jones recalls that at a labor meeting, a woman had protested that she could not freely speak her piece as long as women "haven't a vote." Mother Jones replied, "I never had a vote . . . and I have raised hell all over this country! You don't need a vote to raise hell! You need convictions and a voice!" (*Autobiography of Mother Jones*, ed. Mary Field Parton [Chicago: Charles H. Kerr and Company, 1925], pp. 203–4). Though Sanger considered women's welfare her cause, she too rejected women's suffrage as an effective means to her end – that of eradicating society's "negative attitude toward women" and securing women's control of their "generative" functions (*My Fight for Birth Control*, p. 74).

39 Jelinek concludes her survey of women's autobiography with an accolade to experimental American women writers who are "enriching and expanding the genre's possibilities." She cites in particular "creative" and ethnic women – for example, Maxine Hong Kingston, Maya Angelou, Annie Dillard, Ntozake Shange, Lillian Hellman, and Judy Chicago (*The Tradition of Women's Autobiography*, pp. 189–90). Sidonie Smith finds the "most radical promise of difference" for women's autobiography articulated, not surprisingly, by French feminists who believe in the possibility of a language yet to be written by women yet to be liberated from "the phallologocentric *écriture* of Western culture" (*A Poetics of Women's Autobiography: Marginality and the Fictions of Self-Representation* [Bloomington: Indiana University Press, 1987], p. 58). Smith herself sees the possibility of new decentered forms emerging from the margins that, she believes, women and women writers usually inhabit; she too considers Maxine Hong Kingston an exemplary figure in the development of a women's autobiographical tradition, and points to others like Gertrude Stein, Virginia Woolf, and Anais Nin for whom "the masculine autobiographical mode is passé" (p. 175).

Panel III: On Mystery

Quand bien nous pourrions estre sçavans du sçavoir d'autruy, au moins sages ne pouvons nous estre que de nostre propre sagesse.

Montaigne

Ethel Wilson has long been one of my favorite Canadian writers, perhaps because she seems to me one of the most urbanely elusive. Like Willa Cather, she achieves a graceful simplicity of style that suggests simplicity of meaning. The suggestion is misleading. As the essay The Hidden Mines seeks to show, Wilson's meanings are complex, deep, and, like explosive mines, potentially dangerous to discover. I had not anticipated discovering the dangers when I was asked to give an American perspective on Wilson's fiction. That was for a conference held at the University of Ottawa and attended almost entirely by Canadians, almost all dedicated Wilson scholars. I subtitled the essay An American Cat among Canadian Falcons for reasons given in the first note to the essay.

I had wanted to incorporate the note in this introduction as a way of presenting the essay's particular intention and slant. I decided, however, to leave The Hidden Mines as it was. In its original form, it stands, I think, as the simplest and, perhaps, most tenable kind of cross-cultural criticism. Its theoretical assumption is commonsensical, namely, that I was reading in the ways to which I had been conditioned by my academic, personal, and cultural experiences. In current jargon, I was reading as a . . . or reading from the position of a . . . . I could fill in the spaces easily, and I did. As the essay states, I was reading as an American woman critic, someone I found simple to locate, since this reading *I* was a self I had, for a long time, taken for granted. Whatever I excavated from the hidden mines in Wilson's fiction, I had done in this triple identity as a literary critic, an American, and a woman responsive to the inflections of gender.

The perspectives of the essay may have struck a Canadian audience as unusual, but its form was conventional, shaped by a comparison of the similarities and differences I saw between Wilson and American writers of her time. Writing from my own perspective, I seldom drew upon other critics, so that The Hidden Mines is sparsely documented. I considered loading it with a barrage of notes to make it symmetrical with the other essays, but I decided to leave it as written. As it stands, it is the least wayward and resistant essay in this volume, the most willing to carry out a straightforward assignment. It gives an American reader's account of a Canadian writer. Its reckonings caused me few misgivings. Issues I would find troubling when I wrote Days of Reckoning did not bother me, and why should they? I was asked to say what I saw, and I did. I still see the same dangers and beauties in Wilson's work – and more.

The Capitalistic Will is the most recent essay, written for this collection as a complement to The Hidden Mines. I had tentatively tried out the idea of a comparison between Wilson and Cather several years back, first in a call for cross-cultural studies of Canadian and American women writers that questioned the relationship, if any, between gender and nationality; then in The Hidden Mines; later, in a cross-cultural critique given in Toronto at the 1989 joint conference of the American Studies Association and Canadian American Studies Association; and still later in 1990, in a presentation made, not without trepidation, at the Willa Cather Fourth National Seminar at Santa Fe. The trepidation came from telling an audience of Cather scholars that the fiction of their much adulated writer was, in my opinion, steeped in materialistic values, that sustaining this fiction's lofty romantic ideals and driving its plots was a character's irreducibly mundane desire or need for money. Moreover, I was basing my claims upon a reading of a late Cather novel, *My Mortal Enemy*, that was at the time usually ignored or considered an aberrant, misguided, or failed work. That view has been changing, and even after I finished (or thought I had finished) writing The Capitalistic Will, new studies of Cather's late fiction have appeared to offer new and not necessarily benign readings that make my critical views seem less dissonant than they did a few years ago.

Drawn to the intricacies of polyptychs as I was writing Days of Reckoning, I thought I would complicate the structure of the book I imagined as a literary triptych by making its third panel a composite of two essays. This literary diptych would have an integrity of its own as an American–Canadian cross-cultural critique, and it would be integral to the reckonings of the volume as a whole. In the diptych, questions about the truth of fiction, discussed in Days of Reckoning, reemerge because Wilson raised them explicitly, as The Hidden Mines shows, and because both she and Cather, as I read them in The Capitalistic Will, were juggling certain truths about their characters they refused to admit and yet would not, or could not, conceal. Their attempts at obfuscation produced unresolvable mysteries in *My Mortal Enemy* and *Love and Salt Water*. I found these novels' mysteries intriguing, as mysteries usually are, and my reading sought not to dispel them, but, rather, to explain their necessity. The explanation required a process of excavation, described in The Hidden Mines as a close reading that delves beneath a text's surfaces to discover what interests lay in its depths. In this last essay, I discovered capitalistic interests to which the writers would not admit.

Indeed, they could not admit that the art they wanted to imbue with timeless universal values was interpellated by the values of modern capitalism. In *Love and Salt Water* and *My Mortal Enemy*, they dramatized what I have called "capitalistic will" – a will to accumulate and maintain control of capital and money. The will becomes manifest in legal wills that characters make or refuse to make. Thus, the essay's polyvalent term, *the capitalistic will* has personal, cultural, and legal meanings, all coalesced in the character of rich old men who seek to exert their will even after they are dead. Inheritance – or rather, disinheritance – becomes a central issue in *My Mortal Enemy*, and while a disdain for inheritance suggests it is merely peripheral to the interests of *Love and Salt Water*, the essay comes to a different reckoning of its importance. The reading of both novels is revisionary and based upon my own understanding. The massive panel of endnotes provides supplementary material, interesting in itself, I hope, while supportive of the essay's argument. I tried to avoid *le pendantisme* by storing all I had garnered from this supplemental secondary material in a separate place; there I cite and acknowledge my intellectual debts. But while I have learned from the learning of others, I have tried – essayed for – wisdom of my own. I take to heart, here as elsewhere, the words of Montaigne: "Quand bien nous pourrions estre sçavans du sçavoir d'autruy, au moins sages ne pouvons nous estre que de nostre propre sagesse." I wanted to end the essay – and the volume's literary reckonings – with the romantic notion that reading was a personal act, and that the modicum of wisdom I brought to the texts, from my own person, was an appreciation of their mystery.

The Hidden Mines
in Ethel Wilson's Landscape
(or, An American Cat among
Canadian Falcons)[1]

"I had handled dynamite," Frankie Burnaby thinks at the end of Ethel Wilson's novel *Hetty Dorval:* "I had handled dynamite, and in so doing had exploded the hidden mine of Mrs. Broom to my own great astonishment. . . . "[2]

I start with this image of a hidden mine in Ethel Wilson's fiction because I am an American reader, accustomed by my literature to explosions of violence in the novel and also to abundance, to the presence within a vast and varied landscape of rich deposits – the inexhaustible resources of art. Canadian critics, as they describe the abundance contained in Wilson's fiction, its richness of natural and social detail, have praised the surface serenity of her art: the detached tone; the compassionate and comic insights into the foibles of the great human family; the faith that remains unshaken even when these foibles, our seemingly innocent but obsessive meddling with each other, turn into destructive or coercive acts, violations of each other's freedom. I wish to excavate to a depth hidden beneath the surface sustained so beautifully by Wilson's style and tone and the seemingly casual meandering of her form; I wish to dig for the dynamite I suspect she has concealed. By her own image she has alerted us to the possibility of hidden mines and so validated the process of excavation, which I take to be the critic's essential act. First of all, I want to extract from Wilson's fiction the violence that lurks beneath its serenity. In these dangerous depths, I expect to find also abundance, a rich subterranean treasure of motives and meanings that constitute the source of Ethel Wilson's art.

To the critic, surface and depths evoke complementary images of light and darkness, the contrast integral to Wilson's art and to her vision of the duplicity of life which allows us brilliant evanescent moments whose meanings are shadowy and elusive. In a striking passage, Wilson describes a fluidity of light passing over the landscape of British Columbia and defamiliarizing the "daily look" of mountains and forests. Falling obliquely upon mountain slopes, light "discloses new contours"; in forests, it "discover[s] each separate tree behind each separate tree."[3] Then it fades, leaving us with unforgettable images. The light I bring to Wilson's landscape is also oblique; but I hope its illumination, coming

from an unfamiliar direction and moving into an unexplored darkness, can discover aspects of Wilson's art – images of hidden violence and of abundance –
that we will remember long after the critic's light fades.

Obviously, violence in Wilson is much more muted, much less shocking and
perverse, than in the fiction of William Faulkner and Ernest Hemingway, not
the most brutal but the most famous male American novelists writing as Wilson's contemporaries. American women writers also shed blood more unspar-
ingly than Wilson. Murder, rape, mob vengeance, and war erupt in Flannery
O'Connor and Katherine Anne Porter; and in Willa Cather, violence assaults
the peaceful Nebraska landscape with the suddenness of locusts. In Wilson's
novels, a child can slip into a turbulent ocean in one unobtrusive sentence, a
beloved mother die almost parenthetically, a wife submit to her husband's "hate-
ful assaults" as a nightly aside to daily life, and a war, or two wars, fit incidentally into the unimportant gaps within a family's continuous life. If in these wars,
a man's hand should be "blown off," neither he nor his family "look[s] upon
this as anything out of the way."[4] Nor do we, for Wilson somehow disposes of
the violence she has released, tucking it away among the details of daily life,
which resumes its ordinary course after an explosion; or else she separates us
from violence, as Frankie is separated from war-torn Vienna, by a convenient
"wall of silence." In Wilson's stories, however, the violence contained within
the beautiful Canadian landscape cannot be concealed by silence, hardly allow-
able in the short story's urgent form, or by dense details that attract our attention in the novel, distracting it from hidden dangers. The "humped" body of a
murdered woman lies exposed on the dyke in "Hurry, hurry"; the blood of an
innocent Chinaman flows from repeated stab wounds and a gunshot in "Fog";
blackness and the sea pour into a reeling boat that strikes a reef and splits, spilling
four people into death and causing the suicide of a pregnant woman in "From
Flores"; and in "The Window," a would-be murderer stands with "a short blunt
weapon in his hand," arrested in his deadly assault only by the shocking image
of his own imminent violence.

Violence held in arrest by its own image seems to me a stunning effect of Wilson's art. At the moment when the would-be murderer sees *himself*, his hand is
halted, perhaps (to use one of Wilson's favorite words) only temporarily, but
long enough for Mr. Willy's life to be spared. Violence thus allows for providential rescue, common in Wilson's fiction; and rescue influences our perception of life, of its indifference to human needs or its concern, its accidental nature
or design. With these polarities we plunge to the depths in Wilson's fiction,
reaching her bedrock thematic issue. Has human life ultimate meaning, or is it
simply like – Topaz Edgeworth's life – a succession of "sparkling dots" unin-
scribed in a "significant design"? Nihilism and belief struggle for supremacy in
Wilson's fiction, which like the darkened window of her story reflects the interior space of the mind – or perhaps it is the soul – where significant human action takes place. When the murderous thief brings violence into Mr. Willy's

living room, the consciousness where life is centered, he cracks the darkness that is slowly enveloping Mr. Willy; he allows in an unexpected slant of light that can show Mr. Willy where meaning may exist in an apparently meaningless life. To recognize the danger of irrational, unpredictable, undeserved violence seems in Wilson's fiction a necessary preliminary to believing in providential design. Such recognition, however, brings one precipitously close to the Abyss, the empty darkness that Mr. Willy sees outside and within his window when night effaces the day's stirringly beautiful Canadian landscape. However abundant and variegated external nature appears in Wilson's lavish descriptions, human reality enacts its drama in an interior private living room – in the heart and head, as Nell Severance tells us in *Swamp Angel*.[5] Any human being isolated in this room, cut off from significant relationship to others, must find his or her thoughts mined (or undermined) with dangerous elements: a fear of nihilism, a suspicion of life's ultimate meaninglessness, a sense of the fortuity of encounters that may end in death or in permanent scarring such as Ellen Cuppy will suffer in *Love and Salt Water*. If we dig deeply enough into Wilson's fiction, we strike against the Void; and when Nothingness lies below us, leaving us unsupported, then life and fiction may catapult us into a violence as sudden and meaningless as that which engulfs the odd assortment of men who drown together in the death-drenched story "From Flores."

Like the waters into which a Wilson character may at any whimsical moment sink, the desert represents an endless Void. Thus, aridity recurs as Wilson's thematic term for deprivation of meaning, an invidious form of violence that can enter a room impregnable to a thief. In "Tuesday and Wednesday," Victoria May Tritt (who has more of a name than an identity) lives "in a parched way," lost in a "desert of loneliness" created by time – "the desert between now and sleep." Water and desert sand, both vast, elemental, and seemingly empty, both dangerous for women and men to traverse, especially alone, stretch before the reader as irradicable images of a cosmic void. "Do we always live on a brink, then," Nora asks in *Love and Salt Water* (p. 192). Wilson's fiction shows us that "we do," while every urbane aspect of her style and tone, so admirably discussed by her Canadian critics, tries to pull us back from the Void, providing us with a calm or comic or collected perspective that diverts us from the emptiness of spirit into which anyone, particularly anyone of our modern world, may fall. If oblique means of preventing us from exploding the hidden mines of nihilism, means of formal control, seem inadequate, then Wilson openly moralizes against despair, insisting upon the "beautiful action[s]" of which human beings are capable, acts of compassion, performed by Maggie Lloyd in *Swamp Angel,* of loyalty and love, exemplified by Morgan Peake and George Gordon in *Love and Salt Water,* of self-discipline developed by Lilly in her story, and miraculous rescue produced by "dirty, old" men like Mr. Abednego.

A profound fear that man may be an island, a desert island, the fear that leads Mr. Willy to despair over the "aridity" of his isolated life (rather than to exalt over his freedom) makes Wilson insist, I believe, upon the integrity of the human family. This insistence, however, raises my anxiety, and like Lilly in "Lilly's Story," I grow afraid of unforeseen "Trouble." For since we are all related, enmeshed though we cannot know how in each others' lives, I worry about effects upon my own life that may come from gratuitous and unfathomable causes. I feel myself treading over hidden mines, any one of which may accidentally blow up in my face and leave me, like Ellen Cuppy, scarred. How can I tell what "arrangements of circumstance" have been prepared for me by those nebulous agents of causality in Wilson's fiction, "life and time," which are fusing all of us into one continuous family, relating me to generations past or distant whose effects I can neither know nor avoid? Occasionally the long-range fortuitous effects of family ties will be amusing. In *The Innocent Traveller,* Rose attends the theater (and develops "a taste for . . . the deceits of beauty") because ten years earlier her Great Aunt Annie and a famous actor had met as shipmates, in an encounter arranged by chance. But when chance becomes causality, linking together a chain of events we find incongruous but destructive, I fear its vagaries. If they affect my life – as they effect Mort's death in "Tuesday and Wednesday"[6] – then life itself seems random, without intrinsic order. Wilson tries to mollify the fear of chaos she arouses by showing how families maintain order as they transmit from one generation to the next a pattern of manners, traditions, and beliefs. Families provide a context of relationships which give a woman (in particular) a meaningful role in life, as mother, wife, daughter, sister, cousin. *The Innocent Traveller* celebrates these roles, but also undermines them, I believe, by showing Rachel as a woman held in perpetual if loving servitude, and Topaz as a "youngest child" held in perpetual helplessness. Always cared for by her family, Topaz seems extraordinarily lucky in her hundred years of cheerful idle life; but even she may not have escaped the explosions of hidden mines. Triviality may be one; helplessness, another. The loving family that pampers Topaz also infantilizes her, I believe, by accepting (if not fostering) her helplessness; in her comic way, she remains forever helpless, a child even when she reaches venerable age. Though family ties are tenuous in "Tuesday and Wednesday," they do hold together Myrtle's ego, but also they bind Myrtle forever to her cousin's life. If in this novella Wilson parodies family life, creating an aunt who is a "Kitten" and a "conveniently anonymous" cousin, she nevertheless reveals its profound ambiguities which her most serious fiction cannot resolve. In *Swamp Angel,* Maggie Lloyd's surrogate family focuses the heroine's new identity, but also infuses it with new anxieties and problems; and in *Love and Salt Water,* Nora Peake's loving sister nearly wrecks Nora's life.

Wilson also celebrates and undermines marriage, which stultifies characters to whom it brings the only fulfillment possible. Married men and women run away

from each other in *Swamp Angel,* "The Window," "Beware the Jabberwock";
wives dream of freedom, and husbands of "slugging" or even murdering their
wives. In "A drink with Adolphus," Mr. Leaper notes in his secret diary that a
man "is undergoing trial for the murder of his wife. The thing that impressed
me [he writes, thinking of his own marriage] was that he and his wife had *seemed*
to live a devoted and harmonious life together."[7] I emphasize *seemed* because appearances conceal the truth of family life in Wilson's fiction; or the fiction itself
conceals the truth it makes us suspect, hiding it beneath the surface of serenity
so that we see the Edgeworths, or Cuppys, or Forresters as "ideal couples," much
as Vicky May saw that irascible pair, Myrt and Mort. In *Swamp Angel,* Maggie
experiences marriage at its best (but death ends her happiness) and at its most
crimping. In the same novel, Nell Severance understands that her marriage,
never sanctified by law, only by love, required her to hurt her only daughter.
This daughter, at first fearful of marriage, finds in it her fulfillment; but happiness demands her submission to another, and Wilson's women typically say they
wish to be free. Thus family relationships involve so many complexities they
elude understanding or judgment. They become mysterious though ordinary;
and mystery engenders fear. If a woman, in a moment of carelessness, might
cause her nephew's death, then sisters and aunts, no matter how loving and well
intentioned, have ominous potential. Wilson never lets us forget the harm we
might do each other within the family; and since she insists that family bonds
(the commonplace phrase implies imprisonment as well as security) somehow
connect all of us to each other, she implies that the invidious effects of human
relationships are general and inescapable. Within the great human family are hidden subterranean links that no one can discern because they are buried like an
enemy's mines where one would least suspect their presence and where one
would be sure to tread.

The enemies to human happiness are often coincidental circumstances that
defy rational explanation. How can we find meaning in life, the "belief" that
Mr. Willy seeks to rescue him from the aridity of his desert island, the faith that
Nell Severance magisterially declares in *Swamp Angel,* when we see that at any
moment coincidences may spring upon us as the hoodlums sprang upon old Mrs.
Bylow, precipitating her heath in the aptly named story "Fog"? Coincidence,
sheer coincidence, brings together Eddie Hansen, Mort Johnson, and Victoria
May Tritt at the corner of Powell Street, from where the men march to their
accidental death and Vicky to her unexpected apotheosis as a teller of tales. What
I call accident other readers may consider providential design, a view we can justify when we see fortuity as part of a comprehensive plan to educate characters
to their responsibilities and to love. In *Love and Salt Water,* family members meddle with good intentions in each other's lives, but the results are almost disas-
trous. Though she is a strong swimmer, Wilson's repeated metaphor for a
self-reliant, courageous woman, Ellen Cuppy nearly drowns, and worse, she
nearly causes the death of her beloved nephew Johnny. From this experience

Ellen learns that "she had better mind her own business. Everyone had better mind their own business" (p. 188). But in a family where everyone's business is inherently connected, bound together by inextricable and untraceable human ties, letting others *be,* an allowance that is surely one equation of love, may prove impossible. Acceptance of others does lie within one's capacity. Ellen learns to value Morgan Peake and to trust George Gordon's love, which her terrible accident could not jeopardize. *We* learn a lesson I find frightening: that the "circle of life is extraordinary," including relationships among people widely separated in space and time whose lives touch by coincidence, by accident (or design? what design?), in ways that may affect them "perhaps temporarily," Wilson equivocates, "or perhaps permanently and fatally" (p. 133). Wilson's uncertainty catapults me into an unknowable world where, I suspect, only caprice rules. We may be trapped: we may escape. We may be rescued: we may die. Whatever happens seems beyond control and beyond reasonable prediction. We do not know where the hidden mines in life are buried and which will explode when.

If I were to imagine Edith Wharton taking over Wilson's novel *Love and Salt Water,* I would feel certain that fate would be cruel. Once Ellen and Johnny fall into the sea, I would expect them to drown,[8] for again and again Wharton shows that life is so constituted that rescue never comes when we need it, when we are trapped by the capacious web woven by circumstance, by small choices, weak mistakes, fortuitously untimely encounters, by a lapse in the manners or break in the traditions that, like Wilson, Wharton fastidiously portrays. No one rescues Lily Bart in Wharton's inexorable novel, cruelly entitled *The House of Mirth.* Lily dies, probably by her own hand, and Selden arrives, when he arrives, too late. Only death releases Lily from the despair that time makes inevitable. Sometimes, Wharton will not allow even death to give her characters respite from pain. They live on in *Ethan Frome,* caught in an incredible web woven of human passion and irrational accident. Perhaps I am saying that for all the similarities between them as keenly observant novelists of manners, Wharton as an American has a vision of life somehow inaccessible to Wilson. Providential rescue from seemingly inescapable dangers, like those besetting Oliver Twist, belong to the tradition of the Victorian novel with which Ethel Wilson's fiction seems to me continuous. Though Wilson creates for her readers (and for an American reader especially) a magnificently highlighted Canadian landscape, her vision of life seems as unconditioned by this landscape as her famous travelers, characters who retain in the new world an "innocence" they acquired in the old, whose innocence consists precisely in their preservation of English traditions in the new Canadian city of Vancouver where they come to live with family connections intact. In *The Innocent Traveller,* when Sister Annie looks at the vast Canadian country passing elliptically outside the railroad window, she says: "We shall have to try and learn new ways . . . and I for one am quite ready."[9]

But almost immediately, as she sees the "same sheep, same cows, same horses as in England," she dispels thoughts of a new life and thinks instead, "I am rather old . . . to be able to assimilate great change" (p. 111). But her daughter Rachel is not too old. Yet though Rachel falls in love with the Canadian landscape, responding mystically, ecstatically, to its "dark endless prairie," she lives in Canada the traditional life of filial responsibility she would have led in England. We all know that the Canadian landscape figures in Wilson's fiction as a constant source of wonder and beauty, giving to her themes of nihilism and faith, isolation and love, randomness and providence, a richly symbolic representation through abundant indigenous detail. Moreover, her characters need the *space* of the Canadian continent both to effect their escapes from confinement and to discern "the miraculous interweaving of creation as the everlasting web" that engenders their faith in God's boundlessness. Ultimately, however, Wilson uses a uniquely Canadian setting to universalize human experience, to arrive at truths that transcend place or time. To say this is not to diminish her stature as a Canadian writer, but to praise her, as she praised "great" writers, for being "both regional and universal."[10]

Willa Cather, the American writer to whom Wilson seems most comparable, also sought for universal meanings, those expressed in the cycles of nature and the passage of time. But when Cather dealt with time, she focused upon change — upon development, maturation, and decline; upon history. She recalled, with nostalgia, a past associated specifically and uniquely with the transformation of America from an inchoate land — "the material out of which countries are made"[11] — into a country. In *A Lost Lady,* a novel to which *Hetty Dorval* bears almost startling formal resemblance, the fate of a beautiful woman melds inseparably with the fate of the American West. Marian Forrester disillusions young Niel Herbert as Hetty Dorval does Frankie Burnaby; but the American woman's betrayal of the ideals of honor with which, Niel (and Cather) believes, a great country was created represents a crisis in history, the passing of an old chivalric order to make way for a new crass society represented by such grasping men as Ivy Peters. When the "lady" of Niel's visionary dream of the West becomes "lost," an entire community dependent upon her civilizing force suffers. Mrs. Forrester understands the cultural role that requires a woman like her to personify a dream and purvey grace, beauty, and manners to a crude, primitive people living through a time of historical transformation. Even when she is depleted, without money, friends, or honor, Mrs. Forrester tries with her dinner party to bring civilization to the stolidly impervious young men of Nebraska. Like Ántonia in *My Ántonia* and Alexandra in *O Pioneers!,* Marian Forrester's destiny intertwines with the future of the American West, and as time diminishes her brilliance, it also fades the dream that, Cather believes, imbued the American past with heroism.

In Wilson's novel, Hetty Dorval's fall from grace carries no such historical connotations. Frankie's changed perceptions of Hetty invite no thoughts about the destiny of Canada. The context of Wilson's drama is a moral world in which chance arranges for the convergence of two lives that momentarily flow together, like the conjoined Fraser and Thompson Rivers, and then separate, leaving a young woman to ponder the unfathomable mystery of human relationships. Hetty's amorality remains unattached to historical or even psychological causalities (though we might infer that her fatherless childhood, which she thought also motherless, may have conditioned her to the sense of isolation that becomes merely selfishness). Hetty appears gratuitously in Lytton and later in London as a wanderer who brings disorder because disorder is inherent in life and will make its presence known even when it is hidden behind the face of beauty. Marian Forrester belongs to her particular time and place; and when she suffers displacement, her loss entails the loss of Captain Forrester's heroic dream of the future, of Niel Herbert's romantic dream of the past, and of the pervasively shared American Dream. Even Hetty's end in the novel seems adventitious as she disappears into a country where she is a stranger. But Marian Forrester remains an irradicable part of the land in which her husband and her honor lie buried. She survives in Niel's consciousness as "a bright, impersonal memory,"[12] the memory of the glorious "promise" that life extends to youth and to young countries. Hetty Dorval, like Topaz Edgeworth, both sharply defined but atomistic characters, can be forgotten.

In her own wrong way, Hetty seeks freedom and security, the goals of all Wilson's women, incompatible goals perhaps and perhaps not susceptible to clear definition. By freedom, Hetty means a life without complications or consequences, the latter term a familiar one to American readers because it recurs thematically in Ernest Hemingway's famous collection of short stories, *In Our Time*. Unlikely as a comparison between Wilson and Hemingway may seem at first, it discloses contours in Wilson's landscape that perhaps the oblique light of an American perspective can best reveal. Both writers were consummate stylists who used style to curb meanings too turbulent to release. Both were masters of understatement: of irony – each creating a discrepancy between tone and meaning; and of elision – each leaving narrative gaps implicit with meanings, often terrible meanings, we must infer. Both sense the tension between natural beauty, which endures, and human vulnerability: "you are walking along through the grass on the cliff top, admiring the pretty view, when – crack crack."[13] Either could have written this sentence (though "pretty" would have had a special ironic intonation in Hemingway), for both have been alerted to the profound insecurity of human beings who may at any moment be surprised by violence. Their unsurpassed fishing scenes dramatize a concern with surfaces and depths, as well as a love of the art of fishing, of nature, and of the possibilities for self-possession in solitude. Like Hetty Dorval, Nick Adams in "Big Two-Hearted River," the greatest of American fishing stories, seeks to escape human complications, but unlike her, he has already felt the world crack beneath him, literally, and shatter as the bombs of war exploded. The wounds he suffers end his innocence as a young traveler. A traumatized hero, hurt physically and emotionally, he wants to be alone so that he can be *let* alone and perhaps recover the balance he has lost. He needs to hold himself "steady," like the big trout in the depths of "deep, fast moving water" who resists the current that could sweep him away. Hetty's avoidance of complications is different, an effect of laziness, indulgence, or egoism. She wants to be alone to do as she pleases because she considers herself an island, free from any intrinsic connection with others who share her human state. She desires only sensuous ease, at least superficially; perhaps beneath this desire lies fear of the possibly dangerous currents of life. Like Nick, though for different reasons and to a different degree, she feels the tenuousness of her control over her own destiny. How little it would take to throw her off-balance – only some shipboard gossip. "I want security," Hetty says, "I want it badly"; and though Frankie and her mother suspect Hetty of artfulness, they believe that her plea for security is real, that Hetty is truly "frightened" (p. 52). She does not know, of course, all that she has to fear in an impending war that "life and time" are arranging. After Nick crawls inside his tent, "the good place," he thinks "Nothing could touch him." Eventually, however, or inevitably, he will have to enter the swamp and fish in its "tragic" waters. Neither he nor Hetty can remain safe. *Hetty Dorval* ends in uncertainty, the milieu that, I believe, Wilson, like Hemingway, finds as natural to us as rivers, forests, mountains, and sky.

"We have no immunity," Mrs. Severance tells Maggie in *Swamp Angel,* saying in effect that life cannot be ordered and that in its disorder, it allows no one to remain secure. Though Wilson's characters travel and run and hide, trying to escape from "Trouble," they can never rest at "the good place." Where is it to be found, her women ask, the place where they can be secure? Is it by the Similkameen River, where Maggie hides from the meanness of her husband only to become threatened by the jealousy of Vera Gunnarsen? Is it at Comox on Vancouver Island, where Lilly remains isolated with the Butlers, or in the Fraser Valley, where she merges into the order of the Matron and her well-run hospital? But here, inexplicably, a strand of her former life as a hunted creature reappears, woven fortuitously into the web no one can elude. The Chinaman Yow arrives in the Valley, and once more, Lilly is on the run, seeking in the anonymity of Toronto the security now imperiled by this figure from her past. Love and marriage seem to promise security; but the happiest of marriages, like those of the Cuppys in *Love and Salt Water* or the Burnabys in *Hetty Dorval* or the elder Edgeworths in *The Innocent Traveller,* may be terminated abruptly by death. Impersonal forces as well as people threaten any woman's security at any time. So do one's own emotions, especially the welling of loneliness. Even Vicky May Tritt recognizes the danger of "insupportable" insights into one's isolation, insights that threaten the security she tries so carefully to create through the meagre "arid" routine she calls her life. Like Lilly, like Hetty, Victoria May wants to be safe. But "at unexpected times" (chosen, one guesses, by chance), she cannot help catching a "frightening" glimpse of "something vast" that is usually "concealed," something always "there" – like "the sorrow of humanity" (p. 68). To protect herself against the pain of "revelation," Vicky May "averts her gaze" and waits until what she cannot bear to see is once more concealed. But she cannot deny this revelation of human sorrow, and neither can Wilson's fiction, though it persuades us also to avert our gaze from the suffering it reveals. Like Wilson's women, we want security and see it jeopardized by life's hidden mines. How can we avoid them, the destructive emotions of others, jealousy, meanness, the will to oppressive power, and the accidents of chance?

What little protection we have comes, it seems, from an innate human impulse toward order; and when we share the order we create, we perform the beautiful act of charity. It occurs almost always in Wilson's fiction in a clean well-lighted place, to use one of Hemingway's famous phrases. Again and again, Wilson shows that we may find safety in an interior. a room, made comfortable by human hands, though when this safety remains unshared, it seems pathetic if not simply ludicrous. Vicky May's room, illuminated by one small naked bulb, is not a well-lighted place, but when Vicky is there, reading her old newspapers or her movie magazines and munching on her apple, she feels "safe": "Here in her room she was at home and secure" (p. 77). In her diminished way, she has found the good place for which all the homeless, alienated characters of American fiction yearn. Perhaps because I have often identified myself with these homeless, insecure Americans, I particularly appreciate the recurrent image in Wilson of a small, protected world that human hands create. If a "room lit by a candle and in a silent and solitary place is a world within itself,"[14] it is one that the human being makes and offers as a refuge to other members of our oddly assorted human family. When Vera, near death, enters Maggie's room in *Swamp Angel,* Maggie thinks that warmth, not words, should communicate between these two estranged women: "it seemed to her the least important thing that she should speak and make words, and the most important thing that a fire should burn and warm the cabin and then there would be, somehow, a humanity in the room" (p. 147). Maggie warms Vera as she has warmed Mr. Cunningham, rescued by her hands from death. She instructs Angus "to start the fires everywhere" when they return to open up the camp. She understands that a clean, well-lighted place offers us the only security we can expect in a vast and impersonal, complicated landscape that could overwhelm us with its immensity as well as its indifferent beauty, its inevitable darkness, its dark waters, its fog.

Earlier, alone in a cabin at Chilliwack, Maggie had retrieved her own life, repossessing herself in a room that she had first to hold private and inviolate so that later she could share it with others who come to it ravaged by the sea and by life. "The cabin was a safe small world enclosing her" – this image of security is appealingly regressive: it takes Maggie back to a former and authentic identity; to a place still untouched by time; to a primitivism that historical change will challenge and in time destroy; to elemental needs, like the human need for warmth, touch, food. Maggie cooks, and Lilly cleans; and both women, by responding to elemental needs, create order in a world that can fall quickly into chaos. "It seemed as if order flowed from her fingertips," Mr. Sprockett thinks, watching Lilly straighten out his hotel room.[15] Intuitively, he feels she will bring order into his life, disrupted and left in confusion by his wife's death. Making Mr. Sprockett comfortable becomes Lilly's equation of love as she earns her right to respectability and marriage through years of self-discipline spent in creating a clean, well-lighted place for others. If the world were not intrinsically chaotic, asks the American reader, why would we so delight in women who bring order? If it were not so menacing, so full of imminent "Trouble," why would we seek refuge in a solitary warm room; why would women who can bring order into others' lives be on the run, seeking for themselves a security that has been denied? If the world were not indifferent to our needs, why would we turn again and again to another for comfort and compassion, so highly valued in Wilson's fictional world?

As an American reader who is also a woman, I respond ambivalently to Maggie cooking at camp and Lilly making Mr. Sprockett comfortable, though I celebrate their ability to care for others. I like the desire of Wilson's women for self-possession, and I am not always pleased at their acquiescence to a servant's role, no matter how much I admire the order they bring into others' lives and by this means into their own. Guiltily, I enjoy Myrtle's merciless domination of her employer; but at the same time I am annoyed at simpering weak Mrs. H. X. Lemoyne who "was terrified by Myrtle's eyelids, and could be disciplined any minute that Myrtle chose."[16] What an invention – those formidable drooping domineering eyelids and those outlandish soap-opera instantaneous lies! Wilson makes me laugh, and for the sheer pleasure of laughter I am grateful. Laughter may also instruct us, and Wilson's funny satiric treatment of Myrtle sets into perspective for me the serious impelling need almost all her women have for freedom. Myrtle does not want anyone to dominate her – but neither do other characters. Ellen Cuppy initially refuses George Gordon's proposal of marriage in *Love and Salt Water* because she did not "want to be controlled by him or by anybody" (p. 108). As soon as he proposes, freedom becomes essential to her, and marriage seems, mistakenly as it turns out (or so we imagine), "a prison far away with a stranger." Mrs. Emblem, though "formed for" male companionship, resists another marriage, having discovered that one of "the joys of privacy" is that "she now owns herself." For a hundred years, Topaz Edgeworth has remained irrepressibly herself. Oddly, of all the characters in *The Innocent Traveller,* only she sees Canada as offering its immigrants freedom. She suggests a quintessentially American theme: that of a new life in a new land. "This is a free country, isn't it," Topaz asks insistently, as she crosses the prairies on her way to Vancouver; "We've come to a free country, haven't we?" (p. 109). But Topaz's idea of freedom (she is here defending her right to enter the gentlemen's smoking car) is, of course, comically skewed. For freedom means to Topaz being her idiosyncratic self – obsessively loquacious, basically idle though busy, dependent upon others and yet detached – a likable and occasionally admirable woman who might fill us with dread at the ultimate inconsequentiality of a human life. Having always been treated lovingly, Topaz responds to life with a continuous interest which effects nothing. On a few crucial occasions, she shows generosity of spirit and exquisite manners – when she defends Mrs. Coffin in danger of being blackballed, and earlier when she withdraws from Mr. Sandbach's dinner party. I like her best when she curses Mr. Sandbach aloud in her bedroom, but that may reveal my secret wish for release from gentility rather than the novel's moral high point. If Topaz remains a free spirit through the Family's financial and moral support, other characters like Maggie Lloyd and Lilly struggle toward freedom through the murky circumstances of desertion, betrayal, jealousy, moral meanness, isolation. Both undergo a "rebirth" in which they act as their own midwives. In her cabin in Chilliwack, Maggie Vardoe is reborn as Maggie Lloyd. In the beauty shop of Miss Larue, Lilly Waller becomes immutably Mrs. Walter Hughes, an identity that permits her a new life as Lily [sic] Sprockett. Wilson tells us that in fitting Lilly with a wig and advising her on wardrobe, "Miss Larue, on a fine creative spree, was assisting at the rebirth of a free woman, Mrs. Walter Hughes." "But will it change me?" Lilly thinks, "Shall I be safe?" (p. 255). Perhaps she can never be safe, but she has become free of feckless Lilly Waller.

Wilson's free characters are also fugitive, running like their American relatives to a territory ahead where they can elude repressive men like Edward Vardoe, Huw Peake, or Yow. They need the space of the Canadian landscape to effect their escape. But while Wilson's sense of spaciousness suggests to me the American theme of freedom (for space and freedom are often synonymous in American fiction),[17] her manner seems alien to American writers, insofar as we differentiate them from the British. Wilson sometimes reminds me of Virginia Woolf, whose consummate novel *To the Lighthouse* she calls to my mind with a work that, apparently, I like much more than her Canadian critics. In *Love and Salt Water* (discussed at length in The Capitalistic Will), Wilson conveys the passage of time through elision, as Woolf had done. Like Woolf, Wilson evokes the menace of the sea and the world of nature to emphasize a human need for home and community, for safety. In *Love and Salt Water*, as in *To the Lighthouse,* a fortuitous death is described but not dismissed in one sentence; and a child's wish-fulfillment – to see the seals, to go to the lighthouse – brings unanticipated realizations and unanticipated terrors. Ellen learns to let her sister Nora *be* – and letting others be (as Maggie Vardoe thinks, her husband "would never have let me be") emerges as the essential equation of love that Woolf works out in *Mrs. Dalloway.*[18]

As I read Wilson, I enjoy her evocation of English literature, her command, her deftness, lightness of tone, her confidence in the quixotic phrase, the wry aside, the moralizing moment. I find in her work both the fastidiousness and the insouciance that belong to one who possesses a native tongue as her birthright. But I miss the struggle contained within American writers like Theodore Dreiser, Sherwood Anderson, or Gertrude Stein. Bereft of a language of their own, they laboriously invent a style that turns out polyglot, awkward, cacophonous, colloquial, confused, but also powerful: a style that confronts, without possibility of easy evasion, the profoundly difficult and unanswerable questions of life. I find Wilson's use of John Donne as a kind of last resort for coping with ultimate problems uncomfortably facile. I brood with Dreiser, whose work is impressed indelibly upon my American imagination, over the possibility that man or woman is an island, a person essentially alone and adrift in life, like Hurstwood or Carrie in Dreiser's ponderous and imponderable novel *Sister Carrie*. Perhaps, as Dreiser shows, we are creatures driven by chemic compulsions that nullify out pretensions to personal freedom. In Dreiser, great economic forces, as well as hormones, are released upon the world to determine not only an individual's fate but also the evolutionary direction of a vast society. When Wilson described the growth of Vancouver, she made it seem, by her simple cartoonish description, almost comic: "Down came the forests. Chop. Chop. Chop. . . . The forests vanished, and up went the city."[19] Wilson does note that "men of the chain-gang" were doing the chopping, but she disposes of their plight and of the implications of power and powerlessness, and of tremendous historical transformations that effected radical social reorderings – of the entire drama of growth, industrialization, urbanization, and their consequences – in three words now rather terrible for modern ears attuned to cries of ecological depletion and economic greed: "Chop. Chop. Chop." Because Dreiser could not be fluent, lacking a literary language and tradition as an American writer, because he could not reach into a bag of past poets and pick out a consummate line that would epitomize a worldview – "no man is an island" – because he had to struggle in his life and in his work, he became enmeshed in the endless web about which he wrote, a web woven by desire, irrational chance, coincidence, natural forces, evolutionary drives, social designs. He cared about his characters in ways that could not allow him to be detached or superior. Never could I imagine Dreiser describing a woman or man as Wilson describes Victoria May: "Insipid," "unimportant," "anonymous," "stupid." Wilson is "cool," but Dreiser heatedly compassionate and committed to his characters.

Though obviously unlike Dreiser, Willa Cather shared Dreiser's absorbing interest in characters, no matter how humble. In *One of Ours,* half-witted, illiterate Mahailey emerges as loving and lovable, worthy of the esteem given her by the family she faithfully serves. None of Cather's women is "insipid." Each is potentially a creator of life, is herself alive, and finds life interesting. A minor character in *Sapphira and the Slave Girl* epitomizes this interest: "Mrs. Ringer was born interested." Though Mrs. Ringer is poor, unendowed, alone, "misfortune and drudgery had never broken her spirit. . . . She had probably never spent a dull day." If her days were never dull for Topaz, they seem so to us; but all the days of Cather's women belong within a large significant pattern in which, whatever they do, they sense themselves a creative part. Nell Severance would have been quelled by them, I think, for they could have articulated fully and precisely the faith she asserted in vague incomplete terms. Even when they lived in Canada, like Cécile Auclair in *Shadows on the Rock,* they sensed themselves part of a process that was creating out of individual and inchoate efforts a whole way of life, creating by preserving and by making anew, by continuing and beginning again, as Cécile continues the French traditions her mother transmitted to her and makes them pristine and permanent by transferring them to Quebec. Unlike Wilson's women, Cather's seldom seek security; rather, they provide it as they make a home and a great nation. A hidden mine that Cather describes is not explosive, except with life, as we know from the famous image in *My Ántonia* of children bursting out of a subterranean storehouse – "a veritable explosion of life out of the dark cave into the sunlight" (p. 339).

A sense of the new in American novels – of a new land, new pulsating cities like Chicago, pristine prairies of color-drenched grass, new railroads, new openings, new beginnings – may stir American readers deeply because they share the writer's concern with a new American language and a new style. Americans know they must create a style that expresses a perennial sense of discovery, dream, and disillusionment. As an American novelist, Dreiser could not rely upon what was said before, because the city he describes had not existed before, and even as he wrote, he saw it grow, develop, and change. He was driven by the historical urgency of capturing a kaleidoscopic scene that would not stay still long enough to be memorialized. Wilson feels neither this urgency – the typical sense of rush that Americans experience as their daily lives – nor Cather's nostalgia over what has been and will be no more. Her anecdotal ease in dealing with the past in *The Innocent Traveller* seems inaccessible to American writers, who invariably regret and long for a past that has disappeared. Think of Cather's *A Lost Lady* or F. Scott Fitzgerald's quintessentially American novel, *The Great Gatsby.* Not without reason, the most popular American book is entitled *Gone with the Wind,* and the greatest Southern writer, William Faulkner, shares with the most widely read, Margaret Mitchell, a passion for the past to which American readers resonate as they typically feel loss and separation as their real experience. In Vancouver, Wilson's characters find continuity: as Annie noted, correctly or not, "the same sheep, same cows, same horses as in England." Beyond the city, in mountains, lake areas, woods, Wilson's characters can recapture their own past, or at least exorcise a present they find oppressive; in unchanged places (of which few remain in America), they can retrieve a pattern of peace they once knew.[20] They cannot "escape" from life, as Nell Severance tells Maggie in *Swamp Angel,* but they can *recover* – recapture the past and recuperate from the present. Nick Adams knows that a wounded American can hope only for a temporary stay against chaos before he fishes in "tragic" waters that Maggie may not have to enter. Maggie will not escape Vera Gunnarsen's jealousy, but Nick will never escape himself. Nor will he find refuge with others, even temporary or turbulent refuge, as Lilly found with the Butlers, and Maggie with the Gunnarsens. Like Wilson, Hemingway turned to Donne for a definition of human relatedness, for directions on how to deny his own bleak vision of life, one which I believe he found, finally, both inviolate and intolerable. Much as he wishes to deny it, he saw that man was an island – separate, alone, adrift. In *For Whom the Bell Tolls,* Hemingway's hero tries to link himself with others in a concerted effort to make shared ideals prevail, but the occasion of his union is war, and the outcome is death. Robert Jordan lies alone, merging himself in lyrical rapture and in terror with the earth. Hemingway's vision of life is ecclesiastical: it contains the vanity of human wishes – including the wish for love, marriage, family – and the eternality of the earth, upon which, with an order denied to chaotic human affairs, the sun always rises.

As a reader of American fiction, I feel buoyed by Wilson's way of tucking war, chaos, and violence into the parenthetical asides of her novels; but unlike Maggie, when she thinks she can swim about obstacles, I feel insecure on surfaces, accustomed as I am to the inevitability of depths. Even while I delight in reading of a happy but thoroughly inconsequential life, like that of Topaz Edgeworth, I cannot help remembering other characters to whom nothing happened. I remember Marcher in Henry James's "The Beast in the Jungle," and then I feel my pleasure adulterated as I consider the life of a woman to whom nothing happened – though everything in the world was happening – and who made nothing happen, who in effect was powerless. Powerlessness, fear of isolation, alertness to violence and acts of violation, the vagaries of chance and indifferent if not malign forces, as well as the urgencies of economic and social inequality which must lead to conflict – so I learn from *The Grapes of Wrath* – how could I not be conditioned by all this which I encounter again and again in American fiction? Abundant as it is, American fiction is deeply mined with skepticism and uncertainity. Its landscape is vast, beautiful, and bleak. I have traveled in it for many years, and to deny its influences, to say I am still innocent and can enjoy without wryness the surface skimming of a waterglider or even the complex skill of a juggler (juggling a weapon of destructive power) would be to deny the power of literature.

Wilson celebrates this power by consciously drawing attention to the creative act of storytelling. Her characters tell stories – are unabashed liars; and sometimes by withholding their stories, they assert their autonomy, their possibility of eluding facts and consequences by refusing to acknowledge that they exist. In *Love and Salt Water,* Ellen Cuppy tries to keep her mother alive by not telling that she had died, and her sister Nora tries to keep her son whole by not telling that his hearing is impaired. In *Hetty Dorval,* Frankie collaborates in the fiction Hetty

Dorval creates by not telling what she knows about Hetty; and Hetty herself remains somehow inviolable because she has not told the truth about herself, by this withholding making herself inaccessible even to Frankie, in whose consciousness she lives. Frankie knows she is inventing the story of Hetty Dorval; this act frees her of Hetty's influence and at the same time, since stories last, makes permanent the influence of Hetty's distinctive beauty and power. Through the art of storytelling, Frankie both dispels the trance in which Hetty has placed her and captures it for all time; and she becomes a force powerful enough to cause an explosion in which another story, Mrs. Broom's version of the past, will be released from the depths of silence in which it lies buried. Frankie makes Mrs. Broom tell the story she has withheld, and we cannot minimize the power she exercises in forcing, without forethought, another's confession. In *The Equations of Love,* characters make up stories all the time. Mort and Myrtle lie unconscionably in "Tuesday and Wednesday" (and all the other days of the week), and by their lies, they subdue others, sometimes each other, and so exercise their wills. The stories that give them momentary victories cannot save them, however, from the fate that coincidence has laid in store; but rescue does come from a most unlikely source, from the story of heroism that reticent, neurotic Victoria May Tritt invents. By telling her story, Vicky frees herself, if only for a moment, from the prison of shyness, insecurity, silence, and a sense of worthlessness; from the inconsequentiality of her life; from powerlessness. She effects a change in how Mort will be remembered, in how Myrtle will feel, and in how an inexplicable accident will evermore be described. She changes her own behavior, her very identity from a silent and withdrawn woman to a purposeful active storyteller, the focus of rapt attention. In "Lilly's Story," also in *The Equations of Love,* Lilly's lies become the truths of her life, the means by which she can possess herself and give a happy, useful identity to her daughter. Through her own fictions, she learns how to serve others, and though she seeks isolation, she belongs to a community that includes the Matron, the hospital, and finally the wide world where she may, perhaps, live as a free woman with the man to whom she brings comfort.

This confusion of lies with truth celebrates the storyteller's power to convince us of the reality of fiction; it also dramatizes the mysteriousness of life whose essence we cannot know with certainty. As Wilson's stories show, we cannot know each other because we present, in everyday life, social faces that conceal a real identity shown only to a friend or lover. Though Mrs. Forrester smiles and talks and entertains in the story "Truth and Mrs. Forrester," her reality exists thousands of miles away from the room where people come and go and where familiar things provide company – thousands of miles away where her husband lies ill, possibly dying. The "true Mrs. Forrester" is the loving wife, not the charming hostess who lies out of politeness and boredom or the helpless employer "in thrall" to her garrulous maid. "Truth is so hard to tell," says Mrs. Forrester, "while fiction is the easiest thing in the world" (p. 11). Certainly, Ethel

Wilson makes fiction seem easy, though the truth of her women is hard to define, hard to tell whether they are utterly traditional creatures finding happiness
only in caring for others, cleaning, cooking, creating comfort, yielding compassion. Is Family their essential need, and marriage, though initially avoided (as by
Ellen Cuppy and Hilda Severance), their ultimate fulfillment? Is Mrs. Emblem,
in "Tuesday and Wednesday," with her pink boudoir and her pink complexion
and golden hair and her three husbands, truly an emblematic Woman as the story
insists? "Vicky Tritt does not know what it feels like to be a woman," the story
tells: "Mrs. Emblem knows nothing else" (p. 56). "Truth is so hard to tell," Ethel
Wilson might answer, and she enacts the difficulty in her equivocal style. She
shows us complexities, gains and losses within a single situation, and generosity
and withholding within a single person: "I knew I was in the web," Mrs. Severance says, in *Swamp Angel,* explaining her desertion of her daughter; "I did the
best I could in the web, and it takes God himself to be fair to two different people at once" (p. 151). One must juggle one's responsibilities, as Mrs. Severance,
a skilled juggler, knows; and one must distinguish between the symbol and the
essence, deciding finally for the essence, though one has become attached to the
symbol as though its glitter were real.

Perhaps the truth is that, like Wilson's characters, we are all storytellers. When
we tell our own story, we come into possession – not of objective truth but of
a reality we imagine: that of the person we wish to become, like Mrs. Walter
Hughes, or wish to retrieve, like Mrs. Maggie Lloyd. Perhaps our own power
of invention is the truth about us, and those who possess this power strongly
imagine a person into being, becoming in fact their own fiction, as Lilly becomes
Mrs. Walter Hughes. Naming one's self represents a quest for one's own truth.
Topaz Edgeworth never changes her name in her hundred years of life, and her
reality as a person becomes evanescent, forgettable, except in the story that Wilson tells. Lilly changes her name several times, and in the end accepts the name
of a stranger in order to become the self whom she has imagined into being.
Kind as he is, her future husband takes possession by reiterating the name he
will impose: "LilySprockettLilianSprockettLilySprockettLilianSprockett." The
name delights him and with it he makes Lilly a character in the story of his life.
"Would you mind me calling you Lilian?" he asks, and Lilly, either entirely secure now in her achieved identity or else willing to relinquish it for another that
promises love, does not mind losing a name that gave her "self-possession." Is
Wilson mocking Lilly when she has her confess her secret at the end of her story
that she wears an "adaptation", or is she rejoicing in the erasure of Lilly's past,
once so full of "Trouble"? The truth is hard to tell, though the fiction, "Lilly's
Story," is easy to read. "Perhaps" or "perhaps not," "I think," "it was impossible to say," the omniscient narrator says again and again in Wilson's fiction, implying that even the all-knowing storyteller does not know the truth. Sometimes
we as readers have a choice, because the narrator, uncertain of the truth, offers
two exclusive possibilities, two adjectives or nouns linked together by *and*

though they require *or*. Perhaps we need faith because we cannot know the truth. This, at lest, is what I think when I read Wilson's fiction, but of course I cannot be sure. Her fiction makes me certain and uncertain.

Of her descriptive powers I have no doubt. Her effulgent images of the Northern Lights, of the perfect V of flying wild geese, of indigenous creatures, changing landscapes, sky and space, are famous. Her short short story, "Hurry, hurry," to which I referred at the beginning, is charged with natural scenery which seems to me translucent. Mountains, trees, slanting rays of light, fog, birds, dog, hawk, heron, bushes, blackbirds, steep grassy dyke – all take on a brilliant and unforgettable urgency, a cosmic meaning whose truth might be so terrible that it eludes us as the image of the "hunched" hawk gives way to that of the "humped" corpse of a woman. Human life and animal life seem internecine. The hawk "with its sharp beak and tearing claws . . . would have mauled the terriers, and they would have tormented it." The hawk stares brightly, and so does man the murderer, compelling the woman to hurry away as "he held her eyes with his eyes." She escapes, running. The murderer shows her mercy, or perhaps only indifference. The woman he has killed lies "beside the salt-water ditch." His tears must be salty as he stumbles along "sobbing, crying out loud." Does he cry in regret or for love lost? Are love and salt water inseparable in Wilson's world? If some lucky ones escape the salt water, if they are rescued from drowning, is it at the sacrifice of others, like the drowned boy in *Love and Salt Water* or the murdered woman in "Hurry, hurry," characters linked with the living in Wilson's great web of life? Meanwhile, the light falls obliquely on the mountains. Each tree stands out separately. We see each clearly. We see each fade. "The light is gone" – the story is over "but those who have seen it will remember." The memory of Ethel Wilson's story lies deeply buried in our consciousness, our imagination. It is a hidden mine that we might at any moment of recall explode with terror and delight.

Notes

1   In her essay "A Cat among the Falcons" (*Canadian Literature* I [Autumn 1959]: pp. 10–19) Ethel Wilson avers that she is not a "qualified critic," not one of the "falcons [who] cruise high above and search the literary plain." Rather, as a country cat, she remains indoors, keeping her literary convictions safely private while she watches the sky where the "formidable and trained" – and contentious – falcons soar. Having been invited to give an American perspective upon Ethel Wilson's fiction at a conference distinguished by Canadian critics immersed in Wilson's work, life, and milieu, I recognize my affinity with the country cat. If I venture out with the falcons, I do so in the hope of making criticism "interesting" and perhaps even "amusing," the effects that Wilson valued in diversity of critical opinion. [The conference I refer to was the Wilson Symposium held at the University of Ottawa in 1981.]

2   *Hetty Dorval* (Toronto: Macmillan, Laurentian Library, 1967, published originally in 1947), p. 86.

3 Ethel Wilson, "Hurry, hurry," *Mrs. Golightly and Other Stories* (Toronto: Macmillan, 1961), p. 106. "Then the light fades [Wilson writes] . . . but those who have seen it will remember."

4 *Love and Salt Water* (Toronto: Macmillan, 1956), p. 152.

5 " 'I don't care for fresh air myself except for the purpose of breathing. I exist here . . . and here. . . . ' Mrs. Severance touched her heart and her head. 'Everything of any importance happens indoors. . . . ' " *Swamp Angel* (Toronto: McClelland & Stewart, 1962, published originally in 1954), p. 149, original ellipsis.

6 "Tuesday and Wednesday," *The Equations of Love* (Toronto: Macmillan, 1974 paperback, published originally in 1952). See pp. 127–8, in which the word *caused* appears seven times, linking together an incongruous sequence of events that "life and time" effect through "manipulations . . . of circumstance and influence and spiked chance and decision among members of the human family."

7 "A drink with Adolphus," *Mrs. Golightly*, p. 79.

8 See The Capitalistic Will for a discussion of the original ending to *Love and Salt Water*, which has the two characters die by drowning.

9 *The Innocent Traveller* (London: Macmillan, 1949), p. 101.

10 See Wilson's letter of July 12, 1953, to Desmond Pacey, quoted in his book *Ethel Wilson* (New York: Twayne, 1967), p. 25.

11 The phrase comes from a famous passage in *My Ántonia* that describes young Jim Burden's first sight of Nebraska: "There was nothing but land: not a country at all, but the material out of which countries are made" (Boston: Houghton Mifflin, 1954, published originally in 1918), p. 7.

12 *A Lost Lady* (New York: Random House, Vintage, 1972, published originally in 1923), p. 172.

13 *Love and Salt Water*, p. 149.

14 *Swamp Angel*, p. 146.

15 "Lilly's Story," *The Equations of Love*, p. 262.

16 "Tuesday and Wednesday," p. 101.

17 In an essay on modern American city fiction, I discuss this relation between space and freedom. See " 'Residence Underground': Recent Fictions of the Subterranean City," *Sewanee Review* 83 (Summer 1975): pp. 406–38.

18 I discussed this thematic meaning of love in Woolf in the essay "Love and Conversion in *Mrs. Dalloway*," *Criticism* 8 (Summer 1966): pp. 229–45; reprinted in *Clarissa Dalloway*, ed. Harold Bloom (New York: Chelsea House, 1990), pp. 86–98.

19 *The Innocent Traveller*, p. 24.

20 For a discussion of the Arcadian motif of escape from the city in Wilson's fiction, see my essay "Ethel Wilson's Absent City: A Personal View of Vancouver," forthcoming in *Canadian Literature*.

The Capitalistic Will:
Women and Inheritance
in *My Mortal Enemy* and
Love and Salt Water

He . . . confronted her with a cold business proposition.
My Mortal Enemy

. . . she could no more disturb him than could . . . shares in a common stock
bought in the open market, then sold, and forgotten . . .
Love and Salt Water

Money is the general equivalent of the value of all commodities.
Late Capitalism

As a venture in cross-cultural literary criticism, this essay is poised between the
certainties of The Hidden Mines – in which a reader purports to know the cultural determinants of her critique – and the inconclusiveness of Days of Reckoning. To be poised suggests tenuousness and wavering as well as balance; and
while the essay maintains an equilibrium between a reader's certainties and the
critic's uncertainties – uncertainties induced by postmodern literary and cultural
theories – it leans toward the latter, tending to lose its poise as it falls into inconclusiveness by raising questions about cultural identity. As we know, such
questions have a long lineage in the United States and Canada, tracing back to
their early history as new and emerging countries. From the first, these countries evoked feelings of ambivalence in writers who wanted to celebrate a land
they loved and, at the same time, to resist confinement within its boundaries as
national or regional, rather than universal, figures.[1] Such feelings troubled the
writers discussed in this essay. Ethel Wilson and Willa Cather both aspired to an
art imbued with universal values and, consequently, both rebuffed adjectival
qualifications upon their identity as artists – precisely those qualifications of national origin, race, sex, and class to which literary critics are now paying attention. Viewing their work from "a long perspective," to use Cather's well-known
phrase, the writers saw the ascription of national characteristics to their art as de-
valuating. Set against British literature, the Americanism of Cather's writing,

however defined, might diminish its worth; and set against British and American literature, Wilson's Canadian stories might seem secondary. Nevertheless, both Wilson and Cather wished to acknowledge the inspiration they had found in native settings – in the pristine prairies of Nebraska that, Cather said, first gave her the authentic material of her art, and in the fluidly changing and lambent landscape of British Columbia that Wilson loved.[2] Both wanted to give literary expression to these spacious western settings, which they saw ignored as subjects of art because they seemed outlying, unsophisticated, or uninteresting places. To heighten their importance, they believed they had to discover in their midst the universal themes that have always elevated art.

The complications that ensued from the desire to repudiate and, at the same time, to recognize a relationship between national cultural identity and art are especially involuted in the two novels compared in this essay: *My Mortal Enemy* by Willa Cather and Ethel Wilson's *Love and Salt Water*. Both novels mystify, and seem mystified by, the equations between personal and cultural values they bring to light. Like national identity, established in the texts only to be dissolved within universal themes, capitalistic cultural values are translated into personal desires only to be denied the agency they are shown to have. The result is obfuscation – a muddling of motives and meanings that produces the effects of mystery. The mystery of "real" mystery stories – those with murderers and detectives – is intentional and not to be confused with the ambiguity of literary texts. Ambiguity makes meaning elusive by equivocation, and mystery by deliberate acts of hiding, though mystery stories may also destabilize and deconstruct meaning because they cannot avoid the indeterminacies attributed to language as a putatively arbitrary symbolic code. In focusing upon mystery and its obfuscations, rather than upon ambiguity, indeterminacy, or self-subversions, I am suggesting that like "real" mystery stories, *My Mortal Enemy* and *Love and Salt Water* provide clues to meanings they have in various ways hidden, but these meanings will be discovered – or construed – by interpretation, rather than by the conclusive revelations with which mysteries end. The clues I have in mind are to be found in a certain murkiness of meaning that, I would argue, marks the site of a cultural crisis the texts create and want to hide.[3] The crisis arises when materialistic values represented as everyday realities show their unworthiness to writers and characters who aspire to moral transcendence – who would exchange money for moral value. But since money sustains the capitalistic culture the texts describe, it cannot be extricated from their plots or satisfactorily explained away. Money can, however, be hidden, literally and metaphorically, though not completely. Having been revealed, money becomes a murky element that the writers whisk from view in ways that, I would claim, have mystified their readers as well as their characters and, perhaps, the writers themselves.[4]

The mystification seems unintentional because both *My Mortal Enemy* and *Love and Salt Water* take pains to interpret the actions they describe. *My Mortal Enemy* delivers homilies on love, life, and money through the retrospective story of a first-person narrator whose voice resonates to and reinforces the authoritative voice of her protagonist, while *Love and Salt Water* depends upon an omniscient and unabashedly intrusive narrator to explain the unpredictable eventualities of its plot. But the very explicitness of the interpretive comments contributes to the novels' obfuscations, since neither the characters nor the narrators who voice them have an impeccable authority; they may not even have credibility. Thus, despite the explicitness in the texts, or because of it, their meanings remain not merely ambiguous or indeterminate, but muddled. I propose to argue that this muddling or murkiness has the oxymoronic effect of shedding light, rather than darkness, upon cultural identity.[5] For I believe that the sites of obfuscation within the texts serve as cultural markers of their duplicity. By duplicity I mean a double and incompatible set of cultural values that the writers establish, hold in tension, and by rhetorical and metaphoric refigurations try to collapse.

In Cather's *My Mortal Enemy,* a rich old man approaches his young niece with "a cold business proposition" that would exchange money for marriage − or rather, for not marrying; and in Wilson's *Love and Salt Water,* the heroine's admirable young suitor thinks of marriage as a common exchange on the stock market. These metaphors seems transparently commercial, involving buying and selling, but their transparency has had the effect of erasure, for the texts and their critics, Canadian and American, see through and beyond the commercialism to transcendent values − to religious redemption sought (and sometimes bought) by characters, to providential design, to the art of living passionately or with grace and good nature. Paradoxically, the very incongruity of equating such moral virtues as goodness and spiritual grace with monetary value permits the texts to make their metaphorical negotiations. In *Love and Salt Water,* metaphors turn marriage and divorce into stock-market transactions, and in *My Mortal Enemy,* metaphors turn family transactions into a "cold business proposition" and money into a means of religious transfiguration. The church that money has "enlarged and enriched" in *My Mortal Enemy* becomes a "body" that seems "to assimilate" John Driscoll's dead body, so that the incorporeal and a corpse become one flesh − or one spirit − in which the strains of Catholicism and financial capitalism merge, not temporarily but, it may be assumed, for eternity.[6] The link between financial and spiritual well-being, crassly forged in *My Mortal Enemy,* is delicate in *Love and Salt Water,* but as necessary to its plot and theme. Both novels use money not only as a general equivalent of commodity value,[7] but also as a basis for social and linguistic exchanges. In this respect, national differences seem secondary to cultural similarities. One could argue that the structures of capitalistic economy, whether instituted in one country or another, in the United States or in Canada, cross geographic boundaries to impress upon people on either side of a border − the Canadian–American border, for instance − the same cultural patterns, the same underlying social values, personal desires, and modes of metaphoric expression.[8]

This argument might have ironic consequences for writers who wanted to be identified by the universality of their art, for it would construe their themes as determined by a force that is transnational but also mundanely economic – the force of what I call here the capitalistic will. I mean by this the fixed and persistent purpose – the will – to accumulate money and capital for profit.[9] A capitalistic will implies a desire for power and control; and since capitalism involves processes of commodification, the will to control the production and exchange of things may become indiscriminate, finding no distinction between a commodity and a human being. In the novels, the commodified human being is not preeminently a worker, though their characters work for wages, but a woman upon whom a rich old man can work his will or, at least, make the attempt. He has the support of laws that permit him to enforce his will through legal documents that inscribe, enact, and perpetuate his desires. Consequently, inheritance and disinheritance figure significantly in the novels, along with legal wills and will-lessness.

In *My Mortal Enemy,* rich old John Driscoll wills his money to strangers rather than the niece who has defied his will by her elopement. Disinheritance thus becomes central to the plot, shaping the destiny of its heroine, Myra Henshawe.[10] Deprived of "a great fortune," Myra comes to believe that her marriage and her life have been blighted, a view she bequeaths to the narrator, Nellie Birdseye. In *Love and Salt Water,* Mr. Platt refuses to make a will because he cannot bear the thought of others possessing his stocks and bonds, his linoleum factory and South American traction company, his oil holdings, leaseholds, and winery.[11] This possessiveness seems inconsequential and comic because the young heroine, Ellen Cuppy, will not let it touch her life. When told that the childless Mr. Platt will probably make her his heir, Ellen replies snappily: "Oh no, he won't. I'll see to that" (p. 89). Her legacy will be the grace, good humor, and love her mother gives her as a gift unencumbered by money, legalities, or will.

Differences in the novels between a woman's legacy and legacies defined by men and transmitted to women suggest that gender modulates inheritance in the novels, that gender makes and marks difference. To be more precise, mothers make a difference. But in both novels, mothering roles are interchangeable between the sexes, and gender differences blurred. In *Love and Salt Water,* the father Morgan Peake attends a retarded child whom the mother, Ellen's sister, never sees and effectively forgets. An interpolated passage recalls his existence as it describes the stolid Morgan patiently feeding his indifferent child spoonfuls of ice cream. In *My Mortal Enemy,* Myra's identification with her uncle, whom she fondly calls "old Satan," disallows a facile assumption that women characters are different from and more benign than men. Myra's husband, Oswald, keeps house – he cooks and cleans – and humbly goes to work as a secretary, a position usually associated with women and, as it happens, the heroine's position in *Love and Salt Water.* As his earnings decrease, he becomes increasingly passive, submitting to the capricious willfulness that expresses a frustration of Myra's cap-

italistic will. Myra has to get what she wants from her uncle and, when he dis-
owns her, from an embarrassed husband. In *Love and Salt Water,* Susan Cuppy's
husband is rich and successful, so that his wife can be unconcerned with money
and his daughter dismissive of inheritance. Nevertheless, Wilson's women characters share with Myra Driscoll-Henshawe a dependency upon a capitalistic will
from which they have been distanced by their sex. To see this will close up, we
need to look at the novels' male characters, first at two old men who have by
murky means amassed a fortune.

II

... greed's okay and avarice ...

in the solitude of his bedroom at the top of a cheap hotel he would murmur
with satisfaction, "I've neether chick nor child"

Love and Salt Water

I begin with Ethel Wilson's Mr. Platt, a minor character usually disregarded by
critics, because he is a capitalistic will personifed. Mr. Platt has no interest, no
purpose or desire – no will – except to accumulate money and capital and turn
a profit. As he tells Ellen Cuppy, at the time his secretary: "I've no use for real
estate what with maintenance and depreciation and repairs but there's a sweet
tempting little proposition in Winnipeg that I'm thinking of getting for quick
re-sale" (p. 90). Quick resale means quick profit, Mr. Platt's single interest in
life. He reaches to Winnipeg from Saskatoon to enjoy a business opportunity as
though the "tempting little proposition" were a prostitute or, at best, an attractive woman. Aside from his secretary Ellen, no woman, or any person, has a
place in Mr. Platt's life; he is too single-minded in his pursuit of profit to care
about human relationships. "I've neether chick nor child," Mr. Platt says, actually gloating over his childlessness because the "specious sorrow" of "a lonely
old man who was not in the least lonely" was a "bargain-price luxury."[12] Thus
the old miser turned penurious isolation to profit.

I call Mr. Platt a miser because his main and only characteristic is avarice. Unlike the openhanded Driscoll in *My Mortal Enemy,* Mr. Platt is a hoarder, his
avarice making him "unique in this generation of spenders." These are the
words of John Livingstone, Mr. Platt's lawyer and Ellen's friend. "I bet you ...
he sits with his bonds and strokes them," Livingstone says of the old man as Ellen
becomes his secretary; "avarice is out of fashion, but ... there's always Platt to
keep up the good old ways" (p. 78). Mr. Platt goes on one notable spending
spree when he has Ellen furnish "two small but magnificent offices" and deco-
rate them with "Art."[13] She also serves as a decoration by "looking beautiful"
and providing Mr. Platt with "a fine front." Livingstone's euphemistic phrase
suggests a criminal duplicity that Ellen finds amusing. Mr. Platt has "a genius for

evasion and . . . dislikes the law," the lawyer says, meanwhile evading the moral issues involved in his acting as the old man's "conscience," a complicitous role not without profit to himself. Like Livingstone, Ellen acts in the interests of a capitalistic will (and her own economic interest) by creating a false fine front to represent – or rather misrepresent – Mr. Platt to the public. I am not suggesting that these characters could have stepped outside of the economic system from which Mr. Platt profits, but rather that Wilson insists they have done so, if only by their detached amusement at Mr. Platt's duplicity in expressing a capitalistic will through will-lessness. Ellen's main function during her years with Mr. Platt is to try to get him to make a will. "Even I have made a will," she tells him (p. 91), knowing that "if she should urge the needs of . . . the human race . . . Mr. Platt would retreat at once from making his will" (p. 90).

Mr. Platt's obliviousness to anyone's needs would seem appalling if Wilson had not made his avarice comic, conventional, and compartmentalized, demonstrating her own "genius for evasion" by creating an obfuscating front for a crass capitalistic will.[14] Mr. Platt becomes laughable in his timeless black suit, now faded green, his misfitting square bowler, and his "gamp-like umbrella" – a stock figure who might have stepped out of a Victorian novel. As the town's "unique" character, he is allowed idiosyncrasies that would seem ominous in someone linked to society. Just as Wilson made isolation innocuous by transmogrifying it into a "bargain-price luxury," she makes avarice comically acceptable as natural hunger by describing Mr. Platt swallowing his investment as a heron, of all creatures, swallows a fish (p. 91). Then, by having the old man drop dead – and dropped precipitously out of the plot – she denies him consequentiality. Neither his life nor his death, she indicates, has affected anyone.

But a character in a novel cannot be meaningless or inconsequential, not to other characters and not to the plot. After all, the hungry heron is not inconsequential to the fish. The few years that Ellen works in the Platt Investment Building show the emptiness within a world devoted to money making, a world in which human beings are commodified. Because she considers Mr. Platt comically alien to the human community in which she believes, Ellen dismisses his commodification of her as an indistinct but useful "Miss Um." Miss Um is an impersonal utility that satisfies needs, while Miss Cuppy is a person with a history of needs and desires of her own to which Mr. Platt, in his self-centered pursuit of profit, remains oblivious. Nevertheless, Mr. Platt's commodification of Ellen is not without consequence, since it contributes to her sense of inner depletion.[15] She begins to find her days empty, while the text duplicitously declares them "full," as though "useless" daily work, trivialized night classes, and meaningless badminton games could be fulfilling.[16] Wilson denies relevance to the empty years she describes in an essayistic passage on the "true years of our life" and forgettable "irrelevant years." Though the passage has troubled critics as a digressive or unnecessary intrusion, I see it as Wilson's proleptic attempt to explain away the strangeness of dramatizing and then denying the significance of a culturally valorized capitalistic will. Mr. Platt keeps this will alive in Saskatoon, but to what purpose, one might ask, except to allow the text to obfuscate its power by declaring it inconsequenial. Ellen's friend Livingstone assures her that "greed's okay" and a capitalistic will is innocuous, but as figured in Mr. Platt, this will reveals its essential inhumanity as it is separated from a "conscience," displaced to a lawyer, and from a social body, represented by a receptionist.

I do not wish to exaggerate the importance of Wilson's comic capitalist, but I should note another peculiar aspect of his character – his lack of a past. Wilson's designation of Mr. Platt as a man without a "pre-history" strikes a discordant note in a text acutely conscious of a historical past that has shaped its setting and its characters' sensibilities. Aunt Maury Peake traces the place-names of British Columbia back to the explorations of Captains Cook and Vancouver, the names, like the digressive asides upon discovery, reminding the reader of a particular Canadian identity achieved through the passage of historical time.[17] But the only history Wilson allows Mr. Platt places him outside of time as he makes his fantastical journey to Saskatoon. We are to imagine lone Mr. Platt dressed in his time-worn black suit and square bowler "stepping inquisitively over the great pre-Cambrian Shield," to the disquiet of its "original inhabitants, the wolverine and the porcupine" (p. 79). The thematic implications of Wilson's decision to situate Mr. Platt outside of history are obscured by his neighbors' indifference to his strange, unheralded appearance: "Where did Mr. Platt come from? . . . Nobody knew and nobody cared" (p. 79). This indifference, atypical among characters usually curious about each other's lives, reinforces the nonentity Mr. Platt already has as a stock character. Stock characters are inherently ahistorical, interchangeable, and always already typical, in these respects, human equivalents to commodities.[18] As a literary commodity, Wilson's Mr. Platt is a paradoxical figure, for he is at once typical and idiosyncratic, or typically idiosyncratic, since "unique" characters are idiosyncratic by definition. Since his particular idiosyncracies are dictated by avarice, a deadly sin in essence unchanged by time, the text can reinforce and foreground his abstract, timeless features while obscuring his historical immediacy as a capitalistic will.

III

He had gone straight to the greater glory, through smoking censers and candles and stars.

A poor man stinks, and God hates him.

My Mortal Enemy

As befits a man of his position, the funeral ceremony for John Driscoll, the richest man in Parthia, is dazzling in its extravagance and glorious light. "A river of colour and incense and organ-tone" carries the black coffin to a high altar lit with hundreds of candles. In a spectacular denouement, the dead man's body rises from "the glory" to which it has been elevated and ascends "through smoking censers and candles and stars" to "the greater glory" (p. 16). This awesome spiritual drama, witnessed by an enraptured audience, contrasts with the unimpressive and almost comic death of Mr. Platt, seen only by a night watchman. Mr. Platt's "small aged body" lies on his desk, disarranging business papers called, irreverently, "his darlings." The "manner" of Mr. Platt's sudden and incidental death elicits "a caustic delight" in Livingstone who, we are now told, "fancied himself an artist." This gratuitous bit of information presumably explains why the lawyer appreciates the *style* of the old man's dying, which he declares has the perfection of art. In death Mr. Platt lives up to an aesthetic standard defined by Livingstone as "a pleasing suitability" of style to substance – or in this instance, lack of substance. For as we have seen, Mr. Platt reifies a will to profit and possess that lacks substantial purpose and that makes his inability to write a will absurd. In the end, he dies intestate, as though by not bequeathing his wealth, he can, in the clichéd phrase, take it with him. Because of his will-lessness he remains for a time "a legal nuisance," but he is "quickly forgotten as a human being" (p. 99).

The casual dismissal of Mr. Platt in *Love and Salt Water* contrasts with the portentousness of Driscoll's glittering death in *My Mortal Enemy*. Though Cather calls the death an ascension and "translation," implying a spiritual apotheosis, she ladens the scene of ascent with materialistic detail, as though money translates into descriptive richness. Everything is costly and in excess: the priests' "gorgeous vestments," the altar's "hundreds of candles," the extravagant masses of flowers. The ostentation displayed at Driscoll's death fits the manner of his life, so that the funeral service seems to achieve the perfection of art ascribed to Mr. Platt's death. I say *seems* because Cather's metaphor of translation – of a change in form but not in nature – cannot sustain the identity between spiritual and materialistic values that it implies.[19] Cather's narrator, young Nellie Birdseye, describes a rich and ruthless man entering heaven with an ease unauthorized by the tenets of his religion which has sanctified the poverty Driscoll profaned. These religious inversions make the moral values of the characters and the text murky, if not unreadable. We could, of course, read Nellie's hyperbolic description as ironic by distancing Cather from a narrator who sees materialistic excess as the sign of spirituality, and the buying of religious favor as freely given grace. Nellie effects these exchanges in a romantic language of ineffability, a questionable medium for translating perceived actions into realistic social meanings. In contrast, Driscoll makes his meanings clear and empowering in a legal language that translates his will into action and, through this translation, gives expression to his inordinate pride.

As acts of moral transgression, pride and avarice seem antithetical, but as elements of plot, they produce surprisingly similar effects upon two dissimilar characters, miserly Mr. Platt and money-spending Driscoll. Both accumulate fortunes but end up alone and loveless, and if lack of love signifies destitution, both are destitute creatures.[20] No one mourns for Driscoll at this funeral; every-one comes as a spectator eager to see and gasp – or so Nellie would have us be-lieve. She describes objective features of the funeral devoid of subjective feelings other than awe at the extravagant display. As an adult re-viewing the "pomp and dramatic splendor" she remembers from childhood, Nellie relives her original feelings so vividly that she reassigns the "romantic part" she had always given Myra to her uncle: "John Driscoll and his niece had suddenly changed places in my mind, and he had got, after all, the more romantic part" (p. 16). This ex-change equates romance with display, and because the display appears at a fu-neral, death seems to Nellie "better" than life – at least than Myra's life.

Such a strange inversion (or perversion) of values identifies Nellie with other Cather characters who share her desire for a transcendent *something* that she is trying to realize in, and through, her story. The story takes ironic twists and turns, displacing the romance of love with money, using money to satisfy a yearning for escape that underlies romantic desire, and since death effects an ul-timate escape, turning to the theme of mortality. Death becomes a muddled af-fair in Nellie's description, but the muddle has appealed to many Cather characters who share Nellie's view of death as romantic transcendence and who would undoubtedly have been as mesmerized as she by Driscoll's translation and as dismayed by Myra's double chin.[21] Cather's characters intuitively assent to val-ues that imbue death with romance not because these values are clear, but rather because they have been mystified by murky equations of death with a timely es-cape from life's mundanities and love's demands.

Whether love ever figured in Driscoll's life is questionable. Nothing in his distant past suggests a love interest. In fact, Driscoll has no distant past. Like Mr. Platt, he appears one day out of nowhere, a man without a "pre-history." All that is known of him is that he left Parthia a poor boy and returned with a for-tune mysteriously amassed by "employing contract labour in the Missouri swamps" (p. 10). His money has a more unsavory source than Mr. Platt's, which may have come, as befits an English Canadian character, from service as "a gen-tleman's gentleman" (an occupation that may, or may not, have produced his initial "fortune of twenty thousand dollars"). Of course, neither character re-quires a pre-history to validate his place in the novel's plot; each needs only money. Nonetheless, without a history, both characters seem strangely autoge-nous rather than products of a society inscribed with materialistic interests. The texts try to obscure these interests by vacillating between their historically real-istic foreground and a background in which a character's destiny is determined by impersonal timeless forces – fate, chance, or providence – or by literary con-ventions.[22] Love subjects Myra to these mysterious forces by making her the heroine of a story fashioned from the stock elements of melodrama, fairy tale, and family romance, forms with a common plot involving forbidden love, elopement, and disinheritance.[23] The story begins in Parthia where, we are told, Myra and Driscoll had been an ideally happy couple. Driscoll enjoyed his niece's "racy" wit, and she "appreciated" the "coarse old codger"; the two were bonded in nature by a "blood-tie." Oswald's appearance in Parthia as a penniless young wooer disrupts the father–daughter relationship and reveals its hidden bargains and exchanges: Myra is to gratify Driscoll's pride in exchange for money and ease, and Driscoll is to exchange money for gratification.[24] Driscoll's "cold business proposition" clearly establishes his superior bargaining power as he threatens to cut Myra off from his money unless she renounces the man she loves. Thus, a relationship that had seemed based upon family affection suddenly reveals its financial nexus and, in effect, redefines Myra as an employee who has ceased to please her employer or, put another way, as an investment that has failed to bring a profitable return in gratification of pride and in filial obedience. Driscoll may have considered obedience a daughter's duty, though as represented in the text it may strike the reader, or so it strikes me, as a bought and paid for commodity. The old man had calculated the price of this commodity so that he knew what he wanted of Myra and what he would pay.

Why Driscoll disapproves of Oswald is not clear. His reasons are obviously compelling and crucial to the plot, but characteristically murky. Driscoll "persecute[s]" Oswald because of an "old grudge of some kind" against his father, a "poor and impractical" schoolmaster whose wanderings land him briefly in Parthia. Since parental opposition to a daughter's lover is a literary commonplace, Cather may have seen no need to elaborate a motive for Driscoll's hatred of Oswald; on the other hand, she may have intuited that Driscoll could not have approved of any man who would take Myra from him because he needed her to gratify his pride.[25] Cather obscures the crassness of this need by aestheticizing Driscoll's money. Though she traced his fortune to a swampland, making its source ugly if not dishonest, she translates his money into beautiful things – a "fine house" set in a "ten-acre park of trees," silver musical instruments, paintings, jewels – and into gaiety and youth. Like another mysteriously self-made American, Jay Gatsby, Driscoll gives magnificent parties and gathers about him a spurious display of vitality, the energy of his niece's young thoughtless friends who will betray him by helping her elope. Nellie succumbs to the glamor of the events that once took place in Driscoll's mansion, all trite elements of popular romance. Her view of the past has been handed down by a convenient nonentity, her Aunt Lydia, who believed that Myra had "everything" a woman could want: "dresses and jewels, a fine riding horse, a Steinway piano" (p. 19). The people of Parthia have a high regard for money and material things which Myra, for all her aesthetic pretensions, openly shares, and which Cather seems unable to disregard or discredit. Indeed, she has construed a story that gives credibility to Driscoll's cynical words: "It's better to be a stray dog in this world than a man without money. . . . A poor man stinks, and God hates him" (p. 13). This ugly dictum, Driscoll's legacy to Myra, creates a crisis that My Mortal Enemy struggles in vain to resolve, unable to deny or affirm its truth or to reconcile its cynicism with ideals the text seeks to realize.

IV

"Ah, but she isn't people! She's Myra Driscoll, and there was never anybody else like her." . . .

My Mortal Enemy

"Ellen is Ellen and different from other people."

Love and Salt Water

When Myra Henshawe says "It was money I needed" (p. 62), she seems to distinguish her need from that of other boarders at the shabby west coast hotel where she and Nellie are reunited. The ten years that have elapsed since their Christmas together in New York are elided in the text as though, like Ellen's "few years," they were irrelevant. In fact, these years mark a crucial decline in the fortunes of the characters that an altered vocabulary reflects. Nellie's key adjectives in the first part of *My Mortal Enemy* are *gorgeous, fine, beautiful, splendid, proud, rich*, words replaced in the second part by *wretched, ugly, shabby, humble, poor*. "I was very poor," Nellie says, "Things had gone badly with my family and with me" (p. 49). *Things*, a general term with colloquial overtones, seems self-explanatory – everyone knows *things* can go badly – but its effect is to obfuscate specific circumstances essential to the creation of a historical context.[26] If given specificity, *things* might include the great depression of 1893 which struck a multitude of people who found they too needed money. Myra sees herself as unique among these needy people (invisible to her), and Oswald supports her self-centered view when he says of his wife that "there was never anybody else like her."[27] The text, however, subverts this uxorious claim by introducing women of great achievement who overshadow Myra, a "queenly" actress (Helena Modjeska), an acclaimed poet, and a magnificent opera singer – artists whose talents Myra appreciates but does not share. Like Thea Kronberg in *The Song of the Lark*, these women have the capacity to create rare and incomparable moments of beauty. Such a moment occurs at Myra's Christmas party when Nellie hears a young Polish woman sing Bellini's *Casta Diva*, while Myra sits in the shadows.[28] Nellie never forgets the moment, though she always associates the song not with the singer but with Myra and the fascination of her dark elusiveness for which, she says, "I had no name."[29] Nellie never considers that this nameless *something* may be nothing, or nothing more than a projection of her self-mystifications. Nellie almost wills herself to believe that the woman she had been taught to romanticize has in her nature something "compelling, passionate, overmastering," qualities Nellie finds romantic, though they seem to me ominously coercive. In an unintentionally apt phrase, Nellie epitomizes the secret of Myra's personality as a "hidden richness" she hopes to uncover, but a desire for disclosure must be frustrated in a text committed to obfuscation. When Nellie seems on the verge of putting into words the secret qualities that make Myra unique, she loses narrative power. Instead of describing Myra, she reproduces her impressions as a bedazzled spectator. Observing Myra interacting with a woman poet, Nellie finds her "brilliant and strangely charming"; her conversation is "extraordinary"; the friends said "fantastic things about people, book, music – anything" (p. 35). But what was said remains unsaid in Nellie's narrative, which can reproduce Myra's tirades but cannot give expression to qualities inherently inexpressible as a transcendently romantic *something*.

Though Myra "isn't people," as Oswald says, her needs are, nevertheless, those of countless women in life and literature who have little control over their fate, their fortunes rising or falling with the men in their lives. Among literary characters, her story is a commonplace of plots that Myra herself could have recognized in operas and plays she knew, and among Cather's characters, she is surely not alone in her need for money. By having Oswald insist upon Myra's uniqueness, Cather seems to be trying to reinstate a romantic story she has mercilessly demolished. Oswald obfuscates the cynicism that has shattered this story by presenting a romantic vision of a world in which unique individuals prevail against all forces, even against death. Like her uncle, Myra achieves absolution and apotheosis through a death she has willed. So Nellie would have us believe, and so Oswald asserts when he says of the ailing Myra, "She can do anything she will" (p. 79). Myra herself may have believed this when she likened herself to powerful and wicked kings, but she is powerless to alter her uncle's will or to get the money she needs. In such powerlessness, she is far from unique.

Like Oswald Henshawe, George Gordon in *Love and Salt Water* is a man in love who believes his chosen woman is unique. "Ellen is Ellen," he thinks, "and different from other people" (p. 95). The omniscient narrator apparently agrees as she declares Ellen's social conformity superficial: "Her outer life easily conformed . . . but her inner life became question and answer, question and no answer" (p. 92). However, this inner nonconformity has little perceptible effect upon a life patterned as much by chance as by choice, and eased by social privileges. Ellen's father can afford to take her on an ocean voyage that helps them resume their lives after her mother's death, and a well-placed friend (lawyer Livingstone) helps her get away from a broken engagement in Vancouver by finding her a job in Saskatoon. Her various "preoccupations" keep her busy while she approaches a future which she assumes holds love and marriage, though she has fleeting "premonitions of age" and spinsterhood, fears common enough to women of her class. If Ellen is not unique, she is, nonetheless, distinctively spunky, reflective, and unembittered by loss. She has suffered the loss of her mother (as had Wilson), of a financé, and through his remarriage, of her father; she almost loses her beloved nephew and her life. She accepts the possibility that her face may be permanently disfigured and that she may lose the man she hopes to marry. Courage and common sense make her admirable, which is not the same as unique.

At the end of *Love and Salt Water* Ellen still has the social privileges that Myra had lost and the prospect of a happy combination, denied to Myra, of love, marriage, and money. George Gordon affirms the power of love when he wants to marry Ellen even though her face is partially scarred and disfigured, perhaps for life. He is an ideal suitor, patient, humoring, providing a love that does not alter when it alteration finds. Thus, unlike *My Mortal Enemy*, *Love and Salt Water* ends, as it begins, with marriage. In the opening scene Ellen's sister Nora is preparing for her wedding; in the closing scene, the scarred and chastened Ellen is embraced by her future husband. Love prevails and marriages are happy though "chequered" by life's combination of shadow and light. All the characters have enough money to live as they wish. Nevertheless, they have troubles. The death of Nora's first child, the mental retardation of her second child, and the impending deafness of her third are fortuities. Nora's responses, however, reflect her privileged social position. She can remove the knowledge of her damaged child from her consciousness because her husband's money removes him from her presence, and she can pamper her third child. However, she cannot escape the vagaries of accident – nor can anyone in the novel. For in their ordinary daily lives, Wilson's characters are confronted less by chances to exercise personal will, than by chance itself – accidents, fortuities, and coincidences that arrange one's life. The novel is full of "arrangements," its key word, but most arrangements have been made by happenstance, and those devised by characters have unforeseen consequences. Ellen's mother arranges a birthday celebration for her daughter, feels unwell, and dies. She might have been stricken at any time, just as Ellen's rowboat might have been capsized by any ocean tide. As the narrator points out, "salt water is salt water whether it be in the Atlantic Ocean or the Pacific Ocean" (p. 169).

Ellen's nearly fatal accident at sea closes "a gap" in her understanding that had been created by pride. Having come close to "great ultimate sorrow," Ellen becomes humble, and her sister Nora, magnanimous. Humility, forgiveness, and compassion, qualities alien to the declining Myra Henshawe, attenuate the chaotic effects of chance. Before the near-drowning, Ellen had been a "superior onlooker" who thought her arrangements better than her sister's. Afterwards, she learns that "she had better mind her own business. Everyone had better mind their own business" (p. 188). The cliché is oddly inappropriate, since business as an enterprise of exchange and profit seems extraneous to Ellen's fate (as it is not to Myra's) and to the moral order Wilson's novel envisions as life's ultimate "arrangement." This is a troubling order because the relationship between mistakes and their consequences is markedly askew. As Ellen's brother-in-law Morgan observes: "The price of casual negligence and danger often comes . . . disproportionately high" (p. 192). The disproportion suggests that the forces determining one's fate are impersonal, uncontrollable, and ultimately unfathomable, and that the individual, confronting such forces, must submit herself to a will greater than her own. In accepting humility as the lesson of profoundly affecting experience, Ellen undercuts the cult of personality that sustains Myra's pride in *My Mortal Enemy* and that gives many of Cather's characters their "uniqueness." Corollary to the theme of humility is respect for the otherness of others, Wilson's synonym for love. Husbands and wives can love each other while honoring the distance between them, a distance that is actual when Frank Cuppy leaves his wife Susan to seek for oil in far-flung countries, when Morgan Peake leaves Nora for Parliament sessions in Ottawa, when Dick Peake cannot join Aunt Maury on Galiano Island. The love affair between Ellen, living at the time in Saskatoon, and George Gordon in Montreal seems enhanced by separation and distance. Like occasional silence and separation, distance fosters amiable human relations. Aunt Maury realizes this when she appreciates the canyon that separates her from old, dirty, gossipy Mr. Abednego, the neighbor who providentially rescues Ellen and her nephew by minding their business as his own. Mr. Abednego's inquisitiveness is tolerable and comic because it is disinterested, distinct from a will to arrange or dominate the affairs of others; he personifies a pointless and unpossessive human curiosity.

Such disinterest is difficult for Cather's characters, who cannot maintain distance from each other because they need to arrange, dominate – meddle. Nellie's Aunt Lydia meddled when she passed love letters between Myra and Oswald, and she continues to meddle by lying for Oswald to his wife: "something" about the Henshawes, Nellie says, "would have discouraged me from meddling, but it did not shake my aunt" (p. 45). Myra describes herself as "an old woman who eggs on courtships" and then vows "never to meddle again" (pp. 40–1). Nevertheless, she meddles fecklessly in Nellie's life by foisting upon her a set of depleting lessons as she makes the young woman her confidant, disciple, nurse, and successor.[30] Nellie describes her first encounter with Myra in ominous terms as an appropriation, almost a business takeover: "Her deep-set, flashing eyes seemed to be *taking me in* altogether – *estimating* me. For all that she was no taller than I, I felt quite *overpowered* by her – and stupid, hopelessly clumsy and stupid" (p. 12, emphasis added). Even when Myra implies that fifteen-year-old Nellie is interesting, she violates her by making her into an object of her gaze and gossip. She brings Nellie to her poet friend, lying upon her couch like a young Elizabeth Browning, because, she says, "I want her to see you so that we can talk you over" (p. 53). Talking people over signifies an act of appropriation that allows characters to *use* each other, sometimes to their mutual advantage – as when Driscoll uses Myra to gratify his pride and she uses him as her provider – and sometimes to disadvantage. Using people does not make Cather's characters unique, either in novels or the actual world (nor does it necessarily make them reproachable), but the text's euphemisms for *use* or commodification obscure the coldness underlying its human relationships. Driscoll reveals this coldness in his "business proposition," though he preferred to be seen as warm and generous. Myra presents her domination of Nellie as guidance to an unsophisticated girl who needs someone to "improve" her manners and speech. Everyone uses Myra, making capital of her vivifying presence and residual story. She adds interest to everyone's life.

The church takes on a peculiar use, providing characters not with guidance, but with escape from moral judgment and from the darkness of death. When "the church went to him" and assimilated his body, Driscoll effectively "escaped the end of all flesh" (pp. 15–16); and when Myra went to the church, at the end of her life, she sought to escape the disappointment of unrealized desires. In a much-quoted and argued phrase, Myra alludes to a view of religion she can use to justify her own unfulfilled life, "in religion, desire was fulfillment" (p. 77) – and Myra is practiced in desiring.[31] As death draws near, she turns to a naive young priest for comfort, having no further use for Oswald, now her "enemy." Lacking a spirit of forgiveness, charity, or humility, she seeks absolution from the Church, implicitly viewing religion as she views social relationships, from the perspective of an autocrat who commands, calls, and dismisses, leaves or takes what she wants. At the end of her life, she wants a reconcilation with her uncle and with Catholicism – a coalescence of material, spiritual, and aesthetic benefits that would satisfy a desire for the wealth of Driscoll's niece and the absolution of Driscoll's Church. She finds religious support in young Father Fay, who contributes to the obfuscations of the text by articulating an absurdly anachronistic view of Myra. Speaking "boyishly," as though to mark the naiveté of his statement, he says, "I wonder whether some of the saints of the early Church weren't a good deal like her" (p. 76). Were the early saints, in a reversal of chronology, really like Myra, or was Cather merely trying to modify the impression she had created of "a greedy, selfish, worldly woman . . . [who] wanted success and a place in the world"? (p. 62).

In *Love and Salt Water*, religion cannot be abandoned or reclaimed because it creates human community. As Ellen's mother explains: "The prayer doesn't say 'Give *me* this day my daily bread', it says 'Give *us* our daily bread' . . . and that means all of us" (p. 104, original emphasis and ellipsis). *Love and Salt Water* describes "a circle of life" that includes and integrates all humanity. Prayer "makes us all one family," the mother says, articulating a sense of community that contrasts with the individualism of Cather's characters – a contrast which, arguably, can be traced to cultural differences underlying Canadian and American national identity.[32] Susan Cuppy leaves her daughter a legacy of inner "graces" – "patience, good temper, and gratitude" – and more important, the possibility of spiritual growth through prayer: "Prayer was a legacy that Susan left to her younger daughter . . . often prayer was to Ellen as though the windows and doors of her spirit were opened wide" (p. 94). While *My Mortal Enemy* ends with a foreclosure of possibilities for Nellie, whose heart turns cold at the thought of love and union, *Love and Salt Water* describes Ellen opening her mind and heart to the manifold equations of love.[33]

When Frank Cuppy takes his daughter on a long sea voyage they both discover that love can return to a receptive heart and bring a healing grace. Cuppy meets the woman who will become his second wife, and Ellen matures to a reconcilation with loss. However, a sudden storm at sea that sweeps a beautiful, guileless boy to death reveals the insufficiency of love against the forces of destruction. Ellen ends her voyage with a sense of inescapable subordinacy – inescapable because she lives surrounded by dangerous salt waters that can, and do, make unpredictable incursions upon her life, and because she lives also in the shadow of another country that can, and does, draw away those she loves.[34] The voyage shows Ellen that even affluent and leisured people must accept their own secondariness, for "on a deep-sea freighter . . . [passengers] are of no importance whatever, and their movements are conditioned entirely by the freight which the ship will pick up or deposit. . . . They discover that they are unimportant and are only the pawns of the tinned fruit and grain and borax, which are important" (p. 32). The thought that she might be unimportant – less important than borax! – could not occur to Myra Henshawe, identified through the novel's metaphors with kings, rulers, and despots (though she may simply be a stereotypical American individualist). Myra believes in power and in the coalescence of power with money, art, and religion. The intrusion of money in this equation would make *My Mortal Enemy* seem a surprising novel in Cather's canon, unless one reads the canon, as some critics now do, as more dissonant than assumed, more culturally regressive, and more "American."[35]

Nellie's vignette of Madison Square, "the real heart" of New York, demonstrates how the text makes a peculiar muddle of materialistic and aesthetic values. The very locale is at odds with itself, having "a double personality, half commercial, half social" (p. 21). Left to herself in the moonlit square, Nellie imagines "a winter dancing party" or "a reception for some distinguished European visitor" – social scenes that link gentility with money. As in a Whistler painting, the scene is monochromatic, colored in variants of regal purple with "violet buildings," "violet sky," and "English violets." Here, Nellie feels, "winter brought no desolation"; even the "trees and shrubbery seemed well-groomed and sociable, like pleasant people" (p. 34). Good grooming, good manners, pleasant people, parties, and music meld into a vision of gracious living that includes the services of strangers. Elderly street sweepers clear a bench for Nellie and, in the background, a thin, coatless boy plays upon his pennywhistle. *Thin, coatless, penny* – unobtrusively, these three words appear to suggest a winter desolation that Nellie has denied and that she will escape (as the thin, coatless boy cannot) by entering the Henshawes' Fifth Avenue apartment. Here comfort is enhanced by contrast with the cold outside: "snug fire-places" make the room cozy and warm; high ceilings, wide doors, and deep windows make it spacious; and plum-colored velvet drapes make it regal. Nellie feels herself luxuriating in a gracious extravagance.

Extravagance is a key thematic term in *My Mortal Enemy,* implying the presence of excess or surplus.[36] Nellie gives the term a double meaning when she says, "My aunt often said that Myra was incorrigibly extravagant; but I saw that her chief extravagance was in caring for so many people and in caring for them so much" (p. 35). Nellie mystifies the materialistic interests in her story by shifting the tenor of its terms, modulating the meaning of extravagance from excessive expenditure of money and emotion – Myra's spending sprees and "violent nature" – to generosity and friendship. Myra adds to the mystification by distinguishing between money set aside "for unearthly purposes" and money used for "the needs of this world" (p. 70). But even this distinction becomes muddled because Myra thinks she can satisfy spiritual needs by buying a mass for the soul in the same way she would buy worldly things. Equating need with want, Myra needs things, services, and self-gratification: furs and feathered hats and jewels; quiet rooms elegantly decorated with velvet drapes and a private carriage; servants; and gracious friends she can lavish with gifts.[37] Perversely, it would seem, Myra has displaced need from a struggling working class to the leisured *nouveaux riches* who, like her, are unsuited to deprivation because they have enjoyed luxury. When Shakespeare's Lear was being stripped to necessity, he cried out, "O reason not the need!" Myra echoes the cry; she wants "things superfluous," to use Lear's term for extravagance, the needs of a woman who, in her own words, is "greedy, selfish," and "worldly." At the same time, she wants to be surrounded by "people of gentle manners" and "courtesy" – people she might attract with money (pp. 62–3). Thus, Myra makes and muddles distinctions between money and manners, sometimes equating them, other times separating them (as when she spurns her husband's rich New York clients), and still other times, appropriating (that is, misappropriating) what she thinks is the manner of a working-class woman.

"All old Irish women hide away a bit of money," Myra tells the surprised Nellie as she uncovers a secret hoard of gold coins she has hidden in her trunk (p. 69). In a gesture that inverses that of the text (which hides what it reveals), Myra reveals what she has been hiding: money, social class, and ethnic identity. At her will, she evokes an Irish working woman as a secret self who reveals vulgar and violent inclinations repressed by the aristocratic Myra Henshawe. This old Irish woman abuses her husband and, with a mocking brogue, humiliates a friend: "It's owing to me infirmities, dear Mrs. Casey," she says in dismissing Nellie, "that I'll not be able to go as far as me doorwid ye" (p. 73). Myra enjoys making theatrical gestures and assuming social roles as they serve her purposes, the washerwoman releasing her spite, and the grand lady enacting her aristocratic largesse. Myra theatrically stages her appearances, and Cather represents scenes as though they were taking place on the stage. In the Madison Square scene, she creates stock characters in an encounter that impresses an audience, also on stage in the person of a young and impressionable observer. Nellie sees Myra as a grand lady in furs who graciously gives a coin to a "thin lad with a cap and yarn comforter but no overcoat" (p. 22). The social classes encounter each other in a relationship which the scene makes proper by showing Myra charitable and the boy in his place, playing his penny-whistle and evoking a third stock character by his tune, *The Irish Washerwoman*. Later, other theatrical stereotypes emerge in Myra's dramatization of herself as the victim of a "palavery kind of

Southerners . . . gush on the surface, and no sensibilities whatever – a race without consonants and without delicacy" (p. 56).

Oswald excuses his wife's cruel indelicacies as an *act*. When he realizes that Nellie has overheard Myra's quarrel with him, he comforts her by saying, "Myra isn't half so furious with me as she pretends" (p. 42). Myra theatrically stages her actions to dramatize a mundane bourgeois life and to distance the aristocratic lady she aspires to be from the common woman who expresses her frustrated will. Money plays a key role in her theatrics, serving as a costume, the "cloak [that] can buy one . . . dignity" (p. 57). Lack of money uncloaks the actress and reveals a bitter and violent woman who strikes at those who love her – at Oswald, excusing insult as an *act,* at Nellie, bewildered by a washerwoman, and at Aunt Lydia, finally "sick of Myra's dramatics" (p. 45). Readers have shared Aunt Lydia's exasperation, but I wonder what alternative to dramatics Cather has allowed a woman in Myra's historical circumstances who seeks aesthetic self-fulfillment but lacks art or talent and money of her own.

V

His eyes, however, were dark and soft, curious in shape – exactly like half-moons

My Mortal Enemy

"What kind of father are you that doesn't even listen to his own daughter!"

Love and Salt Water

At the end of *My Mortal Enemy,* Oswald Henshawe lights out, like the perennial American hero, for the territory ahead. He will disappear into the landscape of Alaska, America's last frontier, remaining, to the last, elusive. As Myra's husband, he had pursued money, faltered, and failed. He could have taken "a small position" after a big business takeover had wiped out his superficially prestigious post as private secretary, but Myra's pride, the Driscoll inheritance, had rejected such a lowering of the self.[38] As a result of her meddling (and his passivity), he ends up in "a humble position, poorly paid, with the city traction company" located on the west coast. From there, he moves to Alaska as a final retreat from the world.

Oswald's downward spiral (unfortunately, familiar to contemporary Americans) describes the fate of countless others, but Myra cares only about her losses. As always, she ignores the working poor whose plight she now shares. Though she will project herself upon the landscape of *King Lear,* she cannot see the "houseless heads and unfed sides" that become visible to a fallen king once blinded by "pomp" and "superflex," the extravagance of a privileged life. Oswald is also oblivious to the social implications of the changes in his life, perhaps because he harbors within him a secret inner self impervious to circumstance –

or so Nellie believes. For her own mysterious reasons, she has imbued Oswald with qualities time cannot touch, an "indestructible constancy . . . almost indestructible youth" (pp. 83–4, original ellipsis). Precisely when Myra's husband visibly shows the effects of destructive change (the phrase is usually a tautology in Cather's fiction) – when he is old and discredited – Nellie makes him symbolic of a romantic stasis that holds youth, loyalty, and identity in arrest. As he tells Nellie after Myra's death: "These last years it's seemed to me that I was nursing the mother of the girl who ran away with me. Nothing ever took that girl from me. She was a wild, lovely creature" (p. 84). Of course, the girl he ran away with had no mother, and his fantasy of "nursing" a mother is murky, to say the least. His parting statement is a testament to romance and a reiteration of an underlying assumption in the text, that characters can repudiate the reality they see and know they are seeing. Oswald sees how embittered Myra has become, how she is here and now, in the present, but he enjoins Nellie to think only of the past, of there and then: "Remember her as she was . . . I wish you could have seen her then" (p. 84). Remembering "Molly Driscoll," he forgets Myra Henshawe, a woman who ages and dies, leaving a box of ashes as a legacy. His last act, a fulfillment of "a clause in Myra's will," is to bury the ashes in the sea. Thus he completes Cather's equation between love and salt water.

Though Nellie has idealized Oswald as a chivalric figure of unchanging loyality and love, she subverts the image she has drawn by the cynicism of her final words. They express a fear of love and marriage that implicitly indicts Oswald as a man who led a rich and happy young woman astray. In effect, Nellie endorses Myra's accusation of betrayal by the man who should be her rescuer. "You ought to get me away from this, Oswald," Myra says, pointing to their poverty; "If I were on my feet, and you laid low, I wouldn't let you be despised and trampled upon" (p. 61). Pride speaks, as well as Myra's pain, and both demean Oswald as a husband who has failed to provide money. Instead, he offers the services of a wife, serving meals, washing dishes, working at a lowly job. Marriage has reduced both characters and repressed the romantic *something* Nellie had seen in Oswald. Perhaps this *something* existed only as a projection of her own desire or, as likely, of Cather's need to reaffirm romantic values she confusedly undermines in creating a figure of disjunct features. Oswald's face visibly represents disjunction, his hard cheekbones contrasting with curiously "soft" eyes shaped in half-moons (p. 7). Like Nellie, Oswald seems a "moon-struck" character, attracting young women who aspire to the romance he seems to promise, while he wants a woman who demands wordly things. If he confuses the reader, he has also confused Nellie, leaving as his legacy a cold amethyst necklace and a disillusionment with love that is thematic to Cather's fiction.

In *Love and Salt Water,* Wilson's Frank Cuppy is an extremely attractive figure, loved by his wife and children and successful in his career. To see in him an expression of the capitalistic will that drives queer little Mr. Platt (or obdurate Driscoll) seems at first outlandish, and yet a will to pursue the possibility of profit constantly separates him from the family he believes he loves, as perhaps he does or – to equivocate like Wilson – perhaps not. His lively wife Susan understands that her husband "cares most for me and the children – and, of course [why of course?], for finding oil" (p. 16). An "absentee husband," Frank Cuppy visits his family when he is not on expeditions to countries far and near: "Mexico or Persia or New York . . . Alberta . . . Northern Saskatchewan" (p. 15). The demands of his business are imperative: "he *had* to go to Terehan" (p. 23, emphasis added). To compensate for his absenteeism, Cuppy gives his family expensive gifts, "a nice new roadster" for his wife and "strange and beautiful presents" that make his mind "easier" about his children (p. 17). At the end of the novel, he is living in New York, "near to the heart of things," the clichéd phrase associating heart, that is, sentiment and vital force, with business affairs or things. Money and things may be more important to her husband than Susan Cuppy allows herself to think, though the narrator slyly evokes questions about his values. "He did not *at first* really care about money," the narrator notes (p. 16, emphasis added). But what of *later*? a reader might ask. Perhaps, in time, Mr. Cuppy might come to care for money, just as he cared for another woman within months after his wife's death. In time, his remarriage and, more importantly, his pursuit of "potential oil fields" separate him from the daughters he professed to love. Even when the family was happily together, as in the early Stanley Park scene, Cuppy's thoughts were elsewhere and on business. His wife knew that her husband "habitually thought of other things," but since she could not change him, "she did not mind *much*" (p. 18). I emphasize *much* because it represents a typical Wilson qualification as it asserts what the words deny, and denies what they say. As a child, Ellen can be forthright in demanding her father's attention: "Listen! Listen! Answer me at once! . . . What kind of father are you that doesn't even listen to his own daughter!" (p. 18). This is a question the text poses only to leave unanswered.

If in his own way, Frank Cuppy is enigmatic, this quality does not indict him as a husband or father. He is an appealing character who elicits in the reader, as he does in his wife, an affectionate indulgence. Like the European explorers named and admired in the novel, he sets off for faraway lands, known and unknown. Perhaps he too loves adventure, but his purpose is to make money by exploiting nature's resources. Through him, Wilson acknowledges the economic matrix of her novel and shows that the capitalistic enterprise which defines his way of life makes him indistinguishable from any go-getting American businessman. He himself recognizes that his appropriate setting is not Vancouver, removed from the world's financial axes, but New York. Moving to New York signifies his success at capitalistic venture, just as Oswald Henshawe's departure from the city signifies his failure. Frank Cuppy's deracination conforms to the logic of capitalism as an international or transnational enterprise and shows this logic stronger than the bonds of family and country. His move to New York may suggest also – the suggestion is slight but inferable – a complementary relationship between assimilation and appropriation, as Cuppy assimilates the culture of capitalistic America, and America appropriates the economic future of Canada. Thus, the text comments obliquely upon Canadian capitalistic development and the widely recognized hegemonic relationship between the United States and its border country. This is a more serious comment than its passing references to stereotypically "affluent" Americans "going about their business" while idly noting "that Coca-Cola refreshes and that bigger and better cars are on their way" (pp. 35–7).[39] Frank Cuppy may not have become an "American" when he went to New York, but he had followed the mandates of a capitalistic will that many Canadian social theorists believe has directed the development of Canadian economy.[40] Wilson's seemingly extraneous Mr. Platt represents a stripped, caricatural image of this development and of the absurdity of devoting a life to making money or to finding oil. Frank Cuppy does both; he finds oil and makes money, tucking marriage, family, and love into the convenient moments when he does not *have* to be in Mexico, Persia, or Teheran. Meanwhile, life makes its own arrangements and delivers sudden death to his beloved wife Susan while he is away.

VI

It is not an "American" book.
Ethel Wilson letter

I used to wonder whether . . . I could not see the American scene as it looked to other Americans.
Willa Cather letter

I've nothing to hide – nothing.
Agatha Christie, *Cards on the Table*

In Agatha Christie's mystery story, *Cards on the Table,* a murderer tells the investigating detective, "I've nothing to hide – *nothing.*"[41] The outright lie of Christie's young Englishwoman is different from the obfuscations and self-mystifying of the American and English Canadian storytellers I have been describing, writers and characters who believe they are telling the truth. Truth becomes clear in Christie's mystery as the writer, who has known it all along, lays her cards squarely on the table. The lying murderer also lays cards on the table, actually, in a game of bridge that becomes a clue to her identity and, inadvertently, in an attempted second murder that reveals her secret self. Mystery stories finally disclose the lies characters tell and the secrets they hide; thus, they arrive at a single indisputable truth which the polyvalence commonly attributed to the novel would confound. Even when they resemble mysteries, novels create uncertainty and a lack of consensus because their overt disclosures tend to conceal as much as they reveal, and because the secrets discovered by readers often seem artifacts of their interested readings. Moreover, the cards that the writer lays on the table inevitably are from a stacked deck.

What final disclosure does *Love and Salt Water* or *My Mortal Enemy* make about the cultural identity of its characters? Is Wilson's handsome, successful, oil-seeking Frank Cuppy a Canadian or an American in disguise, his identity hidden from himself even as he gravitates to New York? Is he a fleshed and likable version of solitary, avaricious Mr. Platt, like him driven by a will to make more money? Is Mr. Platt, who refuses to make a will, an unrecognized and unintended but nevertheless revealing caricature of willful John Driscoll? And is Driscoll – a self-made man with a murky past, a fortune, a great house in which he gives grand parties meant to captivate a beautiful woman – an older, distorted version of Jay Gatsby (who is Fitzgerald's distorted version of the quintessential American, Benjamin Franklin, somehow conflated with a "pioneer debauchee" of the American West)?[42] What cards can the critic lay on the table that will begin to address, even if they cannot settle, questions of cultural identity raised by commonalities among characters – and writers – of different national origins?

If national origin is a biographical fact verifiable by official state documents, national cultural identity is an elusive and much argued concept implicated in theories of history and language and potentially subversive of the idea of origination upon which it seems to rest. Can the origins of a national cultural identity be traced back to historical realities that preexist to shape its definition? If so, then the term *cultural identity* would have a definite and knowable referentiality usually denied to language by postmodern linguistic and cultural theories. On the other hand, if culture is an artifact of language, as postmodern cultural theories contend, one may ask what relevance it can have to a cross-cultural criticism of literary texts. And what is the relevance of a literary text, clearly an artifact, to definitions of cultural identity?[43] Needless to say, these questions raise political as well as theoretical issues of far-ranging and general significance which must remain peripheral to a practical criticism centered upon two novels viewed as expressions and enactments of a capitalistic will.[44] A context that focuses upon a will to accumulate wealth legitimizes a critique of texts concerned with private fortunes, legal wills that dispose of fortune, and inheritance and disinheritance as expressions of will. This context reveals strategies for concealment necessitated by what I have called the duplicities of the texts, a double set of cultural values that cannot be denied or collapsed into each other, though they can be obfuscated. Strategies for representing and obscuring these duplicities overlap in the two texts, both of which rely upon an evocation of timeless literary traditions to distract the reader's attention from the historical and cultural circumstances they have shown embedded in capitalistic society.

By emphasizing the literariness of their texts through allusions, conventional plots (love and marriage), and stock characters, Cather and Wilson sought to situate characters bound by historical circumstances within a supposedly timeless background that reduced circumstance to mere contingency. From this background, the writers sought to abstract literature's universal subjects: *time, pride, avarice, love, death, redemption,* and the workings of *will* – the human will and God's will. Thus, they could recess the historical exigencies foregrounded by the realism of their novels to a background against which Everyman – everyman and eternal woman – played out a timeless drama of human life. The drama was highly conventionalized because its plots were unchanging and its characters engaged in perennial struggles. Once enacted within realistically defined historical and geographic settings, however, this timeless drama blurred the boundaries between the particular and the universal in ways that mystified the novels' mode of representation – by vacillating between realism and romance and by simultaneously valorizing and subverting, or transcending, the capitalistic society they portrayed. Mystification of genre, theme, and moral values made anything possible in the novels and everything unpredictable and, paradoxically, familiar. In the realistic world of Saskatoon, a reified, anachronistic, and caricatural figure like Mr. Platt could appear suddenly, usurp the text, and then suddenly disappear – to no one's amazement. In Cather's world, a character like Oswald Henshawe could be a romantic lover, indestructible young and panting, and a failed aging husband cleaning his necktie with benzine. By the same token, a coarse old codger and ruthless businessman could be beatified by money and death. When realistic characters began to reveal the realistic consequences of their pursuit of profit and power (or the failure to pursue), the writers rushed in with romance, comic caricature, or religion to obscure their texts' social revelations and effect their reader's escape from social realities.

Since Cather and Wilson relied upon common literary traditions for their strategies of obfuscations, their novels shared common themes and forms that critics were quick to note and, understandably, attribute to the influence of an established and highly esteemed American writer upon an unknown Canadian woman. But Wilson tried to quell rumors of literary influence, saying in 1947 – the year her first novel *Hetty Dorval* was published (and, coincidentally, the year of Cather's death) – that while Cather was "a fine writer . . . to whom it is very pleasing to be compared," she had read only one of Cather's books, and that "decades ago." Though comparisons with Cather evoked "nice words, sweet words" from her reviewers, Wilson denied any specific connection between *Hetty Dorval* and *A Lost Lady* and any general influence upon her by a writer whom, she said, "I admire and respect . . . but do not know . . . well enough." "I have a memory of delight about *My Ántonia* and *A Pretty Lady* [sic]," Wilson wrote, "and no more because it was ages ago"; and even though she had read *Shadows on the Rock* just the "other day," her memory of it was also so etiolated that she called it the "Quebec story."[45] Wilson may not have been influenced by Cather, but the qualities she chose to praise in her novels show that they shared the same aesthetic values. Both writers valued "simpicity, purity, beauty," qualities Wilson admired in *Shadows on the Rock,* and both valued traditions of restraint and understatement, an art of implication that was delicate, suggestive, and self-consciously literary in its allusiveness. Both wrote with assurance, but liked the uncertainties suggested by the word *seemed,* a recurrent term in their texts that questioned the affirmations they made and contributed to the mystifications they created. They were "*economical*" writers, Wilson's emphasized adjective, who wanted to "unfurnish" the novel – to strip it of immediate social issues and advocacies suitable, they believed, to journalism but not to art.[46] Neither saw this view subverted by the social assumptions in her own writing which took for granted the privileges of class and money and reinforced conventional sexual roles.

Since their women characters have much in common, though they live in different times and places, gender, like genre, seems undefined by national boundaries. In both the American and the Canadian novel, wives depend upon husbands (or fathers) for money and social position, though young unmarried and mobile women easily find ways to support themselves. However, the destinies of the novel's two working women seem chiasmally crossed as the independent Ellen, who had served as a Wren in war-torn London, embraces marriage and domesticity, while the seemingly ordinary Nellie predicts a future that will be self-fashioned, extraordinary, and presumably exclude love. "I know what I want to do," she tells Myra, though she never tells what, precisely, it is that she wants. If Nellie's mysterious vision of herself is proleptically feminist, it is, nonetheless, an expression of disillusionment over the failure of romance she has experienced vicariously. She has lived through Myra's love affair only to end up with an amethyst necklace and coldness, her meager and depleting legacy. "I still have the string of amethysts," Nellie says, "but they are unlucky. If I . . . wear them, I feel all evening a chill over my heart" (p. 84).[47] Repudiating love and marriage, Nellie seeks an ineffable *something* else that society has not yet defined for women and that, paradoxically, definition might diminish. Ineffeability gives a surplus value to Nellie's words – or wordlessness – by evoking in the reader romantic visions of the self that Nellie cannot, or will not, reveal. Those aspects she does reveal show her appropriating Myra's actions as she sits with the ailing Myra and, in imitative gestures of extravagance, brings her flowers she cannot afford to buy.[48] "Mrs. Henshawe got great pleasure from flowers," Nellie says, "and during the late winter months my chief extravagance . . . was in taking them to her" (p. 59).

As Myra's secret sharer, Nellie may be a mortal enemy – an enemy of mortality who keeps Myra alive through her story, and Myra's enemy who finds a voice a friend would have silenced. For Nellie's story is telling as an indictment of a character who equates money with aesthetic self-realization. But the story is also self-indicting as it blurs the boundaries between loyalty and betrayal. Without betrayal, there would be no story, while the story itself attests to a loyalty expressed as the appropriation of Myra's identity. Who Nellie herself is, if she is a person rather than a narrative device, is arguable, although one clue to her identity may be a fleeting allusion to the moon goddess Diana. As a "moon-struck" character, Nellie bears the impress of a mythical figure with multiple and contradictory identities as vestal virgin and goddess of childbirth, huntress and avenger, the hidden and visible figure of night, and the reigning goddess of hell. Like the moon itself, the moon goddess went through transformations that left her with an unfathomable character marked by self-subverting traits. In a lesser way, Nellie also becomes unfathomable, her betrayal of Myra subverting a loy-alty she professes, her identification with Myra subverting a betrayal to which she seems oblivious, and her moon-struck qualities lifting her above the mun-dane world in which women need men and money.[49]

Unlike Nellie, Ellen seems down-to-earth, and yet her character is not as straightforward as it first appears and, I would claim, much more factitious. She is given a childhood that Nellie lacks, experiences that explain her personality, and traditional roles that she accepts by looking forward to love and marriage. She finds her first suitor, Huw Peake, clearly "unsuitable," their courtship a se-ries of petty trials. Her true love, George Gordon, courts her with books, send-ing "Samuel Butler's Note-Books" and promising another "pile of books shortly" (p. 96). Ellen's first response is rejection: "I don't want to be controlled by him or by anybody, books or no" (p. 97). But, as we know, she is controlled by the book in which she exists and the books Wilson has read.[50] For Wilson has placed Ellen within the generic mode of the *Bildungsroman,* making her the heroine of a story of initiation. In keeping with tradition, Ellen leaves home, goes on a long and dangerous "transforming" voyage, takes a wrong road in life (an actual wrong road in a ride up the Fraser Valley with Huw), and finally discovers a so-cially predetermined path to maturity and marriage. Along the way, as though she were on an allegorical journey, she encounters avarice, pride, and blind will, and she acquires humility, forebearance, and love. Unlike Nellie Birdseye, she has an admirable mother to guide her in life – but that she has a life to live is a matter of chance within the novel and of a calculated decision Wilson made in the process of writing the novel as she tried out various ways to bring Ellen's life to an end.

Wilson's alternate ending to *Love and Salt Water* was a double death: Ellen's beloved nephew, left for a few days in her care, drowns and Ellen commits sui-cide. Ellen wanted love, but her life would end in salt water. I have noted that *Love and Salt Water* begins with love and marriage; I should add that it begins also with sudden death – the death of Ellen's mother and of an innocent young boy. Thus, an ending that returns to the beginning with a double drowning would have as much formal and thematic cogency as love and marriage. That love prevailed over death reflects a commercial rather than aesthetic decision, for Wilson's publishers thought a bleak ending would not appeal to the public, and as it turns out, even with its happy denouement, *Love and Salt Water* was re-jected by American publishers. "It is not an 'American' book," Wilson ex-plained, her statement presupposing that she knew – and we know – what an

"American" book is, a definition she elides except to say, almost irrelevantly, that national identity is irrelevant to a novel's "excellence or non-excellence."[51] Vacillating between a need to deny national boundaries to art and a deep loyalty to a landscape she loved, Wilson claimed that she wrote about British Columbia both by choice and by the contingencies of her life, which had brought her to the Canadian province. Wilson was placing herself in another double bind by alluding to biographical facts she wanted excised from literary judgments of her novels. Like Cather, she discovered that her regional settings were "right" for her because they was "rooted" in a deeply felt "association, affection, and apprehension of place and people," because as a Canadian, they were an inextricable part of her life.[52]

In *My Mortal Enemy*, Cather's fleeting allusion to Walt Whitman as a quintessentially American poet initiates an extraordinary association of ideas. Myra thinks of Whitman as a "dirty old man" who reminds her of her uncle Driscoll and his collection of graffiti and "naughty rhymes," memories that unaccountably evoke his "violent prejudices" (which Myra redefines as "real passions") and the cruel codicils of his will (which Myra now condones). Cather's own thoughts of Whitman had evidently been purer and inspirational, eliciting childhood memories of an American past she turned into a creation myth in a novel that appropriated the title of a Whitman poem, *O Pioneers!*. A review of *O Pioneers!* gave Cather pause, not because it was unfavorable, but because it commended her American sentiments. Cather wondered whether she was an authentically American writer or whether, unlike the great American poet, she had somehow betrayed her cultural identity by admiring European literatures and the aristocratic values with which she believed them imbued. Remembering how deeply and how early she had been impressed by a world of privilege and manners she knew from afar and only through fiction, she thought she might have lost the capacity to "see the American scene as it looked to other Americans," as it really was, she seemed to say, to those who saw with an unmediated vision.[53] Her self-questioning raises the question of whether a writer can shed a cultural identity acquired by "association" with a people and place, to use Wilson's words, and then resume it, as Cather believed she had when she wrote her "second first novel," as she called *O Pioneers!*. In her first novel, *Alexander's Bridge,* she had tried to exorcise the influence of European writers by turning to Henry James as an American influence, though James himself lived as an expatriate because he considered America inhospitable to the artist. Obviously, Cather found herself as muddled as Wilson when she tried to sort out her identity as a writer committed to an art that transcended time and place and as an American whose affections and experience were rooted (to use Wilson's word again) in her native land. Cather's strongest and most admired characters identify themselves with a land they nurture throughout their lives and enrich through their deaths, as the soaring conclusion to *O Pioneers!* prophetically proclaims. Myra Henshawe, however, is an unrooted character who moves from place to place, her imagination and values (as her allusions show) shaped by the vision of an aristocratic society mediated through European poetry, plays, and drama. In *My Mortal Enemy,* Cather imagines the American past that Whitman had inspired her to remember in *O Pioneers!* as irretrievably lost and forgotten. It is a legacy from which Myra Henshawe has been disinherited with results as fatefully devastating as those created by Driscoll's will.

As we have seen in the two novels, wills translate personal desire into social co-ercion, allowing the individual to fulfill desires invested in possession, power, and the perpetuation of control. By means of his will, Driscoll maintains control over the disposition of his fortune long after he dies; while by remaining will-less, Mr. Platt tries, impossibly of course, to prevent any disposition, as though he could keep what he possesses forever. Since the law has given individuals the right to possess and in perpetuity pass on accumulated capital, legal wills in the novels (as in American and Canadian society) bear a double imprint as personal desire and social power that parallels their duality as instruments for social justice and for perpetuating economic inequality. In their double inscriptions, legal wills have inherent duplicities that coalesce so tightly with the novels' duplicitous motifs that they provide the "pleasing suitability" between life and art which, as I pointed out, Wilson's lawyer defined as a kind of "perfection" (p. 99).

Legal wills are, of course, the mainstay of murder mysteries, in which love and money – or love for money – frequently motivate crime. They are also integral to historical narratives that trace the fortunes of royal dynasties, financial empires, or ordinary families; and they are indispensable devices of plot within all literary genres. Inheritance and disinheritance figure crucially in every form of literature as expressions of love, hatred, revenge, helplessness, power, oppression, generosity – of timeless human emotions and desires. *My Mortal Enemy* makes intertextual claims to *King Lear* by alluding to its disinherited and deprived characters; such characters, as well as those enriched by inheritance, inhabit the novels of countless writers, among them – to leap over centuries and continents – Jane Austen, Charles Dickens, George Eliot, Henry James, Edith Wharton, and Ernest Hemingway, to name a mere few.[54] Ethel Wilson, as one might expect, made wills and disinheritance comic and inconsequential. In *The Innocent Traveller,* an enraged father soon reconciles himself to his daughter's elopement and reinstates his disinherited heir in his will; and an elderly widow comically refuses an unexpected proposal because marriage would entail the bother of amending her will.[55] Cather's fiction abounds in wills and, necessarily, in dying men who bequeath bountiful wealth upon their heirs: a farm in *O Pioneers!,* life-insurance in *A Song of the Lark,* money for a church in *Death Comes for the Archbishop,* an invaluable invention in *The Professor's House,* and a homestead in *Sapphira and the Slave Girl.* In *My Ántonia,* Cather produces her most bizarre and horrifically comic variation on legal wills with a reciprocal will that induces a man to kill his wife and, after calling neighbors to witness that he has survived to inherit her money, to kill himself.[56]

In both *My Mortal Enemy* and *Love and Salt Water,* wills provide clues, I believe, to the novel's mysteries, to meanings they seek to hide. Wills are meant to be read, and reading these texts as mediated through wills which are at once socially inscribed and personal reveals how money generates a thematic need for moral validation. Since neither text can realistically deny a need for money, both seek ways to disguise a drive that, stripped of its moral veneering, might be called greed, pride, or avarice. And, indeed, the texts call their characters greedy, proud, and avaricious; characters call themselves greedy and proud; and money appears to make the world go round. In acknowledging a profoundly materialistic bias within society, neither text is anomalous in the writer's canon. On the contrary, both make visible, through their stark minimalist form, economic motifs intrinsic to both writers' work and to the novel as a genre linked historically to the rise of bourgeois society. The texts are particularly ingenious, however, in their strategies for hiding what they know they have shown. *My Mortal Enemy* knows that money is hidden away in its trunk and a washerwoman in its aristocratic heroine. *Love and Salt Water* knows that its freighter's lower deck hides its crewmen from the passengers above (p. 35); that a hotel hides its cooks so that guests will believe "nobody works" (p. 139); that a working-class family will hide a brain-damaged child so that his wealthy mother can forget his existence (pp. 120 – 4). *My Mortal Enemy* knows that it is harder for a rich man to enter heaven than for a camel to pass through the eye of a needle, but it represses this knowledge when it apotheosizes willful John Driscoll. *Love and Salt Water* knows that avaricious Mr. Platt has not been inconsequential.

In pointing out thematic similarities traceable to a cultural of capitalism, I do not mean to minimize differences usually construed as signs of different national and cultural identities. Differences I have mentioned (or discussed in notes) include those between American individualism and a Canadian sense of community, a so-called garrison mentality; between America's (imputed) imperialism and a Canadian sense of secondariness that, in its extreme, has been labeled Canadian victimization; between America's history of revolution and violent conquest and Canada's historical accommodations; between an American conflation of financial success and spiritual grace and a Canadian gospel of sanctification through works; between America's self-importance and Canadian self-irony.[57] Such (arguable) differences can be traced in two directions, from their cultural contexts to the texts, or from the texts to inferred (or presumed) cultural contexts. Combining the directions produces a circular logic in which the text leads to culture, and culture leads to the text. The logic is self-validating, while the validity – or truth – of generalizations received or inferred about American and Canadian cultural identity becomes suspended as an issue, though postmodern cultural theories moot the issue by defining the concept of culture as an artifact of writing.

If a comparative literary critique will not yield truths about cultural identity, it will produce recognition. The characters of *My Mortal Enemy* and *Love and Salt Water* are recognizable as traditional figures of Western fiction – as stock characters, caricatures, figures associated with literary genres (the *Bildungsroman*, for instance), or idealizations like the undeterrable lover, (George Gordon and Oswald Henshawe) and the nourishing mother (Susan Cuppy). In *Love and Salt Water*, minor characters can act suddenly to critical effect because their roles are ready-made. Thus, Mr. Abednego appears suddenly – suddenness is intrinsic to his role – as a *deus ex machina* to rescue Ellen and her drowning nephew. In both texts, the characters' factitiousness coexists and competes with their historically realistic features. When Myra Henshawe places herself within a Shakespearean tragedy, or Nellie places Oswald Henshawe within a chivalric mold, they set up a resistance to historical contextualization. However, characters cannot expunge their conditioned cultural values. Myra reaffirms values embodied in her uncle, a man of capitalistic will whose money bought luxuries prized by America's newly rich bourgeoisie, and in *Love and Salt Water*, Ellen Cuppy learns that prayer makes us all one family, while she lives within a nuclear family that is basic to middle-class society. Male characters are made recognizable by their mundane interests – Frank Cuppy's oil interests as a businessman and developer, John Driscoll's financial interests as president of Parthia's bank, and Mr. Platt's sole interest in stocks, bonds, and real estate.

Such commonalities among the characters suggest the theoretical possibility that a culture of capitalism can transcend boundaries by which national identities, and implicitly national differences, are defined. Placed within this transnational context, two novels of different national origins reveal shared cultural values that legitimize their characters' desire for money, profit, and possession, and their translation of desire into action through legal wills. That critics have discussed both *Love and Salt Water* and *My Mortal Enemy* in terms that exclude money, or mention it only to minimize its significance, would support a claim that money is a secret the texts hide and will reveal only at moments of crisis – just as Myra reveals the gold pieces hidden in her trunk only when she faces death. The sign of crisis is obfuscation or, a simpler word I prefer, muddling. When a character's actions or a narrator's comments reveal the power and attraction of money, the text quickly muddles the meaning of money in ingenious ways: it effects a metaphoric exchange between material and spiritual or aesthetic values; and it shifts its attention from a realistically historical setting to an ostensibly timeless background. If this background cannot exclude human avarice and pride, then the texts redefine these irradicable traits by describing avarice as comic and inconsequential, and pride as an intensely "real" and creative passion.

In *My Mortal Enemy*, the reinvestment of passion from secular to spiritual desire seems to me emblematic of a "cold business proposition" the text offers its readers: if, like its characters, they will invest their interest in nonmaterialistic values, they will escape an ugly, mundane reality and enter the empyreal realm of art. This is the escape that Cather believed gave art its transcendent dimension and made it, as romantic artists commonly believed, superior to life. But the proposition made by the text is not as clear-cut as Driscoll's to Myra, which had been calculated to the dollar. For while *My Mortal Enemy* wants to hide the money it has taken out of the trunk, to keep it out of sight, like Myra, it also wants the money to spend; and it implies, or the critic may infer, that money well spent is worth having, and that if Myra had money, she could have had happiness. Perhaps the dream of money is an American dream – or so it has been presented in such quintessentially American novels as Theodore Dreiser's *An American Tragedy* and F. Scott Fitzgerald's *The Great Gatsby,* both published in the same decade as *My Mortal Enemy.* But the equation of money and happiness falls apart in the novels, and happiness remains a mystery hopelessly muddled by money, in effect, by a quantification of desire.

How much money does one need to be happy? And what of needs and desires that cannot be quantified? What of indefinable, supernal yearnings for beauty, romance, and spiritual beatification? In *My Mortal Enemy,* Myra Henshawe needs money for "unearthly" and worldly purposes, which is to say she needs but does not need money. The text supports – but, in good conscience and in good Catholic faith, cannot support – John Driscoll's dictum that "A poor man stinks, and God hates him" (p. 13). To hide its own obsession with money and deny the materialistic values it cannot help underwriting, *My Mortal Enemy* obfuscates the historically realistic aspects of its characters and themes with the romance of art – with allusions to Shakespeare, Heine, Whitman, to great opera, to theater, and to a fairy-tale it recalls only to demolish. To note one final muddle: when Nellie Birdseye passes by Driscoll's great house, she thinks of an unchanging state or a stasis indistinguishable (to me) from death: "I thought of the place as being under a spell, like the Sleeping Beauty's palace; it had been in a trance, or lain in its flowers like a beautiful corpse, ever since that winter night when Love went out of the gates and gave the dare to Fate" (p. 15). If what remains after the departure of Love is a *corpse,* then should not the legacy of Myra Henshawe's story be an affirmation of Life? Love takes Life with it and leaves death behind as a corpse-like palace, but for its own mysterious reasons, *My Mortal Enemy* refuses to affirm romantic love and ends with a chilled heart and intimations of mortality.[58]

That *Love and Salt Water* ends with love and marriage rather than death commits the text to contingency. Death seemed imminent and unavoidable in Active Pass as turbulent tides engulfed Ellen and her terrified nephew, thrown from their capsized rowboat and thrashing blindly in swirling waters. Their rescue, a matter of outlandish chance, equivocates the relevancy of human actions, showing them producing terrible consequences which they can, also, prevent. This pattern of denying and asserting human agency, or asserting and then denying, weaves together disparate views of life which should, logically, cancel each other rather than intermesh. The pattern obfuscates, rather than complicates, the novel's thematic meanings, producing a dizzying oscillation between a view of the capitalistic will that makes its actions inconsequential and a view of life's uncertainties that makes inconsequential actions crucial; between belief in the power of vagarious forces to shape human affairs and belief in the power of human community to obviate the effects of chance. The uncertainties within a pattern of qualification, amendment, exception, and equivocation allow Wilson latitude to affirm an equalitarian gospel of good works which seems to denies hierarchy (implicit in the Catholicism of *My Mortal Enemy*), while she describes a hierarchical class structure that privileges her characters with money and power.[59] Mr. Platt may seem a comically aberrant character within this hierarchy, but in his asocial isolation and his complete socialization (to capitalistic values), he epitomizes the muddled state of being in which all of Wilson's characters are caught. For all embody incompatibilities she has patterned into her text, existing as historically realistic figures and ahistorical stereotypes, as autonomous individuals and interdependent family members, and as socially conditioned beings and pawns of chance and the forces of chaos.

In the novel, these chaotic forces shatter the order of characters' lives and make manifest a cosmic disorder or randomness that disarranges the designs of romance and of providence. The novel's plot moves in a purposeful, linear direction toward a denouement that would complete these designs, while the novel's apparently aimless elliptical form defies design by mimetically suggesting disorder. In a typically muddled ways, a concatenation of discrete events produces both chaos in the characters' lives and calm resolution. Two such concatenations, one begun in Ottawa and another in Montreal, converge to produce the nearly fatal accident in Active Pass. The accident originates almost parenthetically, even comically, with a hitherto unknown Mr. Prendergast, whose "secretary had to telephone the doctor that he was ill, and then telephone Mrs. Prendergast, and the doctor . . . made arrangements at the hospital, and the lives of George Gordon in Montreal and Miss Cuppy in Vancouver were affected, perhaps temporarily, or perhaps permanently and fatally" (p. 117). This disruption of Ellen's plans coincides with a plan that her brother-in-law, Morgan Peake, pursues for political purposes (purposes that turn out unachievable). Chance, coincident, accident, and unnecessary arrangements all seem to signify a lack of purposeful design, and yet an order emerges as love prevails and characters tested by adversity draw closer to each other.

Set in abstract and cosmic terms, the order emergent in *Love and Salt Water* resembles an order defined by contemporary chaos theory.[60] To suggest that contemporary chaos theory may provide a new and illuminating context for a revisionary reading of the text is simply to recognize that critical practice relies upon a disparity between past and present: new ideas formulated in the present lead to new interpretations of works of the past. Contextualized within a new theoretical framework, *Love and Salt Water* discloses a view of life that allows us to shift from the novel's religious perspective to one that is putatively scientific.

I am less interested in the critical value of either perspective than in the volatility of critical practice as it accommodates to new theories, linguistic, cultural, or scientific. In *Love and Salt Water,* an implicit desire to discern an order within the disarray and destruction of human arrangements is susceptible to many interpretations, some propounded by the quizzically omniscient narrator. By suggesting that an interpretation could be based upon contemporary chaos theory, I mean to say that literary texts can, and should, call to question the hermeneutical value of the critical contexts in they have been placed. Wilson herself recurrently questioned the relevance of "Canadianism" to literary judgments. Like Cather, she wanted her novels judged by abstract criteria of excellence she believed to be inscribed in literature that had transcended the boundaries of time and place. Wilson considered her view self-validating, but her critic may think it requires explanation, which is to say, it requires a context. I have noted that a sense of secondariness, commonly attributed to Canadians, might provide a national cultural context for Wilson's ambivalence toward the label of "Canadian" writer, though I offer another context – the culture of capitalism – for her obfuscation of materialistic values she considered in conflict with her moral aspirations. Wilson herself evoked the context of a timeless art in which, like Cather, she sought escape from the vexing questions raised by immediate social realities.

By placing themselves – as they had placed their characters – within ahistorical traditions, Cather and Wilson sought to separate their identity as artists from a personal identity shaped by particular biographical and cultural influences. Both writers sought to keep this identity private, but their biographers made it public and an inextricable part of their art. While a writer's life seems a sensible context for interpreting her work, I would caution that a biographical approach to literary criticism, especially cross-cultural criticism, presents certain hazards. As written, biography itself is a literary artifact and, as such, subject to the skepticism with which many critics approach texts generally, seeing them as the expression of historical and ideological interests rather than of truth. Moreover, biographical explanations of a writer's art presuppose the validity of psychological insights based upon derivative knowledge and of conclusions interesting mainly for their ingenuity. One could conclude, for example, that Wilson created memorable mothers because she had never known her own mother, who died when Wilson was a small child (her father died a few years later). Wish fulfillment might explain why Wilson wrote movingly about mothers and family life though she was an orphan (that is, because she was an orphan), but was Cather – who came from a large and intact family – also fulfilling a psychologically driven wish in acceding to a literary predilection for orphans and motherless children?[61] We have been told that Cather's mother exerted a strong and not entirely welcome influence which Cather may have been rejecting by making Myra motherless and Nellie susceptible to Myra, said to resemble Cather's mother in her autocratic willfulness. Cather's most famous maternal figure, Ántonia Shimerda, transcended realistically hard circumstances by becoming a mythical earth mother or creation goddess, while realistic mothers accepted a servitude that Cather's art made shining and beautiful in old Mrs. Harris (whose lovely daughter, however, a mother of many beautiful children, cried silently over yet another pregnancy, and whose granddaughter, and autobiographical figure, plotted a path of escape from home). To interpret a literary text's twists and turns within a biographical context requires much critical twisting and turning and, in the end, raises as many arguable questions as it may resolve.[62]

To Ethel Wilson and to Willa Cather, their personal lives and their cultural identities – whether defined by their national origin, social class, race, or gender, or settings – seemed irrelevant to their art as an expression of universal human values.[63] To judge the literary "excellence or non-excellence," to use Wilson's phrase, of *Love and Salt Water* or *My Mortal Enemy*, what did it matter, and to whom did it matter, that either novel was the creation of a white woman of a socially privileged class, or that the writer was an American or a Canadian by birth or adoption? This is a question the writers asked and wanted to replace with questions of literary excellence compared to which they thought the historically specific aspects of their personal lives ultimately unimportant. What mattered to them were aesthetic standards they considered universalized within the traditions of the literature to which their writing was indebted. Evoking a background of traditions through conventionalized plots and characters and allusions to literature, myth, music, and religion, they sought to emphasize the universal values in *My Mortal Enemy* and *Love and Salt Water*. Historical specificities were necessary to realistic representation but, both agreed, ultimately necessary to escape. Wilson said that writing provided escape from personal anxieties, as well as "sheer delight."[64] Cather claimed that art had always provided escape and valorized the escape it provided by satisfying the heart's desire for an other empyreal realm of being. What did Cather see about her, in the past and in her own times, that made escape from life a constantly recurrent, a perennial, human need? Perhaps she shared the vision of a crippled and embittered character who saw life as defeating, absurd, and unjust. This is the vision Nellie attributes to Myra, whom she imagines saying, "Ah-ha, I have one more piece of evidence, one more, against the hideous injustice God permits in this world!" (p. 55). If the world we live in allows hideous injustice to become a social commonplace, or if it allows the forces of disorder capriciously to disrupt or end a human life, then perhaps it makes a need for escape urgent, particularly when injustice and disorder make themselves clearly visible. I would claim that the moment of clarity is also the occasion of hiding or obfuscating, and that such moments in the two texts produce mysteries that cannot be resolved by a particular interpretation even though it has been resolute in its ideological position and choice of context. As a child in a real mystery story claimed, "It will just remain a mystery for ever and ever and ever." I find this not a discomforting thought for a critic who values questions. This critic might be sympathetic with a character in another mystery story who said, "I can abide a mystery perfectly well. I have learned that one is not very often happier for having found all the answers."[65] A willingness to abide the mysteries of the text serves the self-interest of critical inquiry as an institution that can continue to probe for meaning and pursue clues to its revelation. More important, it opens the reader to continual wonder – to appreciation of the art for which Willa Cather and Ethel Wilson wanted to be remembered and to serious thought about the world their art illuminated and obscured. In this world, we have been well cautioned to note, "the more important something is, the more it is hidden."[66]

Notes

1   The history of the quest for a national literature, indigenous in material and attitudes rather than derived from Western traditions, is long and enduring in Canada and the United States. Both countries were aware that they lacked a language of their own which would immediately identify them as distinct and different from the countries by which they had been discovered (a dubious term to use these days) and colonized. Both had critics and writers who recognized this lack and argued that each country could, nevertheless, produce an indigenous literature, the Americans declaring their literary independence from England, while Canadians struggled with a complex literary heritage derived from England, France, and the United States. Only a few decades ago, the distinguished Canadian critic (and Cather biographer) E. K. Brown still saw the need to espouse a national literature even though "to write in the English language is to incur the competition of the best authors of Britain and the United States" (*Responses and Evaluations: Essays on Canada,* ed. David Staines [Toronto: McClelland & Stewart, New Canadian Library, 1977], p. 7, reprinted from a 1943 publication). The quest for a national literature in both countries was complicated by the geographic lay of the land, its tremendous span and diversity creating a regional topography that, along with immigration patterns, produced diverse and seemingly autonomous cultural entities. While the geography and history of the two countries may have been similar in certain respects, the problems of self-definition differed: the United States could ignore its proximity to Canada or notice it only to advantage, but this proximity impressed upon Canadians a sense of secondariness to which they became either resigned or resistant. "The famous Canadian problem of identity" – to use Northrop Frye's phrase – has long involved a sorting out of differences from the United States, a powerful nation whose influence and incursions have proved irresistible. Studies on Canadian identity often begin with comparisons with the United States. An unpretentious attempt to explain (in an epistolary form reminiscent of Crève-couer's "Letters of an American Farmer") a Canadian sensibility to a neighbor in the United States begins and ends with the difficulties of self-definition: "We really are quite different from you Americans, even though we talk and dress and look alike. We *have* a distinct identity"; "We know we're not the same but we can't express it succinctly." See Pierre Berton, *Why We Act Like Canadians: A personal exploration of our national character* (Toronto: McClelland & Stewart, 1982), p. 14, original emphasis, and p. 104. Beginning with a citation to Berton, an American journalist, Andrew H. Malcolm, makes his own attempt at defining Canadians for Americans in *The Canadians* (New York: Random House, Times Books, 1985). From the many well-known studies of "Canadianism," each pursuing its own theory of Canadian development and informed by its own political ideology, I mention only a few of the works I have found pertinent to issues surrounding

cultural identity: Harold Innes, *The Fur Trade in Canada* (Toronto, University of Toronto Press, 1956), one of several influential studies by Innes; *The Culture of Contemporary Canada,* ed. Julian Park (Ithaca, N.Y.: Cornell University Press, 1957); John Porter, *The Vertical Mosaic: An Analysis of Social Class and Power in Canada* (Toronto: University of Toronto Press, 1965); *Nationalism in Canada by the University League for Social Reform,* ed. Peter Russell (Toronto: McGraw-Hill Ryerson, 1966); *Close the 49th parallel etc: The Americanization of Canada,* ed. Ian Lumsden (Toronto: University of Toronto Press, 1970). *Understanding Canada: A Multidisciplinary Introduction to Canadian Studies,* ed. William Metcalfe (New York: New York University Press, 1982). In *The Canadian Identity* (Madison: University of Wisconsin Press, 1961), W. L. Morton evokes the American Declaration of Independence to summarize what he sees as a fundamental political and cultural difference between the two countries: "not life, liberty, and the pursuit of happiness, but peace, order, and good government are what the national government of Canada guarantees" (p. 111). Perhaps the most ambitious study of Canadian literature is the three-volume edition, *Literary History of Canada: Canadian Literature in English,* ed. Carl F. Klinck, general editor, and Alfred G. Bailey, Claude Bissell, Roy Daniells, Northrop Frye, and Desmond Pacey (Toronto: University of Toronto Press, 1965). Northrop Frye has written an influential "Conclusion" to the history, which is highly pertinent to this essay (II, pp. 333–61). For a recent rereading of this conclusion, which categorizes it as "characteristically mythopoeic, formal, centralist, Protestant, male-centered, and overwhelmingly English," see Robert Lecker, " 'A Quest for the Peaceable Kingdom': The Narrative in Northrop Frye's Conclusion to the *Literary History of Canada,*" *PMLA* 108:2 (March 1993): pp. 283–93. The essay, written by a well-known critic of Canadian literature, suggests that Frye's views, crucial to the canonization of English Canadian literature, are still important enough to be brought to a sober reckoning. Frye's two collections of essays are also (and still) important to an understanding of the conceptualization of a Canadian national and literary sensibility: *The Bush Garden: Essays on the Canadian Imagination* (Toronto: House of Anansi, 1971); and *Divisions on a Ground* (Toronto: House of Anansi Press, 1982).

Collections of essays on Canadian literature are too numerous to cite here, though I note an influential survey by Margaret Atwood: *Survival: A Thematic Guide to Canadian Literature* (Toronto: House of Anansi Press, 1972). Implicitly, almost all studies of Canadian literature respond to a question raised in the title of a brief essay published in 1929: "Is There a Canadian Literature?" (Douglas Bush, *Commonweal* 11 [Nov. 6, 1929]: pp. 12–14). As an example of how this question persists, even when not explicitly stated, I note an important Canadian critic's fairly recent discussion of Ethel Wilson, which begins by saying that her "concerns" do not make . . . [her] work distinctively 'Canadian' "; goes on to claim that "a demand" for Canadian identity "is irrelevant in any estimate of [Wilson's] literary worth," because her "sensitivity and her stylistic restraint have made her one of Canada's most accomplished novelists, and that is enough" (p. 69); and ends up concluding that though Wilson's vision of life "is not distinctively Canadian," it evidences its national identity by a characteristic Canadian irony" (p. 82). See William N. New, "The 'Genius' of Place and Time: The Fiction of Ethel Wilson," in *Articulating West: Essays on Purpose and Form in Modern Canadian Literature* (Toronto: New Press, 1972; the essay was published originally in 1968 in the *Journal of Canadian Studies*), pp. 68–82.

I assume that I do not need to recapitulate here documentation on the quest for and emergence of an American identity, which traces back to the early writings of Crèvecoeur and de Tocqueville and through such exponents of a national literature as Emerson and Whitman. Strictly speaking, *American* (as used to identify Cather as an American writer) should be an inclusive term, referring to inhabitants of North and South America. But to use the term strictly – in deference to all who might properly claim it – would be contrary to ordinary speech, an affectation more intrusive than helpful. For Canadians, the term *American* conjures so many connotations that another word would entail a loss of profoundly entrenched historical and cultural meanings.

2   I use native loosely, to mean the country and region with which the writer and her work are generally identified, the midwest, and specifically the Nebraska prairies, with Cather, though she was born in Virginia, lived in New York City for forty years of her life, and wrote about the southwest and, not insignificantly, about Quebec. Wilson was born in South Africa, lived for several years in England, and was brought as a child to British Columbia. Both writers experienced deracination in their childhood, Cather being taken from Virginia to Nebraska, and Wilson from England to Vancouver, and both wrote movingly about this experience, Cather in *My Ántonia,* and Wilson in *The Innocent Traveller.*

3   One could explicate this murkiness in Marxist terms as a function of ideology within a society characterized by "hegemonic class domination." For a succinct summary of Marx's definition of ideology, and the qualifications to it made by Antonio Gramsci, see Nicos Poulantzas, *Political Power and Social Classes,* tr. Timothy O'Hagan (London: Verso, 1982, published originally in 1968 as *Pouvoir politique et classes sociales),* pp. 206–10. Poulantzas's restatement of a Marxist conception of ideology, as well as his discussion of "bourgeois political ideology" (pp. 210–21), is particularly pertinent to the argument of this essay. Distinguishing between *"true knowledge"* and the *"necessarily false,"* Poulantzas describes how the "social whole" remains *"opaque"* to its agents (p. 207, original emphasis)–that is, to people acting within their society who, I am suggesting, adumbrate the characters acting within the social world of the two novels. According to Marxist theory, Poulantzas points out, "ideology has the precise function of hiding the real contradictions [within a hegemonic class society] and of *reconstituting* on an imaginary level a relatively coherent discourse which serves as the horizon of agents' experience . . . moulding their representations of their real relations" (p. 207, original emphasis). In different terms, I am describing an opacity (murkiness) that emerges from contradictions between "real relations" and imaginary reconstitutions through re-presentations. Poulantzas's discussion of ideology moves on to include other terms, some emphasized, which are central to this essay: symbolization, mystification, hidden.

    For a view that indicts the mystifying uses of morality to "further the order of capital"– that is, to keep "capitalist domination" entrenched – see Jean Baudrillard, *Simulations,* tr. Paul Foss, Paul Patton, and Philip Beitchman (New York: Semiotext(e), 1983). Baudrillard writes categorically that "capital, which is immoral and unscrupulous, can only function behind a moral superstructure, and whoever regenerates this public morality (by indignation, denunciation, etc. [or by art?]) spontaneously furthers the order of capital" (p. 27). Hiding, concealing, or "dissimulating" is an invidious act, Baudrillard argues, because it serves to regenerate a social system he sees as cruel, ferocious, and immoral (pp. 28–9). I am not suggesting that the literary critic read Cather and Wilson in the light of Baudrillard's devastating views of modern society and its dissimulations (an approach the writers would have found appalling). But readings that extol a writer for bypassing, and so effectively hiding, aspects of social life that impinge themselves upon our consciousness may be challenged by theories of social dissimulation. For example, Phyllis Rose praises

Cather as a "modernist" writer who "sought to bypass consciousness and the circumstantial details with which it concerns itself and to produce an art that appealed to the most elemental layers of our minds" ("Modernism: The Case of Willa Cather" in *Modernism Reconsidered*, ed. Robert Kiely [Cambridge, Mass.: Harvard University Press, 1983), pp. 123–45). Does this mean that Cather ignored what was going on in the world about her, a world caught up in a great depression, a great war, and another great war? An elemental writer might transcend her times and circumstances, but what of a socially oblivious or indifferent writer? She is a figure that Rose seems to me to be evoking by her praise. As noted below, critics are now finding Cather cognizant of social issues of her times, uncovering these issues within and underlying her "elemental" art.

4   See John Berger, *Ways of Seeing* (London: British Broadcasting Corporation and Penguin Books, 1972) for a simple and pertinent definition of mystification: "Mystification is the process of explaining away what might otherwise be evident" (pp. 15–16).

5   To claim that obfuscation enlightens is to disagree with critics who find lack of clarity an aesthetic defect that makes *My Mortal Enemy* enigmatic and *Love and Salt Water* directionless. These defects are sometimes traced to the elliptical form of the novels which, critics complain, leaves them inchoate. Such criticism is not groundless. Even for a writer who said she wanted the novel stripped of its "furniture," Cather creates in *My Mortal Enemy* a strikingly bare and barren work, denied the glorious American landscapes that distinguish her fiction and devoid of its characteristically refulgent memories of childhood and a country's heroic past. (See "The Novel Démeublé," in *Not under Forty* (Lincoln: University of Nebraska Press, 1988, published originally in 1922), pp. 43–51. *Love and Salt Water* creates a curious sense of placelessness, though it recreates the panoramic beauty of British Columbia for which Wilson's fiction is famous. Even as the text lingers lovingly over the places it names – Burrard Inlet, Stanley Park, the Fraser Valley, the Similkameen River, Galiano Island – the fixity of place seems to dissolve as characters feel themselves drifting, literally, because they are at sea much of the time, and socially, because of a besetting sense of placelessness. Placelessness suggests an abstraction from circumstance which Wilson may have intended to reveal her characters' universal qualities but which may, at the same time, point to feelings of marginality as characters sense themselves displaced from centers of power, feelings usually traced to Canada's geographical closeness to and economic distance from the United States. (See notes 34 and 40.)

Since marginality or secondariness has been considered a national Canadian trait, an inferential leap from textual effects to cultural context may be warranted, though it raises methodological questions with which this essay concludes. Nevertheless, we know that inference is common to literary and cultural criticism, and to the criticism of these two particular novels. Critics have found clues to their meaning in specific details or actions, inferred a thematic significance from these clues, extended this significance to a broad literary and cultural context, and almost inevitably, stirred other critics to controvert their conclusions. For unlike clues in real mysteries, the clues seen to lurk in the novels preclude consensus over their meanings, and arguments have ensued even over such seemingly simple matters as the meaning of Cather's title. Cather herself was called upon to tell who the novel's *mortal enemy* was, but her categorical identification merely intensified critical disagreement. Among others, Cather's biographer, James Woodress, cites a 1926 letter written by Cather to her friend George Seibel in which she says that Oswald Henshawe was the mortal enemy to whom Myra referred (*Willa Cather: A Literary Life*

[Lincoln: University of Nebraska Press, 1987], p. 384). Another (and, as I have noted elsewhere, much less authoritative) biographer, Phyllis C. Robinson, quotes an excerpt from
the letter in which Cather confirms Seibel's view that the "enemy" was Oswald; "Of
course you are quite right," Cather wrote, "I can't see much in this particular story unless you get the point of it. There is not much to it *but* the point" (*Willa: The Life of Willa
Cather* [New York: Doubleday, 1983], p. 244, original emphasis). However, the point
must have been considerably less sharp than Cather believed, and arguments over the
identity abound, the various views too numerous to recapitulate here.

One of these many views, given from a cross-cultural perspective, is that of Zhongxiu
He, who begins by stating that "to a reader like myself from a socialist political and economic system, *My Mortal Enemy* is most strikingly a drama of capitalist discord, and the
enemy that Myra Henshawe identifies as destroying her life is poverty" ("Poverty as
Myra's Mortal Enemy," *Willa Cather Pioneer Memorial Newsletter* XXXV, no. 3, [Fall,
1991]: p. 29). Zhongxiu He disagrees with another Chinese critic who sees Myra's "greed
for money . . . offset by her reckless generosity to her friends" and "the negative force"
of money becoming "a positive one because it provides the means for attaining spiritual
fulfillment" (Jean Tsien, "The Fascinating Complexity of *My Mortal Enemy*," *Willa Cather
Pioneer Memorial Newsletter* XXX, no. 3 [Summer 1986]: p. 24). These highly selected and
abbreviated references may suggest why critics consider *My Mortal Enemy* elusive and
why one might claim that in its various equations and capitalist discords, to use Zhongxiu
He's phrase, it is muddled.

Critics disagree also about *Love and Salt Water*, unable to decide whether it is Wilson's
most meager or most philosophical novel. Wilson herself referred to *Love and Salt Water*
as a "small book . . . a temperate affair like the water and climate of our shores" ("Somewhere Near the Truth," a library talk given by Wilson in 1957, printed in David Stouck,
ed., *Ethel Wilson: Stories, Essays, and Letters* [Vancouver: University of British Columbia
Press, 1987], p. 89). In his "pioneer study," as he rightly calls it, Desmond Pacey designates *Love and Salt Water* as "probably the least rewarding of Mrs. Wilson's novels," weak
in its characterization of the heroine and "relatively loose" and unintegrated in its structure, but nonetheless characterized by "unusual subtlety and delicacy" (*Ethel Wilson*
[New York: Twayne, 1967], pp. 159 and 173). In the "Afterword" to the recent New
Canadian Library edition of *Love and Salt Water*, cited below, Anne Marriott calls it "the
slightest of Wilson's novels," but finds its "slightness of plot . . . a special joy" because the
reader "is left free to revel in Wilson's elegant writing style" (p. 177). Casting more fa-
vorable light upon the novel, David Stouck classified it as "a 'romance' in the sense of
Shakespeare's last plays where characters are tested through a series of misfortunes and
misunderstandings before being fully integrated into society" ("Ethel Wilson's Novels,"
Canadian Literature 74 [Autumn 1977]: p. 85). Also with approval, P. M. Hinchcliffe described the novel as Wilson's "most ambitious attempt to combine the world of private
memory with the collective sense of British Columbia's past and to link them to a vision
of the future which is both personal and social. Much more than the other novels, *Love
and Salt Water* abounds in historical reminiscences and topographical vistas, and the
sweeping journeys of all the major characters from west to east and back again are surely
meant to provide a rhythm that will the unify the reader's perceptions" (" 'To Keep the
Memory of So Worthy a Friend': Ethel Wilson as an Elegist," *Journal of Canadian Fiction*
2, no. 2 [1973]: p. 66). Paul Comeau praised *Love and Salt Water* as "Wilson's most philosophical and, coincidentally, her most forgiving novel," fully realizing a "moral dimen-

sion sought after in *Swamp Angel*" ("Ethel Wilson's Characters," *Studies in Canadian Literature* 6 (1981): pp. 35–6).

6 *My Mortal Enemy* (New York: Random House, Vintage, 1954, published originally in 1926), p. 16. All subsequent references to the text are to this edition.

7 This is a standard definition of money restated in a well-known study of contemporary capitalism. See the "Glossary" to Ernest Mandel, *Late Capitalism*, tr. Joris De Bres (London: Atlantic Highlands, Humanities Press, 1975, first published in 1972 as *Der Spätkapitalismus*), p. 594. Mandel is reiterating Karl Marx's view of money as expressed in *Capital*: "The first chief function of money is to supply commodities with the material for the expression of their values, or to represent their values as magnitudes of the same denomination, qualitatively equal, and quantitatively comparable. It thus serves as a *universal measure of value*" (*Capital: A Critical Analysis of Capitalist Production*, ed. Frederick Engels, tr. Samuel Moore and Edward Aveling [Moscow: Foreign Languages Publishing House, 1958, originally published as the 1887 English edition], I, p. 94, original emphasis). In defining money as a measure of value (as distinct from money as a standard of price), Marx traces value itself back to a single original source: "Money as a measure of value, is the phenomenal form . . . assumed by that measure of value which is immanent in commodities, labour-time" (p. 94). As we know, Marx believed that human labor produced not only value, but also surplus value, the basis for a capitalistic system predicated upon the making of profit. In his study of late capitalism, Mandel emphasizes the profit motive, or what I have called here the capitalistic will, as he distinguishes between "simple commodity production and capitalistic commodity production" (p. 96): "Under capitalist production it is not merely a matter of obtaining an equal mass of value in another form – be it that of money or some other commodity . . . but it is rather a matter of realizing as *much surplus-value, or profit*, on capital advanced for production, as any other capital of the same magnitude" (p. 97, original emphasis). In setting out to describe "what capitalism has actually been like in practice," Immanuel Wallerstein defines "historical capitalism" as a "social system" in which "the goal of the holder of capital [is] the accumulation of still more capital" (*Historical Capitalism* [London: Verso], pp. 13–14). Reflecting upon this goal, Wallerstein describes himself face to face with the "patently absurd" aspects of capitalism: "One accumulates capital in order to accumulate more capital. . . . The more I have reflected upon it, the more absurd it has seemed to me" (p. 40). In Wilson's *Love and Salt Water*, the absurdity of capitalistic accumulation becomes manifest in Mr. Platt, discussed later on as a reification of the capitalistic will. On the other hand, if contextualized within a system of circulation and exchange, Mr. Platt's actions make sense both when he buys only in order to sell and when, as a "miser," he hoards. See for instance Marx, *Capital*, II, pp. 492–3 and passim.

8 Among the many discussions of the literary implications for Canada as a border state, I cite two collections as examples of traditional literary cross-cultural criticism: *Crossing Frontiers: Papers in American and Western Literature*, ed. Dick Harrison (Edmonton: University of Alberta Press, 1979); and a special edition of *Essays on Canadian Writing*, entitled "Canadian-American Literary Relations," 22 (Summer 1991).

9 To enter into arguments over the precise definition of capitalism would take me far beyond the scope of this essay. I am concerned with a fundamental aspect of modern capitalism on which there is general consensus: that it is impelled by a profit motive – by a will to make and accumulate capital and to keep possession and control of its accumulation. For a succinct discussion of the primacy of the profit motive and its economic

and political implications, see Robert L. Heilbroner, *The Nature and Logic of Capitalism* (New York: W. W. Norton, 1985). Pursuing the political consequences of capitalism as an economic system, Heilbroner declares that "the winning of profit . . . represents the successful exercise of a basically political relationship. Profit is the life blood of capitalism, not merely because it is the means by which individual capitals obtain their wherewithal for expansion but because it is the manner in which the relationship of domination is evidenced" (p. 76). Of the countless studies on capitalism, one particularly pertinent to this essay is Albert O. Hirschman, *The Passions and the Interests: Political Arguments for Capitalism before Its Triumph* (Princeton, N.J.: Princeton University Press, 1977). Hirschman traces within the history of ideas a translation (or sublimation or, I would say, mystification) of unruly human passions – evinced in personal desires for power and profit – into "virtues" or dispassionate interests of social value. I discuss later on how Cather tries to make a similar translation in *My Mortal Enemy*. Hirschman's historical perspective leads him to discuss avarice, a subject pertinent to my critique of *Love and Salt Water*. Wilson's novel arrives at the same discovery with which *The Passions and the Interests* concludes: that "human actions and social decisions tend to have consequences that were entirely unintended" and that intended effects often "fail to materialize" (p. 131, original emphasis). Writing about an early period of American capitalism (roughly, the time in which *My Mortal Enemy* is set), Martin Sklar defines capitalism in comprehensive terms "as a system of social relations expressed in characteristic class structures, modes of consciousness, patterns of authority, and relations of power" (*The Corporate Reconstruction of American Capitalism, 1890–1916: The Market, the Law, and Politics* [Cambridge: Cambridge University Press, 1988], p. 6). Wilson and Cather may see art as separate from this system, but their two novels, I am arguing, are faithful to its fundamental configuration of class, consciousness, authority, and power, all among many and more elements Sklar identifies with capitalism, whether viewed as a mode of production, property, business – or in any way at all. (I realize that I am not citing as thoroughly as one could – and undoubtedly should – the monumental works of Karl Marx and Friedrich Engels, figures crucial, of course, to any understanding of capitalism; nor I am citing such revisionary Marxists as T. W. Adorno, Louis Althusser, Georg Lukács, Antonia Gramsci, and others who come quickly to mind; or Max Weber, R. H. Tawney; or Herbert Marcuse or Walter Benjamin; and among contemporaries, Eric Hobsbawm, Raymond Williams, Terry Eagleton, and Fredric Jameson – the list could go on and, obviously, for the interests of this essay has to be drastically elided.) Two recent studies which relate capitalism to American literature in important and illuminating ways are Richard Godden, *Fictions of Capital: The American Novel from James to Mailer* (Cambridge: Cambridge University Press, 1990) and "Mark Seltzer, "Physical Capital: The American and the Realistic Body" in *New Essays on The American*, ed. Martha Banta (Cambridge: Cambridge University Press, 1987), pp. 131–67.

10   Cather indicates that Driscoll had a legal ground on which to disinherit Myra because "he had never adopted her" (p. 13). Obviously Cather knew that because "adoption is only permitted by virtue of legislation, no rights of inheritance exist unless there have been proceedings in strict compliance with the statutory provisions." Myra might have supported a legal claim to an inheritance if she could have shown that Driscoll had promised to adopt her, since "some courts . . . imply from a promise to adopt, that there is also an enforceable promise that the child should inherit, though there was a failure to carry out a legal adoption." On this matter, see Thomas E. Atkinson, *Handbook of Law of*

Wills and Administration of Descendents' Estates including Principles of Intestate Succession (St. Paul: West, 1937), pp. 69–70.

11   *Love and Salt Water* (Toronto: McClelland & Stewart, 1990, published originally in 1956), p. 101. All subsequent references to the text are to this edition.

12   Mr. Platt refers to his childless and chickless state four times on one page (p. 90). Ellen's retort is pointed and humorous: "If you really want chickens I'll get you some. If you want young children the Children's Aid needs funds" (p. 90). A man without chick or child but with a private fortune, Mr. Platt could have been a public benefactor in Saskatoon, as Driscoll was in Parthia. According to a historian writing about Saskatchewan only a few years before Wilson published *Love and Salt Water*, the province would have needed Mr. Platt's money because it lacked " 'millionaires living or dead' to endow places of learning or institutions of culture," depending upon "taxpayers" to support its "expanding university." See J. F. C. Wright, *Saskatchewan: The History of a Province* (Toronto: McClelland & Stewart, 1955), p. 278.

13   Even this apparently incidental gesture toward the beautification of a business office can be said to have cultural implications. See, for example, the discussion of "Art owned by and in the service of capital" in Wolfgang Fritz Haug, *Critique of Commodity Aesthetics: Appearance, Sexuality and Advertising in Capitalist Society* (Minneapolis: University of Minnesota Press, 1986, tr. Robert Bock, published originally in 1983 as Kritik der Warenästhetik), pp. 122–31. Haug argues that "capital, with art at its disposal . . . adopts the lofty illusion that it is the highest creation of the human spirit, and not profit, which is its determining aim. Thus everything good, noble, beautiful and great, *seems* to speak for capital" (p. 129). I emphasize *seems* to point to the duplicity and mystification that Haug attributes to a capitalistic appropriation of art for the marketplace.

14   I discuss Wilson's use of evasive strategies in The Hidden Mines, to which The Capitalistic Will is a complementary piece.

15   David Stouck notes that Mr. Platt "depersonalizes Ellen by calling her 'Miss Um.' " Stouck implies that Mr. Platt is not an entirely inconsequential character, since "he represents the furthest point reached by Ellen in her withdrawal from human concourse" ("Ethel Wilson's Novels," p. 86).

16   I might note here that the difference in the way Ellen spends her time in Saskatoon and Nellie spends time in New York connotes a class difference, if – as Bourdieu claims – taste reflects class. Refuting an assumption that taste is "a gift of nature," Bourdieu sees taste and consumption practices as products of a process of cultural acquisition, of learning cultural codes; the aesthetically sensitive " 'eye' is a product of history reproduced by education" (pp. 2–3). See Pierre Bourdieu, *Distinction: A Social Critique of the Judgement of Taste,* tr. Richard Nice (Cambridge, Mass.: Harvard University Press, 1984, published originally in 1979 as *La Distinction: Critique sociale du judgment*). While Ellen plays badminton and avoids books, Nellie goes to the theater, listens to fine music and quotations from great literature, visits a poet, and spends time with artists, all the while being educated to the values of an aristocratic leisured class that, putatively, Myra represents.

17   See, for example, the divagation on Captain George Vancouver (pp. 143–4) and many interspersed geographic and horticultural descriptions, some of which, like that of the arbutus tree (p. 155) or that of the continent's span (pp. 87–9), seem gratuitous. But Wilson's omniscient narrator legitimizes these descriptive passages by claiming that "the formidable power of geography determines the character and performance of a people; it invokes understanding or prejudice; it makes peace or war: (p. 89). Like her character

Aunt Maury, Wilson romanticized a past in which young Captain George Vancouver had given place-names to the distinctive locales of the city that was named after him. She guides the reader through the city in a fond tribute to its eponymous "great navigator" in "A Monologue to a Stranger," *Bulletin* of the Community Arts Council of Vancouver Summer 1957: pp. 22–3. (Cather had provided readers with a guided tour of her midwest landscape in a piece she called "Nebraska: The End of the First Cycle," *The Nation* 117:3035 [September 5, 1923], pp. 236–8). In a volume entitled *The Culture of Contemporary Canada,* a Canadian critic provides a rationale for Wilson's seemingly digressive passages on the geography of British Columbia by arguing that "description fits our national character," for "in a new country . . . there is much to describe": "Canadian novels are filled with description" because writers need to "explain" the country to themselves and to their "international" readers. See Roy Daniells, "Literature: Poetry and the Novel" in *The Culture of Contemporary Canada,* ed. Julian Park (Ithaca, N.Y.: Cornell University Press, 1957), p. 26. The volume begins by asking if Canada has "a national culture" – a question that acknowledges the "diversity" of the country, which might mitigate against a national culture; the colonial past, which might make its culture derivative; and "the nearness of the United States," which might undermine its "individuality" (Park, "Preface," p. v). In an essay entitled "Self-Conscious Canadians," Hallvard Dahlie explains passages on Canadian geography in Canadian fiction as the writer's attempt to shake off a "derivative image" and to speak for and celebrate a Canadian identity. See *Canadian Literature: A Quarterly of Criticism and Review* (Autumn 1974): pp. 6–16; the title of this special issue is "Canadians – Conscious or Self-Conscious?." Dahlie finds some of Wilson's descriptions of the geography of British Columbia fulfilling literary purposes in *Swamp Angel,* and others providing "extraliterary" essayistic explanations that draw attention to Canada rather than the characters and the text.

18 I should note that while a stock character is ahistorical, the meaning he assumes when placed within a historical context may be historically determined. According to classic Marxist theory, the mark of a commodity is repression of the history of the human labor invested in its production within a capitalistic system. In writing on "The Fetishism of Commodities and the Secret Thereof," Marx begins by saying, "A commodity appears, at first sight, a very trivial thing, and easily understood" – a description that surely fits inconsequential Mr. Platt. Marx goes on to say, however, that a commodity becomes "a mysterious thing" as "the social character" it assumes as a product of "men's labour" is taken to be "an objective character stamped upon the product of that labour," with the result that "the products of labour become commodities, social things whose qualities are at the same time perceptible and imperceptible, by the senses" (*Capital,* I, pp. 71 and 72). A sign of Mr. Platt's commodification by the text, as well as within it, is the repression of his history as a past in which he has been "stamped" or conditioned by the culture of capitalism to value a continuous process of exchange the purpose of which is profit. Wilson makes Mr. Platt seem a trivial, if idiosyncratic, figure, who appears autonomously and without a past. Nevertheless, he can be understood as the product of a social formation, even though this is an aspect of his being that the text seeks to make "imperceptible."

19 Money and beatitude seem a common combination in American life, but it is not commonly ascribed to Cather's fiction, which critics praise for excising money from the practices of religion and art. However, in an unsentimental and important early critique of Cather, John H. Randall defined "money and brute power" as the prevailing values of *My Mortal Enemy* and declared its (attempted) coalescence of materialistic and religious values "entirely perverse" (p. 239). Randall strips away pretensions to the religious redemption that Myra believes she has discovered in "desire" and to the apotheosis that Nellie believes she sees in Driscoll's ostentatious funeral service: "It seems clear that the book has no religious overtones whatsoever, but is a brute glorification of the power of money" (p. 237). See *The Landscape and the Looking Glass: Willa Cather's Search for Value* (Boston: Houghton Mifflin, 1960), pp. 234–40 and passim. For a contrary view that sees the "iconography" of *My Mortal Enemy* merging the image of Driscoll with that of God, see John J. Murphy, "The Dantean Journey in Cather's *My Mortal Enemy*," *Willa Cather Pioneer Memorial Newsletter*, XXX, no. 3 (Summer 1986): pp. 11–14. Murphy claims that in Myra's "mind and in the novel's iconography, old Driscoll, who withdrew his favor and made her poor, was like God" (p. 11). By separating herself in a single act from Driscoll, his money, and God and the Church, Myra begins a misguided "pagan life" (presumably, her New York life of theater going, parties, and meddling in love affairs). She must find her way back to Christianity and salvation through "a Dantean journey." I wonder whether a depiction of Driscoll as God is reverent or satiric, and whether the novel has succeeded in hoodwinking a sympathetic reader with its obfuscations. I am reminded that Marx called money "the god among commodities," and this equation may wryly justify Murphy's deification of Driscoll (see *Grundrisse: Foundations of the Critique of Political Economy*, tr. Martin Nicolaus [New York: Vintage, 1973, written in the winter of 1857–58 and published in German in 1939 and in 1953], p. 221). Cather linked religion with art and money in *The Professor's House* and in *Death Comes for the Archbishop*, the novels that precede and follow *My Mortal Enemy*. As Cather's Professor says, in a much quoted passage, "Art and religion (they are the same thing, in the end, of course) have given man the only happiness he ever had" (*The Professor's House* [New York: Random House, Vintage, 1953, published originally in 1925], p. 69). Would not Cather's equivocating parenthetical phrase, "in the end," make almost any equation seem tenable?

20 For a discussion of the contemporaneousness and interrelatedness of sins in their various forms, see Henry Fairlie, *The Seven Deadly Sins Today* (Washington, D.C.: New Republic Books, 1978). Fairlie justifies defining pride or "cold egotism" as a cardinal sin, generating other sins, all of them producing, however, the same effect: "lovelessness." "Given that they [the seven deadly sins] are all loveless," he writes, "they are all as serious" (p. 35), a view that would explain why both Driscoll and Mr. Platt lead loveless lives and which would deny that the latter's avariciousness could be merely comic or inconsequential. While Fairlie argues that the individual has a free will to choose virtue or sin, he also defines sin as systemic to a society: "We may be ultimately responsible as individuals, since we could change societies if we wished, but that they are capable of sinning on their own . . . is beyond any question. If we neglect the poor, it is not only because each of us is avaricious, not even only because those who manage the economy may be particularly avaricious, but because the economic system is founded on Avarice" (p. 25). Since he is writing about sin "today" and, almost ironically, publishing his book in Washington, D.C., one may assume he means by "the economic system" modern American capitalism.

Also writing about sin in the context of contemporary American society, Stanford M. Lyman agrees that central to the seven deadly sins "is their alienating quality. The inhumanity of humanity is located in the sins' capacity to separate man and woman from their kind, and ultimately from themselves" (viii). Lyman seeks to shape a new "rhetoric" of social criticism that "would regard culture, thought, and acts as such . . . and see the precise relationship between values and acts" (viii) – a cultural and sociological rhetoric of sin. See *The Seven Deadly Sins: Society and Evil* (New York: St. Martin's Press, 1978). Marx had already given a cultural context for greed by tracing its etiology to "a definite social development, not *natural,* as opposed to *historical*": "Greed as such . . . is possible only when general wealth . . . has become individualized in a particular thing, i.e., as soon as money is posited in its third quality. Money is therefore not only the object but also the fountainhead of greed" (*Grundrisse,* p. 222 ff., original emphasis).

21   Among such characters, I include romantic figures like Jim Burden (explicitly called a romantic in *My Ántonia*), Niel Herbert (who would have preferred Marian Forrester dead in *A Lost Lady* rather than growing old and corruptible), Claude Wheeler (who never has a chance to grow old in *One of Ours*), and Lucy Gayheart (who dies before she can question her belief in Romance). Bernice Slote, to whom all Cather critics must be indebted, had early established the Romantic matrix of Cather's sensibility and art. See *The Kingdom of Art: Willa Cather's First Principles and Critical Statements, 1893–1896,* ed. Bernice Slote (Lincoln: University of Nebraska Press, 1966). For a recent important study, see Susan Rosowski, *The Voyage Perilous: Willa Cather's Romanticism* (Lincoln: University of Nebraska Press, 1986). For a discussion of Cather's attempt to separate romantic love from Romanticism, see my essay "Movement and Melody: the Disembodiment of Lucy Gayheart," in *Women Writing in America,* pp. 117–44.

22   As we shall see, *Love and Salt Water* shows human life destabilized by forces to which money is irrelevant, like the sea's treacherous tides or a careful person's inexplicable moment of carelessness. Such uncontrollable forces create havoc in Wilson's novel, while economic forces, also shown, are reduced to inconsequentiality. In *Swamp Angel,* an acclaimed Wilson novel, an American millionaire vacationing at the lakeside lodge in British Columbia expresses an almost comic disbelief that a man of his money and power has almost been "conquered" – drowned – by the forces of nature: "that he, R. E. Cunningham, should have been all but conquered, obliterated, by wind, rain and waves on a small lake" (*Swamp Angel* [Toronto: McClelland & Stewart, *1954*], p. 136). Wilson makes sure that the reader knows this capitalist millionaire is an American, as though to imply that only an American would believe himself beyond the forces of nature and contingency. To add to this American's "humiliation," Wilson has him rescued from certain drowning by her heroine, a Canadian woman working at the lodge.

23   Nellie sees this multifaceted plot unfold as she follows Myra from Parthia to New York and then to an unnamed western city (as she might have followed Romeo and Juliet if they had lived on and left Verona). A recent study argues that Nellie pursued the Henshawes (having found out their address from a Christmas card sent to her Aunt Lydia) because she wanted to "supercede Myra" and appropriate her romance; she wanted Oswald. See Merrill Maguire Skaggs, *After the World Broke in Two: The Later Novels of Willa Cather* (Charlottesville: University Press of Virginia, 1990), pp. 85–110. Skaggs considers Nellie "an unreliable narrator" (p. 102), maliciously exaggerating Myra's faults even as she makes them her own. According to Skaggs, Nellie becomes an accessory to Myra's death by rationalizing her refusal to tell Oswald of Myra's suicidal flight to "Gloucester's cliff" with benign motives that serve the despicable purpose of "disposing of Myra, and freeing Oswald" for herself (p. 109). Obviously, Nellie had not figured on Oswald's "betrayal" as he dumped her and headed for Alaska.

24 A sign of Driscoll's commodification of Myra is that the pride he takes in her beauty and wit seems undifferentiated from the pride he takes in his "fine house," persons and possessions being interchangeable to him as sources of gratification (pp. 10–11). When Myra ceases to gratify Driscoll, he evokes a power he always had – the power to give or withhold money. She has no resource to draw upon in an exchange that is, essentially, unequal. As the characters engage in contest of wills, the force latent in capitalistic exchange emerges as a personal power, but this power can be contextualized within social theories of exchange. For example, in describing the dynamics of exchange as it has developed historically in transnational capitalistic enterprises, Immanuel Wallerstein points out that "the apparatus of force came into play only when there were significant challenges to an existing level of unequal exchange" (p. 33). Each unequal exchange (and most capitalistic exchanges are between unequal participants) harbors an "enormous apparatus of latent force," but the force becomes manifest only when the exchange is challenged – as Myra challenged Driscoll, in a confrontations between unequals, when she refused to abide by their contract or to accept his subsequent offer. See *Historical Capitalism* (London: Verso Editions, 1983). As Oswald's wife, Myra can exert force by shutting her husband out of her room, by leaving him, and by withholding love when he fails to provide money, actions that demonstrate the inequality in their relationship by implicitly quantifying love (he loves her more than she loves him).

Cather may have made money a murky commodity in her novel, but in a 1901 article for the Lincoln *Courier* she distinguished clearly between money as a means of exchange and money as power. "After money reaches a certain figure," she writes, "it ceases to be money at all and becomes power. It is not reckoned by its purchasing power any longer, but by its initiative and resistive power" (" 'The Real Homestead,' " in *The World and the Parish: Willa Cather's Articles and Reviews,* ed. William M. Curtin (Lincoln: University of Nebraska Press, 1970], Vol. II, pp. 858–9). Cather's remarks emerge from her description of Homestead, the scene of a brutal struggle between labor and capital that she recalls for her Nebraska readers. The article is interesting for many reasons, not least, the choice of subject and the views on class and power that this subject elicits. Cather begins to sound like Dreiser as she alludes to Herbert Spencer and "a struggle for power" she finds inherent in human history: "The struggle for power is essentially the same whether it is fought with railroad shares or the flint hatchets of the stone man" (Curtin, II, p. 858). Cather attributes the vast discrepancy she sees between rich and poor, capital and labor, to innate differences among men, only some of whom have the ambition to amass a fortune, just as only some, perhaps only a few, have the potential to become "great." The passing glance that Cather gave the Homestead Strike of 1892 seems to me significantly slight, since Cather was close to the actual scene, arriving in Pittsburgh only a few years after the strike, in 1898; moreover, she was extraordinarily close to Isabelle McClung, the daughter of Judge Samuel McClung, who had condemned the would-be assassin Alexander Berkman to a prison term that many considered excessive. Events that figured centrally and crucially in Emma Goldman's life, like the Homestead Strike, became parenthetical asides in Cather's biography. Cather's lifelong companion, Edith Lewis, brackets the sentence that McClung – called by Goldman a "judicial criminal – passed upon Berkman: "(He [Judge McClung] was, incidentally, the presiding judge at the trial of Emma Goldman's associate, Alexander Berkman, who tried to assassinate Frick; and gave him the extreme penalty the law allowed)," (*Willa Cather Living: A Per-*

sonal Record [New York: Alfred A. Knopf, 1953], p. 52). That Lewis takes care to note but not to comment upon the severe sentence makes her text seem duplicitous, at once giving and withholding meanings. Or perhaps Lewis has made her meaning clear, since by the time she comes to her parenthetical remark, she has characterized Judge McClung, father of the woman Cather presumably loved, as "formidable," "stern," "silent," "sardonic," "a man of decided intelligence and ability, with deep and often bitter prejudices," "very conservative in his tastes," and "hostile toward all radicals" (pp. 51–2). According to Lewis, the judge "unbent" to Cather and was "always a kind and considerate friend" (p. 53). I might add parenthetically that Lewis's statement that Isabelle had "no difficulty" in persuading her parents to invite Cather to live in their home contradicts the story that Isabelle had to threaten them that she would leave if they would not allow Cather to stay – but that's another debate that shows the elusiveness of historical truth. What Goldman experienced as the truth of her life and times, Cather turned into material for the writer. For her appropriation and use of Goldman's nephew, David Hochman – a brilliant young violinist killed in the First World War – see my essay "'What was it . . . ?': The Secret of Family Accord in *One of Ours,*" *Modern Fiction Studies* 36: 1 (Spring 1990): pp. 61–78; reprinted in *Willa Cather: Family, Community, and History (The BYU Symposium),* ed. John J. Murphy (Provo, Utah: Brigham Young University Humanities Publications Center, 1990), pp. 85–102.

25   Cather may have implied a realistic motive by noting that Oswald's father was an "Ulster Protestant," which suggests that Driscoll "detested" him because of religious differences. Even so, the reason for such obdurate hatred, which leads to the disowning of his nearly adopted daughter, remains obscure. More murky motives might be inferred if one places Driscoll's prohibitions against Myra's marriage within a literary tradition of father–daughter relationships. Lynda E. Boose describes a historical and cultural context for this tradition in her valuable essay "The Father's House and the Daughter in It: the Structures of Western Culture's Daughter–Father Relationship," *Daughters and Fathers,* ed. Lynda E. Boose and Betty S. Flowers (Baltimore: The Johns Hopkins University Press, 1989), pp. 19–74. Boose notes briefly the peculiarity of Shakespeare's will in which "virtually everything was deeded to Susanna and her already well-to-do husband, while only a dowry portion was left to the second daughter, Judith" – a lopsided bequest that, she believes, may shed light on wills in Shakespeare's texts (pp. 37–8).

In his essay "Strains of Blood: Myra Driscoll and the Romance of the Celts" (*Cather Studies,* ed. Susan Rosowski, Vol. 2 (1993), pp. 169–77), Robert K. Miller traces Cather's allusions to the Irish to currently prevalent racist attitudes (which would suggest that the basis for Driscoll's antagonism to Oswald is neither religion nor incestuous desire, but race). Miller makes some of the points later developed in this essay: that Myra is not unique, as Oswald and Nellie assert, that she engages in "a type of playacting," and that in embodying characteristics commonly attributed to the Celts, she "comes very close to being a stock figure" (p. 172). Like Yongue (cited below), who believes that Cather ascribed a basic "nature" to Myra – an inescapable nature as an "aristocrat"—Miller sees Cather creating wild Celtic nature that Myra could neither escape or transcend. Both views suggest that Myra had no choice in the actions that determined her fate, since nature, fundamental and essential, rules.

26   Cather is remarkably dependent upon indefinite pronouns, often using a word like *something* or *it* to suggest a character's romantically ineffable and supernal desire. As I point out in the essay "'What was it . . . ?': The Secret of Family Accord in *One of Ours*" (cited above), the vagueness of such a *something* can prove portentously ominous. On ineffability as an aspect of both Cather's romanticism and her dismay over the limitations of language, see Gelfant, "Movement and Melody: The Disembodiment of Lucy Gayheart," cited above.

27 In claiming uniqueness for Myra, Oswald paradoxically strips her of uniqueness, for he is attributing to her an individuality that, presumably, identifies the American as a national type. This hypothesized American type is too well known to require detailed description or documentation here. Studies of the American character, as a typified person and as a national trait, have long linked American individualism (not precisely synonymous with individuality, but not completely separable) with distinctive aspects of American history: with its western frontier and, notably, its entrepreneurial capitalism. A recent study restates a common view of the latter linkage by claiming categorically that "in the USA, the dominant national ideology is individualism in all its forms," and that "capitalistic accumulation created the basis for the development of modern *ideologies* of individualism, especially in the USA, where . . . individualism was and remains the defining national ethic" (James O'Connor, *Accumulation Crisis* [New York: Basil Blackwell, 1984], p. 3, 5, and passim, original emphasis). An earlier study traced the American "national consciousness" to an original linkage of universal values with American exceptionalism – "the American way of life" – and with individualism (Yehoshua Arieli, *Individualism and Nationalism in American Ideology* [Cambridge, Mass.: Harvard University Press, 1964]). Cather aspired to an art that combined the elements in this definition of national consciousness: universality, uniqueness, and individualism. In *My Mortal Enemy,* Cather links individualism with a demand for privacy or territorial rights (another common linkage in analyses of the American character) when she has Myra complain bitterly about her noisy neighbors, whose heavy footsteps overhead impinge upon her privacy (pp. 55–7 and 61).

For a view that Cather's characters transcended individuality to merge with monumental elements, see Rose, cited above. That this merging signifies death, as Cather says explicitly, Rose overlooks or ignores. For a Marxist interpretation of how " 'individualism' is constructed out of social powerlessness rather than autonomy" and how this powerlessness is produced by the "capitalistic marketplace" and necessarily mystified (p. 225), see Richard Lichtman, *The Production of Desire: The Integration of Psychoanalysis into Marxist Theory* (New York: Macmillan, The Free Press, 1982). As though to confirm this connection between individualism and powerlessness, Nellie finds Myra still uniquely herself when, as a poor exiled invalid, she seems completely disempowered. However, the original source of Myra's uniqueness, I would note, is money. Money had made Driscoll uniquely different from other people in Parthia, and when Myra walked out on Driscoll's fortune, she became so anomalous that she provided "the most interesting, indeed the only interesting, stories" told in the town (p. 3). The stunningly high cost of Myra's "runaway marriage" added to the story's interest, for disinheritance considerably increased its value as gossip. Through gossip the townspeople made capital of Myra's loss; they appropriated what was not theirs (Myra's life) to profit from her story. (Whether storytelling can proceed by any mode other than appropriation raises issues interesting to pursue in a writer well known for basing her characters upon real people she had encountered. Some, like Annie Pavelka, the prototype for Ántonia Shimerda, were proud of their place in Cather's fiction, and others incensed. Fittingly enough for a novel full of mystifications, the prototype for Myra Henshawe remains a mystery, though Cather offered some

clues to her identity. See Woodress, *Willa Cather*, p. 380 on Myra and passim for references to the real-life prototypes of Cather's characters.)

28   For a discussion of the associations evoked by Cather's allusion to Bellini's *Norma*,
see Harry B. Eichorn, "A Falling out with Love: *My Mortal Enemy*," *Colby Library Quarterly* 10 (September 1973): pp. 121–38; reprinted in *Critical Essays on Willa Cather*, ed.
John J. Murphy (Boston: G. K. Hall, 1984), pp. 230–43. Eichorn's essay is valuable also
for its analysis of Cather's literary allusions, which I discuss later on as creating a strategic
diversion from the materialistic values endorsed in *My Mortal Enemy*. The lines from
Shakespeare's *King John* that Eichorn quotes (different from the line Myra quotes), in
which a niece speaks about her uncle's will plays on words in a way pertinent to *My Mortal Enemy:* "My uncle's will . . . translates to my will . . . ; or if you will . . . "

29   By now, the phrase "the thing not named," which appears famously in "The Novel
Démeublé" (p. 50), has a long and almost notorious history in Cather criticism as signifying Cather's unmentioned (and to her unmentionable) lesbianism. I shall not recapitulate that history here, except to note that Sharon O'Brien called attention to the sexual
innuendos of the phrase in her essay, " 'The Thing Not Named': Willa Cather as Lesbian Writer," *Signs: Journal of Women in culture and Society* 9, no. 1 (1984): pp. 476–99.
Subsequently, O'Brien placed lesbianism within the context of a study of gender as a formative factor in Cather's art. See her influential biography, *Willa Cather: The Emerging
Voice* (New York: Oxford University Press, 1987). Even before O'Brien had given
salience to lesbianism in Cather's life and writing, Helen C. Southwick (Cather's niece)
sought to discount an emerging view of Cather as a lesbian. Southwick focuses upon
Elizabeth Moorhead Vermorcken's early writings about Cather's Pittsburgh years, which
became the source of "errors" in subsequent Cather biographies – errors that "attribute[d] Lesbian overtones to Cather friendships," particularly the friendship with Isabelle McClung ("Willa Cather's Early Career: Origins of a Legend," *The Western
Pennsylvania Historical Review* 65, no. 2 [April 1982]: pp. 85–98). In a biography that tries
"to get all the facts right" (p. xvi), Woodress agrees with Southwick and adds that critics "are stating inference, not fact" when they call Cather a lesbian; "there is no external
evidence to support" the most frequently made claim, that Cather's love for Isabelle Mc-
Clung was sexual (Woodress, p. 141). For a different use of Cather's famous phrase, see
Janet Giltrow and David Stouck, "Willa Cather and a Grammar for Things 'Not
Named,' " *Style* 26, no. 1 (Spring 1992): pp. 92–113. Through "a syntactical and discourse
analysis" of Cather's language, this essay "situates the reader's experience of 'the thing
not named' and the problems of interpretation amidst the linguistic data of the texts"
(p. 91). Deborah Carlin also sees "the thing not named" as a matter of "narrative poetics" (*Cather, Canon, and the Politics of Reading* [Amherst: University of Massachusetts Press,
1992], p. 45). The effect of this poetics, Carlin argues, is an "absence of signified meaning": Cather's technique in the novel "paradoxically claims meaning at the same time
that it asserts the inability of a text to formulate meaning through language" (p. 46). This
paradox produces a "deceptive design," but while Carlin finds mysteries and disjunctions
within this design, she does not relate them, as I do, to the exigencies of the novel's capitalistic values.

30   Meddling may be a displaced expression of energy and will. As a woman of her time
and circumstances, Myra cannot engage in business or politics, two public activities that,
as it were, legitimizes meddling. Men exert power publicly; women meddle in private
affairs. This is a salient arrangement in Victorian novels, as any inveterate reader of Trol-

lope knows. In Wilson's fiction, meddling can have benign effects as an expression of love. As a character in "Lilly's Story" says, "Where I love, I meddle" (*The Equations of Love* [Toronto: Macmillan of Canada, 1952], p. 219).

31   For a refutation of Myra's view that "in religion, desire was fulfillment," see Stephen L. Tanner, "Seeking and Finding in Cather's *My Mortal Enemy*" in *Literature and Belief: Willa Cather Issue*, ed. John J. Murphy (Provo, Utah: Brigham Young University Humanities Publications Center, 1988), pp. 6–38; and for a view that concurs with Tanner, see Eugene England, "Lovers as Mortal Enemies," *Willa Cather: Family, Community, and History*, pp. 125–31. Tanner believes "that Myra's [religious] conversion is more a matter of aesthetics than of theology" (p. 35) and that "the problems of authorial intention in this novel are . . . unsolvable" – that is, that the text offers no basis for deciding whether Cather intended to be ironical when she described Myra "turning to God without turning also to love, humility, repentance, forgiveness, and rejection of worldly values" (p. 36). Critics have carried on a running argument over the issue of "authorial intention," disagreeing about whether it can ever be ascertained and whether it is relevant to interpretation of a text. If the meaning of what Cather has written remains undecidable, a matter of disputed interpretation, so too, I have argued, are the meanings of what the self-mystified and duplicitous characters say in *My Mortal Enemy*. Is Nellie a credible and authoritative narrator (Skaggs, claims otherwise), and is Oswald to be believed when he proudly separates his wife from "people"? Janis P. Stout believes that questions about what the reader can believe and whom to believe may be the result of Cather's "narrative irony" conjoined with her "reticence and tact" (*Strategies of Reticence: Silence and Meaning in the Works of Jane Austen, Willa Cather, Katherine Anne Porter, and Joan Didion* [Charlottesville: University Press of Virginia, 1990], p. 85). This combination of reticence and irony leads to the "interesting" issue of how Cather "manages to raise so many questions, throughout the novel [*My Mortal Enemy*], without voicing them, in a book so terse that readers have sometimes called it incomplete" (p. 86).

32   In his well-known "Conclusion" to the *Literary History of Canada* (cited above), Frye drew together many "impressions" about Canadian literature pertinent to this essay's discussion of Wilson's *Love and Salt Water*. Frye saw in the development of what he called "a garrison mentality" in Canadian frontier communities an historically conditioned national trait that had applicability to "the way in which the Canadian imagination has developed in its literature." His germinal definition emphasizes the importance of community to what he calls "the Canadian imagination": "Small and isolated communities surrounded with a physical or psychological 'frontier,' separated from one another and from their American and British cultural sources: communities that provide all that their members have in the way of distinctively human values, and that are compelled to feel a great respect for the law and order that holds them together, yet confronted with a huge, unthinking, menacing, and formidable physical setting – such communities are bound to develop what we may provisionally call a garrison mentality" ("Conclusion," *Literary History of Canada*, II, p. 342). Frye defines a garrison as "a closely knit and beleaguered society, and its moral and social values are unquestionable" (p. 226) – a definition that might describe the world of Wilson's fiction. I doubt that it would describe Cather's imagined world in which "unique" individuals seek to express their individuality in ways that often ignore the demands of (their) community. I should note Frye's qualifying remark about Canadian identity: "many Canadian cultural phenomena are not peculiarly Canadian at all, but are typical of their wider North American and Western

contexts" ("Conclusion," p. 334). He further problematizes definitions of Canadian cultural identity by saying, "I stress our ignorance of the laws and conditions of cultural history" ("Conclusion," p. 334).

33 In "The 'Genius' of Place and Time," New lists the various "equations of love" that Wilson can permutate. According to his calculations, the following appear in Wilson's collected stories, *The Equations of Love:* "love=a casual affair, love=love of *things,* love=love of home, love=marital love, love=parental/filial love, love=appetite, love=sentiment, love=affection" (*Articulating West,* p. 75, original emphasis).

34 Eventually, Ellen's father is drawn to the United States, as is her rejected suitor, Huw Peake. The sea voyage makes manifest a state of subordinacy that may be Ellen's cultural legacy as a Canadian. Canadian cultural and literary studies commonly attribute to the Canadian character a deeply rooted sense of secondariness or subordinacy. A typical example of such attribution appears in an essay defining nationalism in Canadian literature: "We might expect a feeling of passivity and helplessness, the sense of being on the periphery, to be part of the consciousness of a people accustomed to living on the fringes of the British and American spheres of power." See Frank Watt, "Nationalism in Canadian Literature," in *Nationalism in Canada by the University League for Social Reform,* ed. Peter Russell (Toronto: McGraw-Hill Ryerson, 1966), p. 247. See also note 40 below, on Canadian fear of and attempted resistance to the power of the United States.

35 The coalescence of money and spiritual grace in *My Mortal Enemy* would point to its Americanism if one accepts the well-known view that this coalescence is a cultural legacy of America's Puritan past. On revisionary readings of Cather as a culturally regressive writer, see, for example, Elizabeth Ammons, *Conflicting Stories: American Women Writers at the Turn into the Twentieth Century* (New York: Oxford University Press, 1991), pp. 121–36 and passim; Demaree Peck, " 'Possession Granted by a Different Lease': Alexandra Bergson's Imaginative Conquest of Cather's Nebraska," *Modern Fiction Studies* 36, no. 1 (Spring 1990): pp. 5–22; Eve Kosofsy Sedgwick, "Across Gender, across Sexuality: Willa Cather and Others," *South Atlantic Quarterly* 88 (1989): pp. 53–72; Walter Benn Michaels, "The Vanishing American," *American Literary History* II, no. 2 (Summer 1990): pp. 220–41. Ammons discusses Cather's success in reconciling "the terms *woman and artist*" within a literary form malleable to her conception of gender (p. 128), but race remained "a problem" (p. 133). As Ammons points out, I had also found "Cather's racism" (and her treatment of class and gender) a problem in my essay "The Forgotten-Reaping Hook: Sex in *My Ántonia,*" *American Literature* XLIII, no. 1 (March 1971): pp. 60–82. Peck discerns in Cather's pioneer heroine, Alexandra Bergson, an appropriating and possessive will such as that ascribed to Emerson by Quentin Anderson in his important study, *The Imperial Self* (1971). According to Peck, Alexandra substitutes "the higher law of her will for the law of nature" (p. 18), refusing "to will the land to her brothers" so that "she can will it to herself" (p. 19). As I note later on, the land has already been willed to Alexandra by her father.

36 To point out that excess is intrinsic in capitalism, taking form as the surplus value created by labor, is not to suggest that extravagance is peculiar either to Cather's novel or to modern capitalist societies. Extravagance seems endemic to human history and is sometimes held to effect historical change. The decline and fall of Greece and Rome, for example, have been linked to extravagance by Stanton C. Coblentz in his study, *Avarice: A History* (Washington, D.C.: Public Affairs Press, 1965). Coblentz claims that "wealth and its inheritance, and the luxuries and self-indulgence it encouraged . . . [had] weakening effects" upon Greece, leaving it "helpless and unprepared" before its conquerers (p. 46), and that Roman extravagance contributed to that empire's decline (p. 47). Not surprisingly, Coblentz's study does not include the ethos of minority peoples, among them the indigenous coastal peoples of the Canadian Northwest, whose legends offer an oblique perspective upon Wilson's avaricious Mr. Platt. An early collection of Northwest Indian legends about the landscape surrounding Vancouver names "one vice . . . unknown to the red man . . . and amongst all the deplorable things he has learned from the white races . . . never acquired . . . the vice of avarice." Legend tells us that "the Indian looks upon greed of gain, miserliness, avariciousness and [accumulated] wealth . . . [as] one of the lowest degradations he can fall to." See *Legends of Vancouver,* collected by the Mohawk poet Tekahionwake, known as E. Pauline Johnson, (Vancouver: The Thomson Stationery Co., 1913), p. 49. Wilson was one of the reviewers of *Legends of Vancouver,* which she discussed in a characteristically evasive way: she states her objection to its romanticism and then she understates the objection by diverting the reader's attention to the book's "simple print" and "beautiful small decoration," and to anecdotal memories of Johnson ("The Princess," *Canadian Literature* 9 [Summer 1961]: pp. 60–1). A socioanthropological study of the "culture of consumerism" argues that the meanings of extravagance and thrift are construed differently by different cultures: "Spending only a small proportion of income may in one place and time be called thrifty, wise, and provident; in another it may be held to be miserly, mean, and wrong. Conversely, a high ratio of consumption may be approved as generous, magnificent, and good in one culture, while in another the selfsame behavior may be called spendthrift, feckless, and bad" (Mary Douglas and Baron Isherwood, *The World of Goods* [New York, Basic Books, 1979], p. 26). *My Mortal Enemy's* vacillation over what to call Myra's expenditures reflects its attempt to adjust what it considers aristocratic values to bourgeois American society.

37 Lewis described Willa Cather's tastes as not unlike Myra Henshawe's, though she attributes a necessary "economy" to Cather, in the early days of her career, as well as a selective "extravagance" (*Willa Cather Living,* p. 74). Cather's personal indulgences are well known: good food, elegant clothes, fresh flowers, opera going, theater, parties. Like Myra, she also found "great pleasure in friendship" and enjoyed "being able to make generous gifts to a great many people" (p. 149); she, too, needed – or wanted – "comfort and quiet, a protection from outside intrusion" (Lewis, p. 177). Lewis says Cather "was greatly attracted by beautiful jewels; but she never bought any" (p. 149). Patricia Yongue has documented Cather's predilection for aristocrats in her fiction and in her life. See "Willa Cather's Aristocrats (Part I)", *Southern Humanities Review* XIV, no. 1 (Winter 1980): pp. 43–56; and (Part II), XIV, no. 2 (Spring 1980): pp. 111–25. Yongue's discussion of *My Mortal Enemy* (II, pp. 116–19) equates Myra's aristocrat pretentions with her aesthetic sensibilities. (I note parenthetically that Yongue inadvertently attributes the "worldly" hands of the actress Modjeska to Myra [II, p. 116].)

38 Both Myra and Oswald act upon a self-mystifying notion that they are autonomous agents rather than dependent figures functioning within a social system. On this particular self-mystification as intrinsic to capitalistic society, see Lichtman, "Levels of Mystification," *The Production of Desire,* pp. 108–12. Lichtman's description of the capitalist applies to Myra as she thinks she can exercise her own will in deciding on Oswald's economic choices. Lichtman writes: "The capitalist . . . translates the fact of contractual exchange based on *necessity* into the ideology of *free* movement and individual *liberty*" (p. 108, original emphasis).

39 In a letter written in 1961, Wilson expressed highly critical views of American morality: "How strange Americans are – everyone else may be wicked but they are noble – having committed the greatest crime in history and dropped 2 (not 1) bombs on congested areas, not mountain tops, without (except fatherly) apparent feelings of guilt and remorse. They frighten me with irrationality" (Stouck, *Ethel Wilson: Stories, Essays, and Letters*, p. 220).

40 Canada's writers and social theorists have deplored this development – in effect, the colonization of Canada by the United States – in various ways, of which I give two examples. One contains a sharp rejoinder to U.S. "imperialism" from a *Canadian* socialist perspective: *Close the 49th parallel etc: The Americanization of Canada*, cited above. In this volume, C. W. Gonick reminds the reader that "when we talk about Canada and the American empire, we should keep in mind . . . Canada is a small regional economy within the metropolitan economy of the United States of America. We have always been the hinterland of some imperial system. Our evolution from the British system towards the American system began with the American Revolution but was not completed until the early decades of the twentieth century" (p. 44). In the same volume, see Gerald L. Caplan and James Laxer, "Perspectives on unAmerican traditions in Canada" (pp. 305–20), which argues that "for Canadians who wish to pursue the elusive goal of an egalitarian socialist society, American imperialism is the major enemy," threatening "the very existence of the Canadian nation" (pp. 310 and 306). In a different mode, Margaret Atwood's novel *Surfacing* (Ontario: Paperjacks, 1973, published originally in 1972) describes Canadians becoming "Americans" as they turn to violence against nature, animals, and each other. Americanism is a blight "spreading up from the south" like the disease that is killing the Canadian white birches (p. 7).

41 *Cards on the Table* (New York: Dell, 1974, published originally in 1936), p. 89, original emphasis. As we know, D. H. Lawrence considered lying a usual element of art, writing in his now classic *Studies in Classic American Literature*, "An artist is usually a damned liar, but his art, if it be art, will tell you the truth of his day" (New York: Seltzer, 1923), p. 1. I am not claiming that Cather and Wilson are telling lies, but rather that they are discovering aspects of their capitalistic society – of the determining role of money and class – that they find impossible to deny and yet cannot support, so that they obfuscate or, through metaphorical exchanges, transform what they have seen.

42 See *The Great Gatsby* (New York: Charles Scribner's Sons, 1953, published originally in 1925) for Fitzgerald's allusion to Benjamin Franklin. Fitzgerald's description of Dan Cody as "a gray, florid man with a hard, empty face" (p. 101) suggests how Cather's Driscoll might have looked when he made his cold business proposition to Myra. The novel's narrator says to the conspiratorial Gatsby, "I don't like mysteries . . . and I don't understand why you won't come out frankly and tell me what you want" (p. 72). Perhaps Gatsby does not know what he wants or what he wants is inexpressible. Like Cather – to whom Fitzgerald had written an admiring letter acknowledging her influence upon *The Great Gatsby* – Fitzgerald resorted to ineffability with words like *unutterable, indefinable,* and recurrently, *secret.* While Benjamin Franklin may be a representative American, as indeed he defined himself in his *Autobiography*, Northrop Frye has asserted that there is "no hundred percent Canadian, no ancestral figures corresponding to Washington or Franklin or Jefferson" (*Divisions on a Ground*, p. 48).

43 Days of Reckoning discusses the issue of artifactuality – of culture as the product of writing, as a text – and its implication for cross-cultural literary criticism. Here I leave open issues of truth and artifactuality as they pertain to a general understanding of culture because I wish to focus upon the artifactuality or literariness of specific novels.

44 By contracting my focus, I do not mean to replace culture, gender, or race as critical issues, but to place them within the context of social and economic disparity systemic to the American capitalistic society in which, and about which, Cather wrote and to a continuing struggle between socialist and capitalist governments in the Canadian province that is the background of Wilson's life and fiction. I assume that the critic's choice of context is always interested insofar as it will shunt analysis and interpretation onto a track the critic wants to pursue. To choose cultural identity as a context leads, usually, to a discovery of difference that might have been assumed (though sometimes, by an ironic inversion or chiasmic crossing, expected differences will reveal unexpected similarities). One wonders how differences attributed to cultural identity would diverge from those discovered if *Love and Salt Water* and *My Mortal Enemy* were contextualized as women's writings. Indeed, one might wonder what can be said about Cather and Wilson as women writers, epithets both disliked; and what more remains to be said about Cather, whom contemporary critics describe transcending culturally prescribed boundaries of gender. O'Brien's biography, *The Emerging Voice*, weaves arguments about Cather's sexuality into a coherent narrative that shows Cather transcending the gender barriers of her time. Some critics have criticized Cather's use of a male narrator, declaring it in *My Ántonia*, for instance, an evasive strategy that distracts from the novel's implicit homoeroticism; others praise Cather for portraying strong women like Ántonia Shimerda, Alexandra Bergson, and Thea Kronberg. Some years back, in calling for papers on American and Canadian women writers to be published in *Women's Studies,* I asked a question about the relationship between gender and nationality that is pertinent, if peripheral, to this essay: whether "by focusing upon nationality, one could separate, at least theoretically, universal women's experience from those attributable to specific conditions of place" (p. 1). By place, I meant not merely "a geographical area," but rather "a definable, social, emotional, and ideational milieu" – a cultural ambience (p. 1). I concluded the "Call" with a brief comparison between Cather and Wilson that suggests the aporia posed by the relationship between gender as it relates to women's history and national culture, whether one can transcend the other, or whether one or the other is subsuming. See "Introduction: A continuing call . . . ," *Women's Studies: An Interdisciplinary Journal,* Special Issue, Canadian and American Women Writers, guest ed. Blanche H. Gelfant, 12 (1986): pp. 1–6.

Race relations have just begun to emerge as a context for revisionary readings of Cather's canon, while it has not figured in critiques of Wilson perhaps because of a lack of interest in the subject among Canadian critics, or its apparent irrelevance to Wilson's fiction, or the difficulty of pinning down Wilson's representations of race to a prevailing view. Wilson has described some Chinese characters as threatening, like the wonderfully villainous Yow in "Lilly's Story" and others as "a kind of benevolent influence," like the Quong family in *Swamp Angel.* In *The Innocent Traveller,* she placed a black swimming instructor (whom she based upon a popular Vancouver person) at the center of a controversy among white women and had the usually complacent Topaz Edgeworth rise to his defence. These are passing references to race as peripheral as Ellen Cuppy's sudden realization that white people decree laws for Indians they do not know or understand (p.

120). Their peripherality or omission may in itself become an issue in a critique contextualized by race.

As this essay argues, the texts obscure issues of social disparity by both assuming and ignoring the class structure upon which their fictional worlds are based. In an influential essay written several decades ago, a Canadian critic asked his reader to regard the general "silence on the question of class" in Canadian literature as "ominous." See Robert L. McDougall, "The Dodo and the Cruising Auk: Class in Canadian Literature," *Contexts of Canadian Criticism*, ed. Eli Mandel (Chicago: University of Chicago Press, 1971; the essay was published originally in 1963), pp. 216–31. McDougall believes that Canadian literature evinces "an abnormal absence of feeling for class and of concern for what the class structure can do in a developing society to make or mar the life of the individual" (p. 217). Among the few works of Canadian fiction that do deal with social class, he includes Ethel Wilson's "Lilly's Story," but what he has to say about it is hardly assuring: "Ethel Wilson writing 'Lilly's Story' is Jane Austen writing Sister Carrie" (p. 225). In his discussion of Wilson, New notes that her character Hetty Dorval lacks "the 'working class reality' of Dreiser's Sister Carrie" ("The 'Genius' of Place and Time," p. 69). Class may have become a matter of manners in Wilson's fiction, but in a Canadian novel written in the years of the great depression (which Wilson – and Cather – lived through), class signifies economic and political disparity and social conflict. See Irene Baird, *Waste Heritage* (Toronto: Armac Press, 1939). Comparing Wilson's treatment of social class with that of the wonderful French-Canadian writer, Gabrielle Roy, Jeannette Urbas concludes that "Mrs. Wilson's working-people are primarily individuals" (who, I might note, can always get a job when they need to), while Roy's characters, notably in *The Tin Flute*, are "members of a working-class community," a self-aware "industrial proletariat" ("Equations and Flutes," *Journal of Canadian Fiction*, I, no. 2 [1972]: p. 70).

45   The letters are reproduced in Stouck, *Ethel Wilson: Stories, Essays, and Letters*. The first letter is dated May 28, 1947 (pp. 139–40); the second, November 2, 1947 (pp. 144–5); and the third, July 25, 1953 (pp. 186–9). As I have indicated, despite Wilson's disclaimers, Canadian critics have discerned similarities between Cather and Wilson which they trace to the influence of the American writer. See, for example, Catherine McLay, "Ethel Wilson's Lost Lady: *Hetty Dorval* and Willa Cather" (*Journal of Canadian Fiction* 33 [1981–1982]: pp. 94–106); and Alexandra Collins, "Who Shall Inherit the Earth?: Ethel Wilson's Debt to Wharton, Glasgow, Cather, and Ostenso" (*The Ethel Wilson Symposium: Reappraisals, Canadian Writers*, ed. Lorraine McMullen, [Ottawa: University of Ottawa Press, 1982], pp. 61–72). Critical accounts of Cather's readings in classical and Western literature (readings which range from Ovid, Sappho, Virgil, and Dante to Shakespeare, Goethe, Keats, Carlyle, Verlaine, Flaubert, Sarah Orne Jewett, Whitman) are overwhelmingly numerous, and the allusions in her writing testify to her conscious and immense indebtedness to literary traditions. Wilson replied to a letter asking about the writers who had influenced her (later she was asked about *women* writers) in her usual evasive way, by first saying, "I am not conscious of being influenced by any writers," and then naming *Tom Jones, Moll Flanders, Roxana*, E. M. Forster novels, Proust, Trollope, I. Compton Burnett, and Osbert Sitwell. The letter succinctly summarizes what might be called Wilson's aesthetic principles (Stouck, *Ethel Wilson: Stories, Essays, and Letters*, pp. 183–5). The letters on influence, or lack of influence, are addressed to Desmond Pacey, who was to write the first book-length study of Wilson (cited above).

46 In a letter referring to *Love and Salt Water* that was published in *Chatelaine*, a women's magazine, Wilson wrote, "I am an *economical* writer . . . and this story is already condensed . . . to a point that would make further condensation impossible – would, in fact, nullify it" (Macmillan Correspondence of the Ethel Wilson Papers held in the Special Collections of The University of British Columbia Library, n.d., original emphasis). On Cather, see "The Novel Démeublé," cited above. In an unpublished story with journalistic overtones, "The Vat and the Brew," Wilson turned to juvenile delinquency as a social vice to be deplored, while as editor of *McClure's Magazine*, Cather expressed her preference for journalism stripped of social criticism. In 1910, for example, she assigned Elizabeth Sergeant (with whom she was to have a long, but sometimes stormy and interrupted, friendship) to write a report on an exhibit in a Berlin museum of devices used to protect working people on the job. "What we want," she wrote on May 31, "is a sort of summing up of the interesting things that have been done abroad for the protection of the laborer." But what *she*, Cather, wanted "was a new way of writing on the old and fascinating subject of 'dangerous trades.' " In a letter of July 6, she expressed her preference for emphasizing the ingenuity of the protective devices rather than the dangers in the workplace; she preferred a diverting and diversionary "story" to social facts. As she said, "Personally, I am afraid I am much more interested in the story of ingenious devices made to protect the workers in dangerous trades, than I am in the usual sort of article on that subject; I mean the articles that tell how many people are killed in this and that trade every year." The letter is held in the Cather Collection of the Pierpont Morgan Library in New York. While Cather here directs a journalist to write like a storyteller, later she expresses disdain for socially conscious storytellers who think they can make art out of the material they gather as journalists – a disdain she traces to her experience as editor of *McClure's Magazine*. As she wrote in 1936, "When I first lived in New York and was working on the editorial staff of a magazine, I became disillusioned about social workers and reformers [who] . . . were making . . . investigations 'to collect material for fiction' " ("Escapism: A Letter to The Commonweal," *Willa Cather on Writing: Critical Studies on Writing as an Art* [Lincoln: University of Nebraska Press, 1988, essays and letters published originally 1920–49], pp. 24–5).

47 Nellie may be missing the point that Myra seems to have made explicit: that she wanted marriage *and* money. Perhaps the combination would have gratified her. Perhaps not. At any rate, she had few choices other than marriage or submission to her uncle's will, since she lacked the talent or art to qualify her for the roles played by a unique woman she admired, the actress Helena Modjeska (or by Cather's great opera singer in *The Song of the Lark*), and she lacked any chance at the roles to which she was probably suited, those of finance capitalist, bank president, and patron of the arts, all assumed by the man she most admired, John Driscoll. Perhaps no part she could have played in bourgeois American society would have gratified Myra since she assigned herself anachronistic roles that were more fictitious than real – the role of enchanted princess pining for her love, of defiant daughter eloping in the night, and, more bizarrely, of spiritual heir to Roman tyrants and Shakespearean kings. Myra's discovery of "Gloucester's cliff" on the Pacific coast is an emblematic fiction of her own making, a fantasy as ironic as it is illusory, referring to a place that has no reality in Shakespeare's play. The cliff was an artifactual product of Edgar's words, and Myra believes – as writers like Cather must have believed – that she, too, could give a nonexistent place reality by giving it a name. Edgar invented the fiction of Gloucester's cliff to inspire a will to live, while Myra Henshawe,

in the blindness she shares with Shakespeare's abused character, named the cliff as the site of her death. By contextualizing herself within great works of art and within self-created dramas centered upon timeless themes, Myra was trying to take herself out of her historical times, and out of time itself as the agent of history. A recent study of human desire places it within an economic context in ways that might help explain Myra's failure to find satisfaction in the social world she inhabits: "the personal longings that arise under capitalism have no adequate object within the capitalist structure . . . [capitalism] continually elicits aspirations that are yet without an appropriate terminus for their movement" (Lichtman, *The Production of Desire*, p. 280). Lichtman comes to this conclusion by conflating Freudian and Marxist insights into human behavior in order to describe a social structuring of the unconscious.

48 Nellie had seen Myra sit with her friend, the dying poet, and splurge on a Christmas holly bush for the actress Modjeska. I would claim that Nellie does more than imitate Myra: she appropriates her very mode of appropriation by presenting Myra, as she had presented Nellie, as an object to look at and "talk over." The title of the novel suggests the act of appropriation, taking its place among other titles that use the possessive form: *My Ántonia, Alexander's Bridge, The Professor's House*, and *One of Ours*. On appropriation as an act of the writer, her character, and the reader, see my essay " 'Art and Apprent Artlessness': Self-Reflexivity in *My Ántonia*," *Approaches to Teaching My Ántonia*, ed. Susan J. Rosowski (New York: The Modern Language Association of America, 1989), pp. 126–33.

49 As Bernice Slote has pointed out, myths about the moon-goddess Diana provided Cather with "one of her most deeply affective and complex symbols," involving a "whole body of associations" that figure in Cather's fiction from the early stories to *My Mortal Enemy* (see *The Kingdom of Art*, pp. 97–103). For a succinct account of Diana's "strange transformation" from a goddess of light to Hecate, the goddess of darkness, see Edith Hamilton, *Mythology: Timeless Tales of Gods and Heroes* (New York: New American Library, 1940, 1942), pp. 31–2 and passim. Described as a goddess who represents the double nature of human beings, Diana might be the tutelary spirit of Cather's doubled and self-divided characters. Critics have been well aware of this doubling and the inner divisiveness it entails, as Susan J. Rosowski has recently reminded readers: "after all, critics have long recognized that the theme of two selves runs through Cather's writing ("Recent Books on Willa Cather: An Essay Review," *Modern Fiction Studies* 36, no. 1 [Spring 1990]: pp. 131–41; I quote from p. 140). Hermione Lee defines the doubleness in Cather's writing in particular ways in her book, *Willa Cather: Double Lives* (New York: Random House, 1989); the title for the original English edition was *Willa Cather: A Life Saved Up*.

50 To say that the book is, in turn, shaped (if not controlled) by a national sensibility that inevitably affected Wilson as a writer would be tenable if one accepts cultural definitions based upon geographic boundaries. For example, one might refer to Frye's description of the historic shaping of "a Canadian sensibility" that is characterized by a "sense of probing into the distance, of fixing the eyes on the skyline" ("Conclusion" to *Literary History of Canada*, II, p. 340). Frye calls this a "presbyopic sense" and traces it to "the vast distances of river and sky [in Canada] that confer nobility on faraway looks." This sense remains as a heritage of "Canadian cultural history," manifesting itself as an "obsession with movement and transportation, the eye that passes over the foreground object, the restlessness that solves all social difficulties by moving somewhere else, the commitment to a society that involves constant movement" ("National Consciousness," *Divisions on a Ground*, p. 50). Wilson's *Love and Salt Water* dramatizes each aspect of the presbyopic sense Frye enumerates: the faraway look as Ellen and her mother watch from their window the movement of distant freighters on the horizon, their vision passing over the foreground of the landscape; the sea voyage undertaken to assuage grief over Susan Cuppy's death; the constant movement of Canadians across the continent that Wilson describes at length, particularly the travel of "western people" who "move and return, move and return, very like birds" (pp. 87–9 and passim). I would suggest that the cultural critic might find a circular verification by moving from context—"the Canadian sensibility," "the Canadian imagination," "the national consciousness," as Frye convincingly describes it – to the text of *Love and Salt Water* and, conversely, from text to context.

51 Wilson declared her withdrawal of *Love and Salt Water* from American publishers in a letter to John Gray, probably dated February 7, 1957. The original letter is in the Macmillan Correspondence of the Ethel Wilson Papers held in the Special Collections of the University of British Columbia Library (reproduced in Stouck, *Ethel Wilson: Stories, Essays, and Letters*, pp. 206–8).

52 Wilson often referred to her regionalism in attempts to mediate between the localization of her fiction within a specific and realistic setting and the universality of its themes and human appeal. She described her rootedness in British Columbia in a letter written in response to a review of E. K. Brown's biography of Cather (mentioned below) in which she asked the reviewer "for a commentary sentence on a certain aspect of writing [on regionalism and nationalism], especially, perhaps, in a young country." (The letter, dated July 8, 1952, is reprinted in Stouck, *Ethel Wilson: Stories, Essays, and Letters*, p. 182.) Wilson claimed in the letter that contingency had led her to write about British Columbia: she said that "though she knew other countries," "she could write at length only about Canada – and only about British Columbia, though she knew "Canada from here to Prince Edward Island." "Everything I attempt to write is Canadian, and even regional, in its aspect," she admitted, but she implied that "aspect" was a superficial feature of her fiction beneath which lay embedded universal themes and values.

53 Cather expressed this doubt about her ability to see America as others saw it in a letter to H. L. Mencken, dated February 6, 1922. In this letter she wonders whether all the Tolstoy novellas she had read and reread when she was only fourteen "had so 'marked' me that I could not see the American scene as it looked to other Americans – as it, presumably, really was." She later tried to contravene Tolstoy's profound influence by immersing herself in Henry James and Edith Wharton. Still later, she tried to exorcise the influence of James, patent in her first novel *Alexander's Bridge*, by writing *O Pioneers!*. I quote from a photocopy of the letter in the H. L. Mencken Papers in the Rare Books and Manuscripts Division of the New York Public Library. The original letter was presented to the Enoch Pratt Free Library in Baltimore. My thanks to Virginia Close, Reference Librarian of Baker Library, Dartmouth College, and to John D. Stinson, Manuscripts Specialist of the New York Public Library for their help in locating the letter. I might add that I wonder which American, in Cather's view, was seeing the American scene authentically, Myra in her furs or a coatless boy playing a penny-whistle. I wonder also if Cather was not misleading in saying she had wanted to see America as others saw it, for she said explicitly that the artist must be an individualist and see her world in her own way, despite pressures upon her to conform to a socially solidified vision. In the thirties, for example, she inveighed against radically oriented critics who would coerce a writer to describe America as they saw it and she called their "revolt against individualism" an attack upon the artist "because the artist is of all men the most individual" ("Escapism," *Willa Cather on Writing*, p. 26). Even when Cather expressed in novels like *A Lost Lady* and *My Mortal Enemy* her predilection for an aristocratic way of life, she sought to escape the ugly social aspects of a past she was evoking, for when Cather remembered aristocratic lords and ladies, she forgot the peasants and serfs whose labor created their lovely leisure (just as she was to forgot the contracted laborers in a Missouri swampland she remembered long enough to mention as the source of Driscoll's money, grand house, and grandiose exit from the world).

54 Henry James's novella *Washington Square* describes a woman deserted by her suitor when her father threatens to disinherit her if she marries him. One wonders whether Myra would have been better off if Oswald had deserted her. She would have inherited the Driscoll fortune, but at the expense of romance and the dramatic gestures it produce – and at the expense of all the stories, including Cather's, fabricated from the romance. *Washington Square* was made into a distinguished motion picture entitled, pointedly, "The Heiress." Edith Wharton disassociates and reassociates money and art in a story about a disinherited art collector. See "False Dawn (The 'Forties)" in *In Old New York* (New York: Berkley, 1981, published originally in 1924), pp. 3–56. Wharton describes an involuted interrelationship between inheritance and disinheritance and the personal, cultural, and monetary values placed upon art. For her protagonist she drew selectively upon the life of James Jackson Jarves, an American disciple of Ruskin, an early American collector of medieval Italian art (unsalable art which he finally gave to Yale University), and an art historian (who idealized art in a way Cather might have approved). In Ernest Hemingway's *The Sun Also Rises* (New York: Charles Scribner's Sons, 1954, published originally in 1926), Robert Cohn inherits fifty thousand dollars from his father (p. 4), and Mike Campbell is "going to be rich as hell" when he comes into his inheritance (p. 38). *The Sun Also Rises* is obsessed with money, which it shows constantly being exchanged in realistically commonplace transactions and in a symbolic "exchange of values" thematic to the text. Of all American writers, Thomas Pynchon turns the literary conventions governing wills and disinheritance to the most imaginative, enigmatic, and idiosyncratic use in his fiction, or so I think. *The Crying of Lot 49* begins with the reading of will that involves its heroine in a mysterious journey of detection that may, or may not, lead to the discovery of a hidden underworld of the disinherited.

55 *The Innocent Traveller* (Toronto: McClelland & Stewart, 1982, published originally 1949), pp. 45–50 and p. 63. Describing the disinheritance of one young woman, the text alludes incidentally to an inheritance passed on to another (to Anne Edgeworth, a main character). Later on in the text, Wilson's exaggeration of the onerousness of changing a will, like that of making a will in *Love and Salt Water*, typifies her comic reduction to inconsequentiality of such serious matters as legal wills and, implicitly, money matters and property. I refer to Mrs. Grimwade's refusal of a marriage proposal from a man she admires, even in his "dotage," because of "the thought of her Will so carefully made, leaving her fortune in Consols to the Missions and leaving small bequests to the young Raphael nephews and their wives. What complications would ensue!" (p. 79).

56 A brief, synoptic view of wills and inheritance in Cather's fiction reveals a gallery of characters, from wicked Wick Cutter to saintly Bishop Latour, who echo Myra's cry for money as the answer to need. This review shows that occasionally Cather allowed men to benefit from a will made by women: in *A Lost Lady,* Niel Herbert inherits a small sum from his mother, and in "Old Mrs. Harris," Mr. Templeton inherits "a few thousand dollars" from his aunt. Usually, however, Cather made women beneficiaries of wills, perhaps because she could devise few other realistic ways to give women characters access to money and power. Given their limited resources, women would find disinheritance devastating, as Driscoll knew when he disinherited Myra and gave the money she might have had to a home for poor and aged women. In her own will, Cather took advantage of a legal right to exercise control over her property long after her death, possibly for perpetuity. By designating her lifelong friend, Edith Lewis, as benefactor and trustee, she passed on to a woman a control of her literary effects that Lewis exercised with stringency, as an early biographer of Cather (a Canadian by birth, as it happens) discovered. See Leon Edel's account of his meeting with Lewis and "the delicate diplomacy" in which he had to engage in order to persuade her, as "guardian" of Cather's papers, to let him complete the biography begun by E. K. Brown and interrupted by his untimely death. See "Homage to Willa Cather" in *The Art of Willa Cather,* ed. Bernice Slote and Virgina Faulkner (Lincoln: University of Nebraska Press, 1974), pp. 185–204. Ironically perhaps, the equation between material and aesthetic values that I have described Cather making and trying to obscure in *My Mortal Enemy* emerges clearly in a phrase in her will that designates her writing, her art, as "literary property." Obviously, Cather knew that art had a cash equivalent, and as Lewis pointed out in *Willa Cather Living,* the income from her novels, after 1929, allowed Cather to live the way she wished and, as noted above, in a style Myra Henshawe would have appreciated and wanted to appropriate. I thank Patricia K. Phillips, Director of the Willa Cather Pioneer Memorial and Educational Foundation in Red Cloud, for graciously sending me a copy of Cather's will. (As an aside, I note that in 1929, three years after the fictional Myra was disinherited, Virginia Woolf described how her sensibility drastically changed when she inherited from her aunt a legacy of five hundred pounds a year to be paid "forever." The money, she says, "seemed infinitely more important" than the vote, which had just been granted to women. See *A Room of One's Own* [New York and London: Harcourt Brace Jovanovich, published originally in 1929], pp. 37–39.)

57   On the garrison mentality, see Frye, "Conclusion" to the *Literary History of Canada;* on the victim as a prototypical Canadian literary figure, see Atwood, *Survival: A Thematic Guide to Canadian Literature;* and on irony as an identifying aspect of a modern Canadian literary sensibility, see Linda Hutcheon, *Splitting Images: Contemporary Canadian Ironies* (Toronto and New York: Oxford University Press, 1991). The differences to which I allude have been argued in various ways and among various critics. Frye has contended, for example, that "a culture founded on a revolutionary tradition, like that of the United States, is bound to show very different assumptions and imaginative patterns from those of a culture that rejects or distrusts revolution. First, an underlying assumption of a successful revolution is 'violence pays' " (*Divisions on a Ground,* p. 46). Elsewhere, Frye made the same point, this time drawing an implication pertinent to an American capitalistic will: "the central fact of Canadian history [is] the rejection of the American Revolution. What won the American revolution was the spirit of entrepreneur capitalism, an enthusiastic plundering of the natural resources of a continent and an unrestricted energy of manufacturing and exchanging them "("Preface to an Uncollected Anthology" in *Contexts of Canadian Criticism* p. 184). Needless to say, critiques of cultural differences abound and an attempt to begin to cite them would exceed the already strained boundaries of

this essay. The essay also cannot undertake to document the studies of Puritanism, a subject pertinent to its interests but beyond its scope. In a survey of Canadian literature that stresses national identity, Ronald Sutherland gives a succinct summary of "the effects and aftereffects" of Puritanism in Canada as different from its effects in the United States ("A Literary Perspective: The Development of a National Consciousness," *Understanding Canada: A Multidisciplinary Introduction to Canadian Studies,* ed. William Metcalfe [New York: New York University Press, 1982], pp. 404–8). Sutherland's essay begins with a common assertion "that Canadian literature has from the beginning reflected a preoccupation with the United States" (p. 402); proceeds with a detailed comparison between the literatures of the two countries; and concludes with an affirmation of its original premise that "a national literature reflects the spiritual quality and growth of a nation," and that Canadian writing reflects "the psychology of the Canadian from colonial or garrison mentality to a new state of multilateral independence and individualism" (pp. 483–4). The long essay is informative for an American reader (though Sutherland conspicuously omits Ethel Wilson from his survey), but it illustrates the problems with an unproblematic critical belief that a text reflects a cultural context and that the context exists ready to be described.

58 Various critics have turned to Cather's life in order to interpret Myra Henshawe's character and the novel's theme. This seems to me a dubious way of interpreting a text, since the biographical material that critics can adduce is itself an artifactual result of interpretation. Later on, I note briefly the complications that ensue from turning to biography in a comparative critique.

59 For a discussion of family influences upon Wilson's views of religion, see Irene Howard, "Shockable and Unshockable Methodists in *The Innocent Traveller,*" *Essays on Canadian Writing* 23 (1982), pp. 107–34. Wilson briefly discusses her religious upbringing in a letter written in 1955 to Mazo de la Roche that describes a "congenital" Anglicanism overlaying a Nonconformist Wesleyan background, which "even if transplanted to British Columbia, carries with it a terrific sense of duty and of personal responsibility" (Stouck, *Ethel Wilson, Stories, Essays, Letters,* pp. 197–99). In an earlier letter of 1951, she had written strongly and at some length about the views of the American "reactionary," William Buckley, whose recently published book *God and Man at Yale* she discusses: "But oh dear, Bill, his parent a very rich and very fine oil man, is *completely* capitalist, confuses Capitalism with Christianity . . . he is a Roman Catholic . . . [whose] strong R.C.ism injects other matters" (Stouck, *Ethel Wilson, Stories, Essays, Letters,* p. 163, original emphasis). Wilson calls the American anticommunist "smear" campaign, in which Buckley is involved, a "snake pit" and says its "extreme hatred . . . terrifies me."

60 For a comprehendible discussion of chaos theory, see James Gleick, *Chaos: Making a New Science* (New York: Viking Penguin, 1987). Gleick describes a relationship between unpredictability, apparent disorder or chaos, and universal orderly designs – matters thematic to Wilson's fiction, which expresses them, obviously, in nonmathematical and nonscientific terms. Critics look for theoretical codes that will help decipher the meanings of literary texts, finding them even in theories that deny the possibility of deciding on meanings. I am suggesting, outlandish as it may seem, that chaos theory provides a possible theoretical code that translates Wilson's themes of chance, providential order, and universal human values into terms that validate them in ways entirely different from those provided by cultural codes. This is not to deny or erase interpretations of Wilson that place her views within the context of traditional religious beliefs – or even

traditional nonreligious beliefs. I find, for example that Wilson's view of providential order conforms to a deistic vision, described by Charles Taylor as an interlocking of the
purposes and functions of "the entities in the world" to create "a harmonious whole,"
an "entire order" (*Sources of the Self: The Making of the Modern Identity* [Cambridge, Mass.:
Harvard University Press, 1989], p. 275).

61 Wilson created appealing good-humored mothers like Susan Cuppy in *Love and Salt
Water* and Ellen Burnaby in *Hetty Dorval* – mothers conceived, perhaps, as wish fulfill-
ments; self-sacrificing mothers like *Hetty Dorval*'s mysterious Mrs. Broom and resource-
ful Lilly Waller in "Lilly's Story"; and eccentric or ordinary mothers like Hilda Severance
and Vera Gunnarsen in *Swamp Angel*. Among Cather's parentless children are Alexander
Bergson, Jim Burden, Niel Herbert, Tom Outland, Cécile Auclair, Lucy Gayheart, and
not unnotably, Molly Driscoll.

62 The lives of the two writers reveal interesting similarities and differences. As I have
noted, both were transplanted at about the age of ten from a place they knew as home
to a western geography still in a pioneer stage. As young women, both earned a living
teaching school, Cather more briefly than Wilson. Both published comparatively late in
life, considerably late for Wilson whose first novel appeared when she was fifty-nine years
old. A crucial difference, of course, is that Wilson married and was, by all accounts, extremely happy as the wife of a distinguished Canadian doctor, Wallace Wilson. Because
of various honorific professional duties, Dr. Wallace was sometimes an absentee husband,
like Frank Cuppy (though unlike Susan Cuppy, Ethel Wilson often accompanied her
husband to his meetings, turning her experiences into a hilarious account of a wife's
(mis)adventures at her husband's convention in the story "Mrs. Golightly and the First
Convention"). Cather has become almost notorious for her portrayal of unhappy marriages, too numerous to list here, and the bitterness of her final portrayal of marriage in
My Mortal Enemy has usually been interpreted in biographical terms. The problems and
complexities of such interpretations seem to me manifold, particularly in a biography such
as Phyllis Robinson's *Willa*, which I have discussed, along with other biographies of
American women writers, in an review-essay entitled " 'Lives' of Women Writers:
Cather, Austin, Porter/ and Willa, Mary, Katherine Anne," *Novel: A Forum on Fiction* 18,
no. 1 (Fall 1984): pp. 64–80; reprinted in *Women Writing in America*, pp. 235–48. See also
the questions raised in my review of Mary McAlpine's biography, *The Other Side of Silence: A Life of Ethel Wilson* (1988), which is called "Fixed Smile," *Canadian Literature: A
Quarterly of Criticism and Review* 128 (Spring 1991): pp. 164–65.

63 To assume, as some critics have, that setting makes a writer American or Canadian
trivializes the issue of cultural identity. Because *Shadows on the Rock* is set in Quebec, an
American critic has called it Cather's "Canadian novel" and praised it for capturing a
Canadian sensibility (though he did not clearly define this sensibility, leaving this matter
to a Canadian critic). See Benjamin George, "The French-Canadian Connection: Willa
Cather as a Canadian Writer," *Western American Literature* 11 (Fall 1976): pp. 249–61;
reprinted in Murphy, *Critical Essays on Willa Cather*, pp. 269–79. George claims that while
certain aspects of Cather's writing "would seem to mark her as a distinctively American
writer . . . she came to hold a close affinity with Canadian ideals and attitudes, pointedly
different from those of her own national ethos"; these Canadian "ideals and attitudes . . .
reach their culmination in her Canadian-set novel, *Shadows on the Rock*" (p. 269). I would
read *Shadows on the Rock* as a typical Cather celebration of the heroic beginnings of a new
country, essentially no different from the celebrations in Cather's "American" novels,

O Pioneers! or *My Ántonia*. Moreover, I would claim that in celebrating the history of Quebec, Cather typically misreads the past not only to glorify a lost Golden Age but also to insist that in Quebec the past has been held in a state of stasis – that time has not changed the city on the rock in which a young daughter has been faithful to the transplanted French traditions of a (conveniently) dead mother. David Stouck, a distinguished Canadian critic of Cather (and of Ethel Wilson) stressed "the static quality" of *Shadows on the Rock* and its underlying "desire to stop time." Stouck's description of French characters clinging to their new home, their old traditions, and to each other as a community – while always aware of and imperiled by a looming wilderness – transcribes Frye's description of a Canadian "garrison mentality" to Cather's text. See *Willa Cather's Imagination* (Lincoln: University of Nebraska Press, 1975), pp. 149–61. While Cather would like to imagine that a city that was to become part of the modern world could remain as arrested as the ancient Native American stone city she described in *The Professor's House*, historians inevitably point to the drastic changes that settlers have effected in the landscape of Canada's populated areas. See, for example, Ralph R. Krueger, "A Geographical Perspective: The Setting and the Settlement" in *Understanding Canada*, pp. 11–79.

64   On Wilson's discussions of "the origins of her books" (p. 81), see "Somewhere Near the Truth," a radio talk given by Wilson in 1957, printed in Stouck, *Ethel Wilson: Stories, Essays, Letters,* pp. 81–91. On Cather's views on art as escape, see her letter entitled "Escapism" in *Willa Cather on Writing,* pp. 18–29. Cather wrote this letter in 1936, as the Great Depression dragged on, to answer socially oriented critics (who had criticized her novels as escapist and irrelevant to the times). She contentiously equated art with escape by asking, "What has art ever been but escape?" (p. 18). In the immediate present, art could offer escape from dire "industrial conditions," a subject, she said, appropriate to pamphlets and propaganda, but not to literature. I might add that Cather's view on the need for escape from ordinary life was shared by the advertising industry, which had been shaped by, and would significantly shape, the culture of capitalism emerging in the United States. While she thought she was inveighing against the materialism of this culture, Cather was articulating in her own terms an argument for escape that advertisers were presenting as a rationale for the mass consumption of material goods. For example, in 1926, the year *My Mortal Enemy* was published, a writer for the trade journal *Advertising and Selling* declared that "people are seeking to escape from themselves" and, consequently, that advertisers could best serve their purpose – sell the most and make the most profit – if they catered to a popular desire for escape from immediate social realities (quoted in Roland Marchand, *Advertising the American Dream: Making Way for Modernity, 1920–1940* [Berkeley: University of California Press, 1985], p. xvii). Of course, Cather would have disavowed any connection between the escape offered by her art and that implicit in commercial advertising. Nonetheless, a coalescence between the visual arts and advertising became explicit in the highly sophisticated ads of the nineteen twenties which drew upon the avant-garde styles of "cubism, futurism, vorticism, impressionism, Art Deco, and expressionism" (Marchand, pp. 140–8).

65   Anne Perry, *Callender Square,* A Victorian Mystery (New York: Ballantine, A Fawcett Crest Book, 1990, published originally in 1981), p. 183; and Anne Perry, *Rutland Place, A Victorian Mystery* (New York: Ballantine, A Fawcett Crest Book, 1990, published originally in 1983), p. 69. Anne Perry's series of Victorian mysteries shows the hideous injustices perpetrated in a society in which modern capitalism was taking shape and exerting its unfettered will. All the mystery stories in the series reveal precisely those aspects of social class and gender that the two novels I have been discussing sought to hide.

66 Guy Debord, *Comments on the Society of the Spectacle,* tr. Malcolm Imrie (London: Verso, 1990, published originally in 1988 as *Commentaires sur la société du spectacle* by Editions Gérard Lebovici), p. 14.

Index

Continued from the front of the book